Reconsidering the Emergence of the Gay Novel in English and German

Comparative Cultural Studies
Series Editor: Tötösy de Zepetnek, Steven

Comparative cultural studies is a contextual approach to the study of culture in a global and intercultural context. It works with a plurality of methods and approaches. The theoretical and methodological framework of comparative cultural studies is built on tenets borrowed from the discipline of comparative literature, the field of cultural studies, and from a range of thought traditions including literary and culture theory, (radical) constructivism, communication theories, and systems theories. In comparative cultural studies the focus is on theory and method as well as application. The monograph series of Books in Comparative Cultural Studies publishes single-authored and thematic collected volumes of new scholarship. Manuscripts of books are invited for publication in the series in fields of the study of culture, literature, the arts, media studies, communication studies, the history of ideas, and related disciplines of the humanities and social sciences to the series editor in a word attachment via email at <ccsbks@purdue.edu>. The series is affiliated with *CLCWeb: Comparative Literature and Culture* (ISSN 1481-4374), the peer-reviewed, full-text, and open-access quarterly published by Purdue University Press at <http://docs.lib.purdue.edu/clcweb>.

Volumes in the Purdue series of Books in Comparative Cultural Studies include <http://www.thepress.purdue.edu/series/comparative-cultural-studies>

James Patrick Wilper, *Reconsidering the Emergence of the Gay Novel in English and German*
Li Guo, *Women's* Tanci *Fiction in Late Imperial and Early Twentieth-Century China*
Arianna Dagnino, *Transcultural Writers and Novels in the Age of Global Mobility*
Elke Sturm-Trigonakis, *Comparative Cultural Studies and the New* Weltliteratur
Lauren Rule Maxwell, *Romantic Revisions in Novels from the Americas*
Liisa Steinby, *Kundera and Modernity*
Text and Image in Modern European Culture, Ed. Natasha Grigorian, Thomas Baldwin, and Margaret Rigaud-Drayton
Sheng-mei Ma, *Asian Diaspora and East-West Modernity*
Irene Marques, *Transnational Discourses on Class, Gender, and Cultural Identity*
Comparative Hungarian Cultural Studies, Ed. Steven Tötösy de Zepetnek and Louise O. Vasvári
Hui Zou, *A Jesuit Garden in Beijing and Early Modern Chinese Culture*
Yi Zheng, *From Burke and Wordsworth to the Modern Sublime in Chinese Literature*
Agata Anna Lisiak, *Urban Cultures in (Post)Colonial Central Europe*
Representing Humanity in an Age of Terror, Ed. Sophia A. McClennen and Henry James Morello
Michael Goddard, *Gombrowicz, Polish Modernism, and the Subversion of Form*
Shakespeare in Hollywood, Asia, and Cyberspace, Ed. Alexander C.Y. Huang and Charles S. Ross
Gustav Shpet's Contribution to Philosophy and Cultural Theory, Ed. Galin Tihanov
Comparative Central European Holocaust Studies, Ed. Louise O. Vasvári and Steven Tötösy de Zepetnek
Marko Juvan, *History and Poetics of Intertextuality*
Thomas O. Beebee, *Nation and Region in Modern American and European Fiction*
Paolo Bartoloni, *On the Cultures of Exile, Translation, and Writing*
Justyna Sempruch, *Fantasies of Gender and the Witch in Feminist Theory and Literature*
Kimberly Chabot Davis, *Postmodern Texts and Emotional Audiences*
Philippe Codde, *The Jewish American Novel*
Deborah Streifford Reisinger, *Crime and Media in Contemporary France*

Reconsidering the Emergence of the Gay Novel in English and German

James Patrick Wilper

Purdue University Press
West Lafayette, Indiana

Copyright 2016 by Purdue University. All rights reserved.

Printed in the United States of America.

Cataloging-in-Publication Data on file at the Library of Congress.
    Print ISBN: 978-1-55753-731-7
    ePDF ISBN: 978-1-61249-417-3
    ePUB ISBN: 978-1-61249-421-0

Cover image: Punch's Fancy Portraits, No. 37. By Edward Linley Sambourne. *Punch Magazine*, 1881. Via Thinkstock, by Getty Images.

To Benjamin

Contents

Acknowledgments	ix
Note on Translations	xi
Introduction	1

Part 1: Religion and Law

Chapter 1
Sin and Crime — 15

Part 2: Greek Love

Chapter 2
Transcending Greek Love — 51

Chapter 3
The "Manly love of comrades" — 71

Part 3: Science and Sex

Chapter 4
The Highest Being Drawn Down into Decadence — 91

Chapter 5
Health, Masculinity, and the Third Sex — 115

Part 4: Wild about Oscar Wilde?

Chapter 6
A Tough Act to Follow: Homosexuality in Fiction after Oscar Wilde — 137

Chapter 7
Das Bildnis des Oskar Wilde — 153

Afterword	171
Works Cited	177
Index	199

Acknowledgments

I would like to acknowledge the debt I owe to Heike Bauer and Joanne Leal, for their guidance and encouragement, as well as that I owe to Robert Gillet and Gregory Woods, whose input was essential to bringing this project to fruition.

I would like to thank my partner, Benjamin Nikolay, for his unending support (financial and otherwise) and unfailing patience.

And, last but by no means least, I want to express my gratitude to Purdue University Press and the entire editorial team for enabling me to make this contribution to the scholarly discourse, and special thanks to the Comparative Cultural Studies Series Editor Steven Tötösy de Zepetnek and to Production Editor Dianna Gilroy for their assistance and suggestions.

Note on Translations

I have used published translations of German texts when possible; when no such translation exists, translations are my own.

Introduction

Responding to a question about "the Love that dare not speak its name" while on trial in April 1895, Oscar Wilde defended same-sex passions from the witness box, citing Lord Alfred Douglas's poem "Two Loves" (1894) (Douglas 297). Although this love might not have dared to speak its name in the face of pervasive social and legal condemnation, it was not for lack of options. Rather, in Wilde's time and in the decades following, names for same-sex love abounded. As scholars and historians of sexuality and homosexuality have shown, the nineteenth century saw the emergence of competing taxonomical and conceptual structures for same-sex desire and sexuality. Concerning the subject of homosexuality, nowhere were the discursive links stronger than between the German- and English-speaking worlds, which took the form of renewed interest in Western traditions of Greek love, the influence of German sexological research into homosexuality on English sexual-reform efforts, and the impact of Oscar Wilde's trials and conviction for acts of "gross indecency" (i.e., sex acts) with other men upon German writers and homosexual subcultures. This dynamic discursive environment provides the backdrop to the first novels explicitly dealing with love and desire between men.

This study reconsiders the "gay" or homosexual novel in German and English. As Gregory Woods writes, "towards the end of the nineteenth century, at very roughly the same time that the existence of 'the homosexual' as a distinct type of individual was being definitely established, the novel started to take over from poetry as the best place in which accessibly to express the quotidian realities of homosexual lives" (*A History of Gay Literature* 136). This shift from poetry to the novel, Woods suggests, was part of larger social and cultural trends and the development of the novel as an art form and as "the pre-eminent 'social' literary medium of the bourgeois-capitalist era" (136). Late nineteenth-century sexological investigation into same-sex sexuality might have played a role. Harry Oosterhuis posits that the self-narration undertaken by homosexual men and women for sexologists, such as the Austrian psychiatrist Richard von Krafft-Ebing, utilized the literary genre of the autobiography: "Krafft-Ebing's case histories can be viewed as a specific version of the modern (auto)biographical genre as it originated in the eighteenth century and came to full development in the nineteenth century" (*Stepchildren of Nature* 216).

It is possible that these nonfictional narratives of gay lives led to fictional ones. Although this would be an interesting question, it is not the aim of this study, though, to offer an answer as to why this move from poetry to the novel took place, but rather to explore the themes common to these works.

Claude Summers defines gay fiction as "the fictional representation of male homosexuals by gay male and lesbian writers; the evolution of conceptions about homosexual identity; and the construction, perpetuation, revision, and deconstruction of fictions (including stereotypes and defamations) about homosexuality and homosexuals" (*Gay Fictions* 11). Summers gave this definition in 1990, and yet, for the purposes of this study, it still has mileage. Of course, here I limit it to the novel—and for that matter so does Summers, who discusses mostly novels and a few short stories. Hence, I use a broad definition of the gay novel: it is the genre composed of novels in which men who recognized their same-sex desire (regardless of whether they would ascribe to this or a similar term) gave voice to that desire. It explores the development of identities based on same-sex desire, which have fed into modern gay identities, and it is particularly poised to challenge stereotypes and (mis)conceptions about homosexuals.

The present study focuses exclusively on gay male novels. Some of the earliest works of fiction to thematize female same-sex love and desire, however, did respond to similar discourses, as in the cases of lesbian novels that incorporate and translate into fiction Krafft-Ebing's or Magnus Hirschfeld's scientific concepts and theories, such as Radclyffe Hall's *The Well of Loneliness* (1928) or Minna Wettstein-Adelt's *Sind es Frauen? Ein Roman über das dritte Geschlecht* (Are These Women? A Novel about the Third Sex, 1901), which she published under the pseudonym Aimée Duc. Nevertheless, gay male novels were responding to distinct, although sometimes complimentary, discourses and stereotypes to their female counterparts. For instance, exploring medical discourse on female sexual inversion, Chiara Beccalossi writes that "late nineteenth-century physicians formulated detailed theories of love and sexual acts between women. Rather than mirroring more sophisticated explanations of male same-sex desires, medical ideas of female same-sex desires had their own rich narratives, and their own multilayered history" (*Female Sexual Inversion* 5). Therefore, an analysis of late nineteenth- and early twentieth-century discourses of female same-sex desire in the earliest lesbian novels is beyond this scope of this book, but it is an area which would no doubt yield fruitful further research.

When I use the term "gay novels" to designate the works I have chosen to study, I recognize that I am using the word "gay" anachronistically. The English word "gay" dates, writes George Chauncey, to the 1920s and especially 1930s when it was used in New York gay subcultures (20–21). It may have made it across the Atlantic during World War II because, according to the *OED*, in the late 1940s and early 1950s "gay" appears in British writing. The German equivalent, "schwul," on the other hand, has a much longer history, and thus it would be appropriate to call the four works of fiction on which I have selected to focus here "schwule Romane" ("gay novels"). Paul Derks's research indicates that by 1900 the word "schwul" was already in wide circulation with the oldest written usage of the term appearing in a Berlin criminological treatise in 1847 (*Die Schande der heiligen Päderastie* 95–96). The term "homosexual" was in usage in both linguistic contexts during this period. The word "Homosexualität" was coined by the campaigner Karl Maria Kertbeny (1824–1882) in 1869 (Tobin "Kertbeny's 'Homosexuality'" 3), and, according to the *OED*, this term found its way into the English language in 1892. This term itself provides an example of the kind of cross-cultural transfer regarding discourses of homosexuality with which this study is concerned.

In terms of scope, this study treats texts of the formative years of the gay novel, revisiting the time of the emergence of the genre to argue for its continued relevance. Since the 1970s, when gay literary studies arose as a field of scholarship, there have been a great number of studies that have focused in part, primarily, or entirely on fiction of this period. Many of these studies discussed openly for the first time homosexuality in the work of established literary figures or rediscovered forgotten early gay-themed literary works. By the 1980s and mid-1990s, a new gay literary canon was being established in studies that include Summers's *Gay Fictions Wilde to Stonewall* (1990), Mark Lilly's *Gay Men's Literature in the Twentieth Century* (1993), Joseph Bristow's *Effeminate England* (1995), and Woods's *A History of Gay Literature* (1998). Since the mid- to late-1990s, scholarship in gay and lesbian literary studies has been, to a large extent, supplanted by queer studies in academia. Nevertheless, critical work on the gay novel genre did not disappear when "queer" came on the scene. This work might be best described as having been incorporated into queer studies. If anything, the field of inquiry in gay and lesbian literature is richer and more diverse than ever before. Important examinations of gay novels have been published within the past decade, such as the 2011 *Cambridge Companion to Gay and Lesbian Writings*, edited by Hugh Stevens. The difference is that the foci of much of this recent work are far narrower than the comprehensive recovery projects of the 1980s and 1990s: take, for example, Norman Jones's *Gay and Lesbian Historical Fiction* (2007), Martin Dines's *Gay Suburban Narratives in American and British Culture: Homecoming Queens* (2010), or Monica B. Pearl's *AIDS Literature and Gay Identity* (2013).

Since such a great deal of scholarly attention has been invested in the emergence of the gay novel, particularly in the 70s, 80s, and 90s, it then must be asked why it should interest us now. The reason, I argue, is simple: because, when approached with a comparative literary and cultural methodology, there are still original interpretations to be made. Unlike many earlier studies, this work does not focus exclusively on fiction from one linguistic or cultural group, neither does it investigate works of fiction from two or more cultural contexts and completely ignore the specificities, the peculiarities, or the inflections of the cultural context in which these works were written. Thus, the contribution of the present study to the field of scholarship lies squarely in its cross-cultural and comparative focus, in its exploration of the transnational legacies and the exchange of knowledge and culture between the German- and English-speaking worlds. This study draws on and links to recent research in related and adjacent disciplines, in particular comparative work in the history of sexuality and sexology (see especially H. Bauer, *English Literary Sexology*; Schaffner, *Modernism and Perversion*; and others), to show how the emergence of the gay novel correlates to broader trends in the development of homosexual identity and culture. This is the "why and how" of the ways in which this study fits into the framework of comparative literary and cultural studies. It is this approach which enables me to make my fresh interpretations of the texts here under scrutiny and arrive at new insights into how the gay novel genre cohered.

I have selected four texts indicative of the rise of the modern gay novel to draw larger conclusions about the formative environment of this genre in these discursively linked linguistic and cultural contexts. These works of fiction are US-American émigré Edward Prime-Stevenson's short novel, *Imre: A Memorandum* (1906); Thomas Mann's classic of homoerotic longing, *Der Tod in Venedig* (*Death in Venice*, 1912); E. M. Forster's posthumously published, gay bildungsroman, *Maurice* (1913–14; 1971); and Scottish-German John Henry Mackay's *Der Puppenjunge: Die Geschichte einer namenlosen Liebe aus der Friedrichstraße* (*The Hustler: The Story of a Nameless Love from Friedrichstrasse*, 1926), a novel set in interwar Berlin's homosexual subcultures. These are among the earliest works to fictionalize love and desire between men and are some of the most open in dealing with the subject.

I do not claim, however, that my selection is comprehensive. Indeed, I must mention that from this era there are various texts that are not included in this study, or are considered only in passing. Among these are quite a number of German works of fiction: Emerich von Stadion's *Drei seltsame Erinnerungen* (Three Strange Memories, 1868), Adolf Wilbrandt's *Fridolins heimliche Ehe* (*Fridolin's Secret Marriage*, 1875), Bill Forster's (pseudonym for Herman Breuer) *Anders als die Andern* (Different to the Others, 1904), the anonymously authored novel *Liebchen: Ein Roman unter Männern* (Darling: A Novel Among Men, 1908), *Zwischen den Geschlechtern: Roman einer geächteten Leidenschaft* (Between the Sexes: Novel of an Outlawed Passion, 1919) by "Homunkulus," and many more. There are English examples as well, such as Forrest Reid's *The Garden God: A Tale of Two Boys* (1905), D. H. Lawrence's "The Prussian Officer" (1914), and A. T. Fitzroy's (pseudonym for Rose Allatini) *Despised and Rejected* (1917). Hence, I have had to reach a compromise between breadth and depth, since the limitations of space prevent me taking a broader selection. No doubt, further investigation with other constellations of novels will provide ever greater insight into the rise of the gay novel.

Imre: A Memorandum, which Prime-Stevenson published under the pseudonym "Xavier Mayne," is the first-person narration of Oswald, a thirty-something Englishman living in Europe, who recounts how, while studying Hungarian in Budapest, he met, befriended, and fell in love with a twenty-five-year-old army lieutenant named Imre von N. *Imre* represents a first in English literature for its happy ending for its two gay protagonists. Although by no means a forgotten work, Prime-Stevenson's novel has received considerably less attention than the others examined here. Much of the scholarship on *Imre* is in the form of overviews of the history of gay writings, which thus do not provide in-depth discussions of the themes presented in the novel (see Austen, *Playing the Game* 20–27; Levin, *The Gay Novel* 18–21; Fone, *A Road to Stonewall* 195–206; Looby, "The Gay Novel in the United States" 419–22). Notable exceptions, though, are James Gifford's *Dayneford's Library* (1995) ("The Athletic Model" 98–117) and Margaret Breen's essay "Homosexual Identity, Translation, and Prime-Stevenson's *Imre* and *The Intersexes*" (2012), upon whose work I seek to build.

By contrast, scholarly treatments of same-sex desire in Mann's *Der Tod in Venedig* abound. Since his diaries and notes began to be published in 1977, Mann's sexuality and sexuality in his fiction have been a regular topic of research. The diaries, writes Hans Rudolph Vaget, gave Mann's literary reputation "a major boost" ("Confession and Camouflage" 568). "They confirm what sympathetic readers have felt all along: in Mann's work, a homosexual sensibility is struggling to come to terms with itself" (Vaget 573). In particular, the novella *Der Tod in Venedig*, Andrew Webber writes, "has identified Mann, however ambivalently, as a pioneering modern gay writer" ("Mann's Man's World" 68). In the novella, respected and recently ennobled author Gustav von Aschenbach is swept away by a sudden pang of *Reiselust* sparked by a homoerotically charged exchange of stares with an unknown man near the Englischer Garten in Munich. He departs for the south, eventually arriving in Venice, where he beholds, watches, and eventually falls in love with a teenage boy of unearthly beauty. Much of the early scholarship on homosexuality in the novella and Mann's other works of fiction, for instance, Ignace Feuerlicht's seminal essay "Thomas Mann and Homoeroticism" (1982), Gerhard Härle's groundbreaking *Männerweiblichkeit* (1988), and T. J. Reed's *Death in Venice: Making and Unmaking a Master* (1994), focuses on the relationship between the literary texts and the author's attitudes to and experience of homoeroticism. Although the fact that for Mann same-sex desire was a major impetus in his work and life is an important concern here, this study contributes to recent work, such as Robert Tobin's essay "Queering Thomas Mann's *Tod in Venedig*" (2012), Philip Kitcher's *Deaths in Venice* (2013), and Jeffrey Meyers's *Thomas Mann's Artist-Heroes* (2014), which grants primacy to the text and its portrayal of same-sex passions without constant recourse to how this reflects upon Thomas Mann, and vice versa.

After Christopher Isherwood received the manuscripts for Forster's *Maurice* and his short stories, he anticipated the watershed their publication would represent, saying of scholarship on Forster to John Lehmann that "Unless you start with the fact that he was homosexual, nothing's any good at all" (Moffat, *E. M. Forster* 20). Despite receiving disparaging reviews and dismissive treatment following their posthumous publication, for instance, in Jeffrey Meyers's *Homosexuality and Literature 1890-1930* (1977), *Maurice* and the short story collection *The Life to Come and Other Short Stories* (1972) have come to secure Forster a place in the canon of gay English writers. As a consequence, ever since Robert Martin's seminal essay "Edward Carpenter and the Double Structure in *Maurice*" (1983), a great deal of scholarly attention has been devoted to the analysis of this novel. This study brings a fresh perspective to the text by analyzing it in relation to its American and German contemporaries. The novel is a coming-of-age story, or bildungsroman. As Maurice Hall passes through the spheres of home, public school, university, and career, he encounters various discourses relating to his desire and his sexual subjectivity and comes under the influence of two distinct homosexual identities. The protagonist would have been crushed by the weight of societal condemnation had it not been for finding love with Alec, with whom he escapes as an outlaw into the greenwood.

The other three works were all written, if not all published, before the First World War. *Der Puppenjunge*, on the other hand, was penned and appeared after that paradigm-shifting conflict. Therefore, Mackay's first six writings, *Die Bücher der namenlosen Liebe* (*The Books of the Nameless Love*), which were published together under the pseudonym "Sagitta" ("arrow") in 1913 and reissued in 1924, might yield a more profitable comparison to *Der Tod in Venedig*, *Imre*, and *Maurice*. Most critical interest in Mackay's homosexual writings is invested in these earlier works (see Jones, *We of the Third Sex* 263–76; Fähnders, "Anarchism and Homosexuality in Wilhelmine Germany" 117–53; Kennedy, *The Anarchist of Love*; Popp, "Zwischen Wilde-Prozess und Eulenburg-Affäre" 95–97; J. Bauer, "On the Nameless Love and Infinite Sexualities"). I too give these writings some attention, but only in support of my analyses of *Der Puppenjunge*. There are comparatively few studies that investigate the 1926 novel (see Popp, *Männerliebe* 32–40, 156–63; Lücke, "Beschmutzte Utopien" 307–12), which is why it is my main focus here. The themes that are developed in the first six *Bücher der namenlosen Liebe* are brought to fruition in the full-length novel and it is owing to this fact that the novel offers such productive comparisons as well as contrasts to the other three literary texts. The title translates literally as "boy-doll" and is a play on the contemporary slang term for a boy prostitute, "Pupenjunge," which derives from the verb "pupen," to fart (Kennedy, *The Anarchist of Love* 38). The novel comprises two intersecting narratives, treating Berlin's homosexual subcultures and male prostitution from differing points of view. The first of these is that of Günther Nielsen, the "boy-doll" of the title, a teenage runaway who comes to Berlin from a northern German village. In the metropolis, he learns a lesson in social Darwinism: exploit or be exploited. The second point of view is that of Hermann Graff, a man in his early twenties, who arrives in the city on the same day as Günther and who falls in love with the eponymous "boy-doll."

As stated above, the originality of this study lies in its comparative—intercultural and interlinguistic—methodology. This work peers beyond boundaries to offer unique analyses of the novelistic responses to comparable social, scientific, and literary discourses, responses that demonstrate remarkable similarities and often surprising differences. By broadening the scope beyond national literary traditions, this project presents fresh insights into these fictional responses to a unique historical moment.

As I explore in part 1, one of the most fundamental affinities between these linguistic and cultural groups is the Judeo-Christian sanction against men lying "with mankind, as with womankind" (Leviticus 18:22, King James Version) which was codified in law in the United States, Britain, and Germany. This is in contrast to France or Italy where there were no laws forbidding sex acts between men since the Napoleonic Wars (see Sibalis, "Male Homosexuality" 117–18). These secularized and institutionalized religious strictures are to a large extent, one may even say primarily, responsible for catalyzing the counterdiscourses that influence the works of literature. Homosexuality was a "German invention," argues Robert Beachy, owing to several vectors in German society, including the fact that intercourse between men was illegal in the German-speaking lands ("The German Invention of Homosexuality" 804). This may also explain why Greek love defense and justificatory strategies were the pursuit primarily of German and British writers; as Christopher Robinson argues, French contributions to this discourse are "rare" (*Scandal in the Ink* 18, 146).

Chapter 1 examines the influence of religious and legal discourse on the four works of fiction. Responses to this discourse which manifests in all four works of fiction are the exile and travel motifs. In *Imre*, Oswald seems to be a fictional example of the itinerant, turn-of-the-century invert that Yvonne Ivory describes in her essay "The Urning and His Own: Individualism and the Fin-de-Siècle Invert" (2003); however, there is enough that distinguishes him from this figure and enough departure from the homosexual exile and travel motifs to argue that this novel questions the efficacy of escape from religious and legal forces. Oswald finds a new homeland with the man he loves, and they take solace from their togetherness. Although they may not consciously take a stand against a homophobic society in the way that Hermann Graff does at the end of *Der Puppenjunge*, by putting down roots they too subvert these forces. In *Der Tod in Venedig*, travel to "the charming south" (202) ("[dem] liebenswürdigen Süden"; 67) liberates the protagonist from the strict discipline that has ruled his existence. The narrative, however, does not straightforwardly endorse the delight he takes in his liberation; instead as the plot progresses, until the final scene, the narrator increasingly distances himself from the protagonist and begins passing judgment on the extremes to which Aschenbach's desire leads. Liberation does not lead to life, but rather to death. In this way, the novella problematizes the motifs of travel and exile in the south. *Maurice* turns the motif of sexual liberation through travel to and in the Mediterranean lands on its head. Rather than finding freedom in Greece, Clive finds only further repression. Exile is still an important theme in the novel, though, but not to the traditional destinations. Rather than flee with Alec to France or Italy, places where a homosexual man "could share with a friend and yet not go to prison" (183), they become outlaws of the greenwood. Finally, Graff is tempted by the south, but after his short prison sentence as a "sexual offender" he is determined to return to Berlin to wage an individual struggle with societal forces, a struggle which is informed by the author's theories of individualist anarchism which he expounds in the writings that Mackay published under his own name.

Part 2 examines the ways in which, in the second half of the nineteenth century, the classics were mobilized to form an essential counterdiscourse to those which characterized homosexuality as sin, crime, or disease. It was the moment of the Greek love apologia, which achieved its most public invocation in Oscar Wilde's defense speech of "the love that dare not speak its name" during his trials for acts of gross indecency (Hyde, *Trials* 201). Chapter 2 explores the two responses in German fiction to "Greek love." Often premodern models and ideals were an uncomfortable fit in the modern era owing to the fact that it was believed that if these relations were to remain "heavenly," they must remain chaste. Mann's *Der Tod in Venedig* is an ambivalent as well as an ironic treatment of Greek love-inspired relations between a man and a youth—even if the "relationship" occurs only in the fantasy of the protagonist. This treatment problematizes the Hellenic ideals grafted onto Aschenbach's love for Tadzio. The novel *Der Puppenjunge* signals a greater break with legacies of Greek love than Mann's novella. Although it depicts the love of a man for a youth, like classical predecessors, Mackay, in his fiction, rejects Greek love justification. The nameless love, the love of a man for a younger, "is a love, like every other" (289) ("ist eine Liebe, wie jede andere"; 333), and thus requires no historical or philosophic apologia.

Some responded to the shortcomings of Greek love by reinventing it. The British writers John Addington Symonds and Edward Carpenter did just that, mobilizing their interpretations of Walt Whitman's the "manly love of comrades" (*The Complete Poems* 150) from the "Calamus" cluster of the American poet's *Leaves of Grass* (1855, first edition). Chapter 3 explores the English responses to Greek love. Although it is not likely that Prime-Stevenson had read much, or any at all, of Symonds's or Carpenter's works, he developed a similar vision of same-sex identity and relations to his British contemporaries, one that invokes the past, revives it with Whitman's verse, and mobilizes it to formulate a masculine identity and lifelong bond between adult men. Forster's *Maurice* is influenced by Carpenter's and Symonds's views on Greek comradeship and, in the narrative, contrasts two forms of Greek love: Hellenism, which is represented by the character Clive Durham, and "Uranian" comrade love, represented by Alec Scudder. Robert Martin, in his essay on Forster's novel, discusses the "double structure" of *Maurice*, which is an essential point of reference for this part of my study. My critique of Martin's thesis is that he places Symonds and Carpenter at opposite ends of a spectrum, with the former representing a nineteenth-century Greek love apologia, and the latter a Whitmanian vision. However, I argue that both theorists contributed to the identity and mode of relations which are depicted in Forster's novel. Therefore, *Maurice* trades one set of ideals for another. I also demonstrate how in the novel, sex and sexual desire outside the bounds of a philosophic framework are portrayed negatively.

Part 3 investigates sexology, or the scientific study of human sexuality, as a means through which many homosexual men and women during this era and later were able to assign meaning to their sexual desire. As the writer J. R. Ackerley recounts in his memoir *My Father and Myself* (1968), the label "homosexual" helped him discover where he stood on "the sexual map" (118). Chapter 4 explores the impact of late nineteenth- and early twentieth-century research into same-sex sexuality on the German works of fiction. Two schools of sexological thought bear a significant degree of influence on Mann's early fiction. First, the influence of the school made up of sexologists who regarded homosexuality as indicative of broader mental and physical degeneration, such as Richard von Krafft-Ebing, manifests in *Der Tod in Venedig* in the metaphor which likens homosexuality to cholera and in the casting of Aschenbach, and other characters, as degenerate figures. Second, the school made up of sexologists such as Magnus Hirschfeld, who theorized that homosexual men and women were sexual intermediate types between the ideal male and female types, exercised some influence over Mann. This is evinced by the positioning of the protagonist as an intermediary figure in terms of gender and sex, something which is communicated most overtly through his intermediate "race." In contrast, Mackay's fiction opposes sexual science, considering these theories "false and dangerous" (*Hustler* 158) ("falsch und gefährlich"; *Puppenjunge* 184). *Die Bücher der namenlosen Liebe* depict same-sex love beyond the medical and sexological paradigm; nevertheless, science plays a key role in Mackay's autobiographical novella, *Fenny Skaller: Ein Leben der namenlosen Liebe* (Fenny Skaller: A Life of the Nameless Love), which was published with *Die Bücher der namenlosen Liebe* in 1913, although this takes the form of the protagonist's negation of this branch of knowledge, empowering him to forge his identity in opposition to these models.

The school of German sexological thought which hypothesized that homosexual men and women represented a third or intermediate sex, a model devised by Karl Heinrich Ulrichs in his polemic writings and developed by Hirschfeld, proves indispensable for the English-language works of fiction. Chapter 5 explores the impact of liberationist third-sex platforms on Prime-Stevenson's *Imre* and Forster's *Maurice*. The novels foreground the health and masculinity of their central characters in order to contradict prevailing theories of degeneracy and underpin their portrayals of homosexual subjectivity with the third- or intermediate-sex theory, which is explicit in the former text and implicit in the latter. Prime-Stevenson's novel complements his study *The Intersexes: A History of Similisexualism as a Problem in Social Life* (1908) and, as such, is the fictive component to his effort to educate the general public about homosexuality and therewith bring about social change. The third-sex concept of Ulrichs and Hirschfeld forms the core to his endeavor. Finding its way to England through Symonds, Carpenter, and Havelock Ellis, the third sex is considered by some scholars as absent from Forster's novel (see Fletcher, "Forster's Self-Erasure"; Booth, "Maurice"). I argue here that it is as central to Forster's depiction of Maurice's and Alec's homosexuality as Symonds's and Carpenter's Whitmanian vision, the two being part and parcel with one another.

Part 4 explores the conflict in novels between foregrounding images of homosexual masculinity and "queer" images which dates from this period, largely in response to the Oscar Wilde trials in 1895, and which is common to both cultural contexts. *Der Tod in Venedig* demonstrates that some writers in Europe were willing to consider the affirmative aspects of Wilde's legacy (another of these writers was André Gide), whereas *Der Puppenjunge* shows that other writers wanted to distinguish themselves from the effeminate Wildean stereotype. Novels in English are less nuanced, reacting, to varying degrees, against this model. They foreground masculine homosexuality and offer their homosexual readers images in contrast to the prevailing stereotypes.

Chapter 6 considers the responses in English-language fiction to Oscar Wilde in the wake of his "queer moment," his trials for acts of gross indecency, which assisted, according to Alan Sinfield's *The Wilde Century* (1994), the effeminate model of homosexuality to cohere. The English novels, on the whole, react to the Wildean homosexual model by foregrounding masculine images of homosexual identity. The more unalloyed of these is found in Prime-Stevenson's *Imre*. In Oswald's discourse on homosexual history, he argues that "the Race-Homosexual" is judged by the "Normalists" for its "countless ignoble, trivial, loathsome, feeble-souled and feeble-bodied creatures" (86). They are the most visible, and thus the stereotype is modeled upon them; however, the vast majority of homosexual men are perfectly "normal," and many are even exceptionally manly, they are "the extreme of the male," "its supreme phase, its outermost phalanx" (86). More subtle in its depiction of homosexual masculinity is Forster's novel. In contrast to *Imre*, where the Wildean figure is rejected and despised, in *Maurice* the representative of Wildean homosexuality, Risley, is an important, although minor, character. He is the "child of light" who helps Maurice along his way toward forging an authentic homosexual identity (see Summers, *E. M. Forster* 148; Summers, *Gay Fictions* 88).

In Germany, in the early decades of the twentieth century, Oscar Wilde's writings experienced a literary rebirth. As a result, as Yvonne Ivory, Wolfgang Popp, and Robert Vilain argue in their respective studies of Wilde's influence in Germany, his impact on German writers, especially homosexual ones, was profound. Chapter 7 explores the ways in which this influence is manifest in the two works of German fiction. Mann's novella is an ambivalent exploration of dandy-aestheticism as rebellion, one which pits against each other what *Der Tod in Venedig* characterizes as the masculine and feminine impulses in artistic creation. The reader might expect Mackay's fiction to be friendly to Wilde's legacy for no other reason than for the apparent debt he owes Wilde for his designation of same-sex love as "the nameless love" ("die namenlose Liebe"). And his novel does indeed attest to the importance of the Wilde scandal in formulating homosexual stereotypes in Germany. And yet, the effeminate model of homosexuality associated with Wilde is repudiated in *Der Puppenjunge*. When narration is distanced, the depiction of effeminate minor characters is neutral, but when the narrator's and Hermann Graff's perceptions merge, effeminate figures seem threatening.

This was the time when "the Love that dare not speak its name" began not merely to dare, but to demand to speak its name. It was the period during which the gay novel emerged. The four works of fiction which I examine here demonstrate that reaching an audience could pose a challenge to speaking about this love. *Imre: A Memorandum* was published privately and under a pseudonym, whereas *Maurice* remained unpublished until 1971. *Der Tod in Venedig* escaped censure, from mainstream critics at least, on account of its ambivalence, and *Der Puppenjunge* appeared during the interwar years when a whole continent of gay and lesbian writings briefly opened, but none of his nameless love books carried the author's name until after his death (Kennedy, *The Anarchist of Love* 22). These four works extended discursive limits and broadened the images and motifs with and through which to discuss and depict love and desire between men. Despite setbacks, the effects of this groundbreaking work would be felt by later writers as well as readers. The gay novel has changed much since the beginning of the last century and has gone through many transformations, from post-Second World War protest novels, to pulp fiction of the 50s and 60s, to the liberation of the 70s and beyond. Indeed, so too have the discourses of male same-sex desire which this study examines. And yet both the gay novel and the discourses are still with us.

Part 1

Religion and Law

Chapter 1

Sin and Crime

When, as a teenage boy during the First World War, the author Beverley Nichols (1898–1983) was found reading Oscar Wilde's *The Picture of Dorian Gray* by his father, it was as if he had been "caught in an illicit act": his father "spat on the book and tore the pages with his teeth. 'Oscar Wilde! To think that my son . . .' Beverley protested that he did not know what Wilde had done" (Connon, *Beverley Nichols* 40). Nichols's biographer questions whether this innocence was feigned, considering the fact that Nichols knew to hide the book and to read it in his bedroom with the door locked. Nonetheless, the admission abated his father's rage. The next morning at breakfast, by way of explanation, he handed his son "a sheet of paper on which he had written, 'ILLUM CRIMEN HORRIBILE QUOD NON NOMINANDUM EST,' which Beverley translated as '*The horrible crime which is not to be named.*' 'That,' said [his father], 'is what the man did'" (Connon, *Beverley Nichols* 40). Nichols's father's (over)reaction to witnessing his son reading *Dorian Gray* is indicative of the currency Wilde held in Britain as a byword for homosexuality in the decades after his conviction for acts of "gross indecency" with other men in 1895 and his death in 1900. And yet this is an association of which young Nichols is seemingly unaware, and so his father must fall back on another naming structure, possibly the only other nomenclature that was available to him, that of religio-legal discourse. Wilde was guilty of the "crime" so horrible that it "is not to be named." He could have also said "sin," as for many at this time the two concepts were synonymous and interchangeable. In contrast to French fiction of the era that fictionalized male-male passions, for instance Rachilde's *Les hors nature* (1897) or André Gide's *L'immoraliste* (*The Immoralist*, 1901), which were written and published in a country where male same-sex acts had not been criminalized since the Revolution (Sibalis, "Male Homosexuality" 117–18), the four works of fiction under scrutiny in this study were produced in countries where such expressions of desire were both condemned by moral-religious authorities and persecuted by temporal ones.

This chapter is in a way an extension of the introduction in that it lays a foundation for the analyses of the literary texts which follow in the three subsequent sections. This chapter considers how same-sex acts came to be known as an "unnatural" crime/sin so horrible that it could not be named among Christians, scrutinizing the formation of what I describe as the societies' "default" discourses: religious and legal conceptions of sin and crime. It first surveys research into the development of religious attitudes from ancient times to the Middle Ages, then contrasts the development of legal strictures as an outgrowth of these attitudes from the early modern period to the turn of the twentieth century in Britain, Germany, and the United States, and finally investigates the literary responses to religio-legal discourse, in the form of the guilt and shame internalized by the protagonists and in the form of the exile and travel motif which was common to much early gay literature. The exile motif was little more than a coping mechanism for dealing with this shame and guilt, whereas the means for challenging it, directly and indirectly, as well as overcoming it lies in the three counter-discourses, which are examined in chapters 2 through 7.

Punishing "unnatural" Desire

It is generally held as a truism that the Judeo-Christian prohibition against male same-sex passions finds its source in the Bible, but the history of these religious strictures is long and complex. Biblical scholars, especially of the past twenty years, have pointed out that references to sex between men in the Bible are few and far between. "The Bible hardly ever discusses homosexual behavior," writes Richard Hays. "There are perhaps half a dozen brief references to it in all of the scripture. In terms of emphasis, it is a minor concern" (*The Moral Vision* 381). Instances of citations of such "wickedness," occur in Genesis 19.1–9; Leviticus 18.22 and 20.13; Judges 19.1–30; Romans 1.24–27; 1 Corinthians 6.9; 1 Timothy 1.10; and Jude 7 (see Rogers, *Jesus, the Bible, and Homosexuality* 66). Of these, the tale of the men of Sodom (Genesis 19.1–9), the Levitical prohibitions, and the pronouncements of Saint Paul (Romans 1.24–27) seem to possess the greatest cultural resonance. In the King James Version, Leviticus 18.22 states: "Thou shalt not lie with mankind, as with womankind: it is abomination." Leviticus 20.13 adds: "If a man also lie with mankind, as he lieth with a woman, both of them have committed an abomination: they shall surely be put to death; their blood shall be upon them." Paul warns against acts that are "against nature" (Romans 1.26): "the men, leaving the natural use of the woman, burned in their lust one toward another; men with men working that which is unseemly, and receiving in themselves that recompence of their error which was meet" (1.27). These sinners, concludes Paul, "are worthy of death" (1.32). The notion that intercourse between men warrants capital punishment derives chiefly from these passages. For Oscar Wilde in 1895, the death penalty was not an option as it had been abolished in England in 1861. Not able to invoke the Levitical mandate that he "be put to death," Justice Alfred Wills handed down "the severest sentence that the law allows," two years in prison with hard labor, which he considered to be "totally inadequate for a case such as this" (Hyde, *The Trials of Oscar Wilde* 272). But why had this abomination, over numerous others listed, become such a site of sexual anxiety?

Robert Allen in *The Classical Origins of Modern Homophobia* (2006) and Theodore Jennings in *Plato or Paul?* (2009) suggest that Western opprobrium predates Christianity and actually has its origins in ancient Greek philosophy. David Greenberg and Marcia Bystryn argue that Christian attitudes towards love and sex between men were forged at two key historical moments: during late antiquity and in the High Middle Ages. First, "early Christian views of sexuality were formed in the context of a broad trend toward asceticism in the Hellenistic and late Roman empire" (Greenberg and Bystryn, "Christian Intolerance of Homosexuality" 517). Thus, Christian intolerance of homosexual acts "reflected a broader rejection of all sexual experiences not intended to lead to procreation within marriage" (Greenberg and Bystryn 526). The Levitical prohibitions gained widespread authority when Roman law adopted the biblical strictures after Christianity became the state religion (Crompton, *Homosexuality & Civilisation* 34). Yet, after the fall of the Roman Empire, most temporal authorities are mute on the subject of sex crimes, which was a domain left to a large extent exclusively to the medieval church (Greenberg and Bystryn 530). The second historical moment which shaped religious attitudes towards homosexuality, reestablishing the boundaries between sanctioned and unsanctioned sexuality, was the Gregorian reforms of the High Middle Ages. "Ecclesiastical denunciations of homosexuality began to reappear in the 11th century, with homosexuality among the clergy becoming a target of persistent criticism" (Greenberg and Bystryn 533). The theologian and reformer Peter Damian of Ravenna (ca. 1007–1072) first used the term "sodomia" in his *Liber Gomorrhianus* (*Books of Gomorrah*, ca. 1050) essentially inventing "sodomy" as a concept "for categorizing—that is, for uniting and reifying, for judging and punishing—genital acts between members of the same sex" (Jordan, *The Invention of Sodomy* 43). Damian defined sodomy as anal intercourse and identified this act as one that "surpasses all others in uncleanness," which causes the "death of the body, the destruction of the soul," and "opens the doors of hell and closes the gates of heaven" (qtd. in Boswell, *Christianity, Social Tolerance, and Homosexuality* 211). The definitive canonical statement on sodomy was made by Thomas Aquinas (1225–1274) in his *Summa theologiae* (ca. 1265): same-sex acts are associated with heresy and are construed as "against nature" because, like bestiality, oral sex, and masturbation, procreation is not the aim (Boswell 318). "By the end of the 13th century," conclude Greenberg and Bystryn, "the major elements in the Christian response toward homosexuality had been created. Scholastic theology had reconstructed sodomy as a sin against nature, far worse than other sexual sins" (542). Ecclesiastical bodies were formed to prosecute persons suspected of this sin at the same time that secular authorities were keen to begin wielding their power in this domain (542). The transition of power in regard to punishing "unnatural" sexuality from church to state in Western Europe is a multifaceted history. The sections below outline key developments in this history in Great Britain, Germany, and the United States of America in order to highlight and offer explanations for the similarities and differences in terms of moral and legal standards between these countries during the late nineteenth and early twentieth centuries.

Britain: From "sodomy" to "gross indecency"

"Buggery" was first brought under the scope of temporal jurisdiction by the Buggery Act of 1533 after England's break from the Roman Catholic Church during the reign of Henry VIII. "Forasmuch as there is not yet sufficient and condigne punishment appointed and limited by the due course of the laws of the Realm for the detestable and abominable vice of buggery committed with mankind or beast; . . . it may be enacted . . . that the same offence be from henceforth adjudged felony, and such order and form of process therein to be used against the offenders as in cases of felony at the common law" (qtd. in Moran, *The Homosexual(ity) of Law* 22). The new law indicates a shift in power, but not a radical reconceptualization of the offence. Jeffrey Weeks writes that the act adopted the same criteria as the church: "all acts of sodomy were equally condemned as being 'against nature,' whether between man and woman, man and beast, or man and man" (*Coming Out* 12). Byrne Fone notes that "The 1533 law secularized both the crime and the punishment"; as for felons, the punishment for sodomites was hanging and the seizure of their property (*Homophobia* 216). Early modern "sodomy" though, writes Alan Bray, differed to modern homosexuality in that it "covered more hazily a whole range of sexual acts, of which sexual acts between people of the same sex were only a part" ("Homosexuality and the Signs of Male Friendship" 41). He points out, moreover, that "it was not only a sexual crime" but "also a political and a religious crime" (41), which explains "the ubiquitous association of sodomy with treason and heresy" in Renaissance sources (42). Seventeenth-century records of arrest and conviction for "sodomy" and "buggery" highlight this fact. The Old Bailey, London's central criminal court, has recently digitized its court proceedings from 1674 to 1913, and a search of the archives for "Sodomy" from the list of "Sexual Offences" between 1674 and 1700 will bring up four cases. Only one of these, though, involves intercourse between men: "Mustapha Pochowachett a Turk, was Tried for committing the most Unnatural and Horrid Sin of Buggery, which is so detestable, and not fit to be named among Christians; which he did on the 11th of this Instant May, upon the Body of one Anthony Bassa, Dutch Boy, of the age of 14 years" ("Mustapha Pochowachett"). The others involve a woman who "did commit Buggery with a certain Mungril Dog," a man who was arrested "for Buggery of a Mare," and Thomas Davis who was indicted for an act of "Assault upon one Charity Parrot, Spinster" ("Mungril Dog"; "Buggery of a Mare"; "Thomas Davis").

Same-sex desire was, like all sins, a potential for any individual. John Dennis's *The Usefulness of the Stage* (1698) identifies sodomy as one of the "four reigning vices" in England along with "the love of women," drinking, and gambling (qtd. in Naphy, *Born to Be Gay* 151). William Naphy notes that it was believed that "some people had 'appetites' that incline them to one sex or another," yet "'giving oneself over' to these appetites was largely a matter of the will and habit" (Naphy 149). Despite the fierce legal and religious condemnation directed at sexual acts between men during this period, many historians agree that a certain degree of tolerance toward same-sex love and the sexual act existed. Randolph Trumbach considers this tolerance more or less universal during the early modern period, citing the scant occurrences of charges being brought against perpetrators (Trumbach, "Renaissance Sodomy" 45). When Mary I ascended the throne, she repealed her father's buggery act, but Elizabeth I reenacted the law in 1563. Most of the few cases that were brought to court in the century and a half after this seem to have been cases of rape against prepubescent boys (Trumbach 50). Rictor Norton concurs, stating that "Laws against homosexuality have never been enforced with full vigour systematically in any country: prosecution always proceeds by fits and starts" (Norton, *The Myth of the Modern Homosexual* 140).

The nineteenth century was an era during which persecution dramatically increased. There was a "widespread conservative reaction across Europe," writes Naphy, which he identifies as a response to the French Revolution and the Napoleonic Wars (Naphy 235–36). Especially sexual vice was targeted by moral crusaders, as H. G. Cocks argues, never "before in the history of Britain had so many men been arrested, convicted, imprisoned, pilloried, and even executed for homosexual offences" (Cocks, "Secrets, Crimes, and Diseases" 107). Charles Upchurch writes that the early decades of the nineteenth century saw a rise in surveillance and a "new uniformity of the police presence," which brought with it a "greater frequency of arrests" and inspired "self-policing" on the part of homosexual men (Upchurch, *Before Wilde* 15). Searching the digital records of the Old Bailey attests to this. From 1674 to 1913 there were 1072 total cases involving sodomy and 96 involving "assault with sodomitical intent." There were, as stated above, four cases of sodomy from 1674 to 1700 with no cases of sodomitical assault. This rose markedly in the eighteenth century to 56 cases of sodomy and 30 cases of sodomitical assault. And the numbers surged between 1801 and 1900, with 668 cases of sodomy and 61 cases of assault with sodomitical intent tried at the Old Bailey alone. The dramatic upswing in uses of the anti-sodomy law is contrasted to the abolition of the death penalty in England for this crime in 1861, but it still carried with it fines, prison sentences, and the pillory.

The prohibition against same-sex acts between men was reinscribed in English law with Section XI of the Criminal Law Amendment Act of 1885. The amendment originally had nothing to do with sex between men but was intended to control brothels by increasing the age of consent for girls from thirteen to sixteen. A section was introduced by Henry Labouchère which reads: "Any male person who, in public or private, commits, or is a party to the commission of, or procures, or attempts to procure the commission by any male person of, any act of gross indecency shall be guilty of a misdemeanour, and being convicted shall be liable at the discretion of the Court to be imprisoned for any term not exceeding two years, with or without hard labour" ("The Criminal Law Amendment Act of 1885" 335). The origins and intention of this piece of legislation, known as the Labouchère Amendment, writes Lesley Hall, "are profoundly obscure and have resisted the attempts of historians to elucidate" (Hall, "Sexual Cultures in Britain" 41). The MP's "aim in proposing the amendment remains unclear," argues Morris Kaplan, who cites Frank Harris, a contemporary journalist, who later suggested that "it was an effort to sabotage the entire bill." Nevertheless, the amendment was added to the act without debate and became law (Kaplan, *Sodom on the Thames* 175). Jeffrey Weeks asserts that the result of the new law was a sharpening of the division between legitimate and illegitimate forms of sexual relations. "Homosexuality was seen as posing a threat to stable sexual relations within the bourgeois family, which was increasingly regarded as an essential buttress to social stability" (Weeks, *Making Sexual History* 25). His interpretation, though, rests upon the assumption that this law made *all* homosexual acts illegal for the first time, whereas before this was the case only for instances where proof of anal intercourse could be established. Norton refutes this oft repeated assertion on the part of some historians. "Before 1885 most of the men prosecuted under the antigay law were convicted of 'attempted sodomy,' a misdemeanour covering behaviour such as oral intercourse, mutual masturbation, frottage, groping, and soliciting" (Norton 141). The phrase "in public or in private" contained in the amendment, argues Norton, did not dramatically expand the remit of the law. On the contrary, "it was always the case that sex between men in private was a criminal offence." The only change, he asserts, is the amendment's term "gross indecency," which is merely a nineteenth-century reworking of the phrase "attempted sodomy" (141). Matt Cook, as well, suggests that the new amendment was in fact a less decisive shift in anti-sodomy laws than Weeks and Ed Cohen suggest in their respective studies (Cook, *London and the Culture of Homosexuality* 42–43; Cohen, *Talk on the Wilde Side* 91–93, 118–19).

The 1885 law, since it did not actually increase the scope of anti-sodomy laws, seems to have actually reduced the penalty for sex between men. The draconian measure of capital punishment for this crime, which was in place at the beginning of the century, eventually gave way to a maximum sentence of two years with hard labor. But for the upswing in conviction, blackmail, and the threat of social ostracism, the Labouchère amendment would appear to be a modest liberalization of the law. In reality, this signals a shift in the practices of policing sex crimes, argues Charles Upchurch, "from a system reliant on relatively rare but brutal displays of punishment on the offender's body to one that sought to reform behavior through a system of observation and regulation." Critical to this shift is a movement away from the public use of the death penalty towards more frequent and consistent enforcement of lesser sentences (Upchurch 7). The first conviction of "gross indecency" at the Old Bailey was that of Edgar Miller on 3 May 1886, who received nine months' hard labor. Between this first case and Oscar Wilde's conviction on 20 May 1895, there were 94 convictions of gross indecency at the Old Bailey ("Edgar Miller"). Apart from the Wilde trials, the highest-profile early application of the law was the Cleveland Street Scandal (1889), with the conviction of two working-class male prostitutes who operated out of the brothel in Cleveland Street near London's West End (Kaplan 168–70; see also Lewis et al., *The Cleveland Street Affair*; Hyde, *The Cleveland Street Scandal*).

Germany: Movements and Setbacks

Until Article 116 of the *Constitutio Criminalis Carolina* (the first criminal code of the Holy Roman Empire), the cities and states within the Holy Roman Empire of the German Nation had no sodomy laws; however, in the late Middle Ages in the bustling and well-urbanized regions that now make up southern Germany and Switzerland, many law courts operated from the assumption that penal codes of the Roman Empire were still in effect (Puff, *Sodomy in Reformation Germany and Switzerland* 27). For the entire German Reich, Emperor Charles V brought sexual decency under temporal jurisdiction in 1532, one year before Henry VIII issued his decree. The *Constitutio Criminalis Carolina* criminalized sodomitical acts ("Sodomiterei") as "against nature" ("wider die Natur") which was punishable by death (Hull, *Sexuality, State, and Civil Society in Germany* 64). "If anyone commits impurity with a beast, or man with a man, or a woman with a woman, they have forfeited their lives and shall after the common custom, be sentenced to death by burning" (qtd. in Puff 29) ("so eyn mensch mit eynem vihe, mann mit mann, weib mit weib, vnkeusch treiben, die haben auch das leben verwürckt, vnd man soll sie der gemeynen gewonheyt nach mit dem fewer vom leben zum todt richten"; Kaufmann, *Die peinliche Gerichtsordnung Kaiser Karls V.* 81). Although this law persisted into the eighteenth century, the decentralized nature of the German Nation, until 1871 with the establishment of the Kaiserreich, meant that regional variations with regard to enforcement and the scope of the law varied greatly. Helmut Puff writes that as "Cohesion between regions different in language, economic output, and level of urbanization was low" (19) and because "the *Constitutio Criminalis Carolina* was subsidiary to customary and local law, it took many principalities and territories more than a century to implement the code" (30; see also Hull 58). The disparity between regions also had an effect on the understanding of what acts constituted sodomy. Maria Boes points out that the definition of "unchastity" or "impurity" ("vnkeusch") could be elastic depending on the time period or location within the Holy Roman Empire. Sodomy could be as broadly conceptualized as to include all nonprocreative sexual acts or even sex between Christians and non-Christians (Boes, "On Trial in Early Modern Germany" 29).

The Enlightenment ideals which pushed for the decriminalization of religious offenses, such as witchcraft, blasphemy, heresy, and sodomy, became reality in France with the Revolutionary criminal code of 1791, which was then confirmed in the Napoleonic Penal Code of 1810 (Sibalis, "Male Homosexuality in the Age of Enlightenment and Revolution" 117–18). Those countries under France's direct sway at this time followed suit by adopting similar penal reforms. The southern German kingdom of Bavaria abolished its anti-sodomy law in 1813, setting a prescient for the German states of Württemberg (in 1839), Braunschweig, and Hannover (both in 1840) to follow. Reform came to the hegemonic powers of Austria and Prussia, but was not quite as sweeping as elsewhere. Austria abolished the death penalty for same-sex acts in 1787, making it one of the first European nations to do so

(Stümke, *Homosexuelle in Deutschland* 11; Eder, "Sexual Cultures in Germany and Austria" 156). In the penal code established in 1803, male as well as female same-sex acts were punished with prison sentences. In the ascendant northern German powerhouse, Prussia, only sex between men was penalized. The death penalty was repealed in 1794 and the "1851 revision of the Prussian penal law defined same-sex acts as only a minor offence, nevertheless imposing prison from six months to four years" (Eder 156; see also Mosse, *The Image of Man* 27–28). As the driving force behind German unification, Prussia asserted its dominance over its neighbors, and extending its anti-sodomy laws was one facet of this. In 1869, the Prussian anti-sodomy law, §143, became law for the entire North German Confederation (*Norddeutscher Bund*) as §152. This was a huge step backward, for example, for the kingdom of Hannover, which had not penalized homosexual acts for nearly three decades. Prussian dominance became absolute when the German Empire was proclaimed at Versailles in January 1871 following the Franco-Prussian War (1870), and §152 was adopted for the entire Reich as the notorious Paragraph 175 (Steakley, *The Homosexual Emancipation Movement in Germany* 21; Stümke 21–23; Sibalis 119). The statute, which for the first time unified German legal attitudes toward same-sex acts, reads: "An unnatural sex act committed between persons of the male sex or by humans with animals is punishable by imprisonment; the loss of civil rights may also be imposed" (qtd. in Grau, *Hidden Holocaust?* 65) ("Die widernatürliche Unzucht, welche zwischen Personen männlichen Geschlechts oder von Menschen mit Tieren begangen wird, ist mit Gefängniß zu bestrafen; auch kann auf Verlust der bürgerlichen Ehrenrechte erkannt werden"; qtd. in Stümke 21). 1871 marked the end of an era, writes Hans-George Stümke, for those German states which for an entire generation had not criminalized homosexuality (23).

Germany holds the special distinction of being the first country to produce an organized homosexual liberation movement. Robert Beachy argues that "the criminalization of male same-sex eroticism and the inclusion of the Prussian anti-sodomy statute as Paragraph 175 in the new German Imperial Criminal Code after 1871" was one of the "four broad vectors of German history" which gave rise to the "invention" of homosexuality (Beachy, "The German Invention of Homosexuality" 804). In contrast to France, where male-male sex acts were not illegal and as a consequence were less often the subject of public debate, in Germany the situation was reversed. Sexology, in particular the liberationist variety, was key in the development of modern homosexuality and "served as an example, sparking homosexual rights activism elsewhere in Europe" (Beachy 836). On 14 May 1897, Magnus Hirschfeld, a physician and sexologist, led the founding of the Scientific-Humanitarian Committee (Wissenschaftlich-humanitäres Komitee, or WhK). James Steakley writes that "The Committee's goal was first and foremost legal reform" (*The Homosexual Emancipation Movement in Germany* 30), so they prepared and circulated "a three-page petition which outlined the scientific and humanitarian reasons for amending Paragraph 175 so that homosexual acts would be punishable only in cases involving coercion, public annoyance, or adult minor relations," which was brought before the Reichstag in December 1897 (Steakley 30; Wolff, *Magnus Hirschfeld* 43). This first, ultimately unsuccessful, petition bore 900 signatures of scientists, lawyers, and highly placed civil servants, and by 1914, Hirschfeld and his followers had collected the names of more than 3000 doctors, 750 university professors, and numerous public figures, among whom were Gerhart Hauptmann, Heinrich and Thomas Mann, Frank Wedekind, and Rainer Maria Rilke (Steakley 31; Wolff 43; see also Mancini, *Magnus Hirschfeld* 87–132). Manfred Herzer argues though that legal reform was merely part of the committee's overall goal, which was the "liberation of homosexuals." Herzer points out that "This rather abstract formulation, in essence a slogan, implied far more than the repeal of a particular law targeting homosexual men. Rather, liberation meant 'elimination of the existing prejudices among the people.' To back up this point, Hirschfeld pointed to his own 'observations in France, Italy, Holland, and other countries, where prejudices continue to exist almost unchanged' despite the repeal or at least reform of anti-sodomy statutes in those countries" ("Communists, Social Democrats, and the Homosexual Movement" 201). The committee faced its first major setback in the Harden-Eulenburg Affair (1907–1909). Hirschfeld, who testified as an expert witness on homosexuality, confirmed that one of the officials, Lieutenant General Kuno Count von Moltke, was indeed homosexual. His strategy had been to win support for his cause by asserting that homosexuality was widespread and existed at every level of society; but his plan backfired, and the financial resources of the WhK almost evaporated as supporters feared exposure and resultant ostracism (Steakley 38–40; see also Wolff 68–87).

In the aftermath of the First World War, the relative liberality of the Weimar Republic, which took the form of freedom of opinion, press, and assembly, led to an outpouring of homosexual writings and publications as well as an increase in the number of organizations and meeting places. This era gave the WhK greater maneuverability in its reform efforts. In the area of educating the public, efforts took many forms, including the new mass medium of film (Eder 158). Richard Oswald's *Anders als die Andern* (*Different from the Others*, 1919) is not only, as James Steakley argues, "the first feature film with an explicitly homosexual theme made anywhere in the world" ("Cinema and Censorship in the Weimar Republic" 181), but also a unique filmic example of an effort at seeking tolerance from the mainstream public and rallying homosexual individuals to the cause of emancipation and legal reform (see also Dyer, *Now You See It* 25–42). Hirschfeld, who appeared in the film and served Oswald in the role of "scientific-medical advisor," considered his collaboration on the project the logical continuation of his prewar activism: "as Hirschfeld himself pointed out in introductory remarks at the film's premiere, his cinematic role was by no means markedly different from the sort of education work he had been engaged in for decades" (Steakley, "Cinema and Censorship in the Weimar Republic" 184). In the film, Paul Körner, played by Conrad Veidt (who would become one of Germany's leading actors), is a famous violinist who is blackmailed for his homosexuality. Denounced to the police, his career and reputation destroyed, he commits suicide. Hirschfeld is the understanding physician who saves the protagonist's friend and protégé, Kurt Sivers (played by Fritz Schulz), from following him into death and encourages him to become active in the reform movement. "The film thus closes not with a double suicide but with a clarion call to redeem Körner's death by political activism" (Steakley, "Cinema and Censorship in the Weimar Republic" 187). The first showing took place in Berlin at the Richard Oswald Film Theater, near the Kurfürstendamm, on 24 May 1919. The film was, writes Charlotte Wolff, a "bombshell" (*Magnus Hirschfeld* 191), one which set off a debate about indecency in film. Steakley writes that censors decided on 16 October 1920 that the film offended "public order and security" and was therefore banned to general audiences, but could be shown to medical professionals in training contexts ("Cinema and Censorship in the Weimar Republic" 192). This and other initiatives led by the WhK nearly bore fruit, culminating in a bill that would have legalized homosexual acts between consenting adults in private, which was approved by committee in the Reichstag on 16 October 1929. A full vote before the entire parliament seemed within grasp until the Wall Street stock market crash caused the bill to be tabled and never to be taken up again (Steakley, *The Homosexual Emancipation Movement in Germany* 85).

The Old Sin in the New World

When European explorers and colonists arrived in North America, what they found among the peoples of the New World, write John D'Emilio and Estelle Freedman, were "Native American sexual customs [that] varied widely" from tribe to tribe and that above all "differed from their own" (*Intimate Matters* 6–7). The earliest records of same-sex activities among indigenous Americans come from Spanish and Portuguese conquistadores. These accounts are very often of questionable reliability, writes Brett Genny Beemyn, as "European observers sometimes characterized other cultures as engaging in sodomy and other 'vices' in order to portray themselves as superior and to justify colonial expansion" ("The Americas" 145). Nevertheless, a great deal of research has been devoted to Native American sexualities, especially the gender/sexual identity *berdache* (see Archer and Lloyd, *Sex and Gender* 103–05). White settlers brought their sexual mores with them, and consequently the thirteen British colonies that would at the end of the eighteenth century free themselves from the rule of mother England all established laws against "sodomy, buggery, or 'the crime against nature'" (see Eskridge, *Dishonorable Passions* 16). As in Britain as well as in Germany, during the early modern period, "sodomy" was "an elastic and dynamic concept" which encompassed various prohibited sexual acts (Eskridge 16; see also D'Emilio and Freedman 30). The laws that the colonies established were essentially extensions of English law, which called for the execution of those found guilty. "The seventeenth-century American colonies adopted a variety of approaches to sexual transgression," writes William Eskridge, "all harsh in theory but less so in practice" (17). For instance, in Virginia's 1610 code, sodomy was a capital offence like rape and adultery: "Men outnumbered women on the colony by a ratio of three to one; the Virginia Company periodically disciplined the randy young men for behavior that upset the public order" (Eskridge 17). However, after the mid-seventeenth century, sex crimes including sodomy were less stringently enforced. The situation was similar in other middle and southern colonies; the hazily defined crime of sodomy called for the death penalty, but, writes Eskridge, it was rarely enforced (17). The situation was slightly different in Pennsylvania, where sodomy was not a capital offense until 1718. Under Penn's "Great Law" of 1682, only murder warranted the death penalty. The punishment for sodomy and bestiality was "property forfeiture, public whipping, and six months at hard labor for the first offense and life in prison for the second"; there are, though, no recorded convictions for sodomy in colonial Pennsylvania (Eskridge 17).

Whereas in the middle and southern colonies sodomy laws sought to maintain public order, the laws in theocratic New England reflected the leaders' concerns over the maintenance of the moral purity of their communities (Eskridge 17–18; see also Oaks, "Defining Sodomy in Seventeenth-Century Massachusetts" 79–83). If the Puritans thought they could flee the "sodomitical" practices that infested the Old World, they soon learned that they were sorely wrong. Despite "severity in punishment" for "sundry notorious sins," writes Governor William Bradford in his history *Of Plymouth Plantation* (written between 1630 and 1651), in 1642 "even sodomy and buggery (things fearful to name) have broke forth in this land oftener than once" (qtd. in Katz, *Gay American History* 20–21). "Upon the examination of this person and also of a former that he had made some sodomitical attempts upon another, it being demanded of them how they came first to the knowledge and practice of such wickedness, the one confessed he had long used it in old England; and this youth last spoke of said he was taught it by another that had heard of such things from some in England when he was there" (qtd. in Katz 21–22). And yet, the Pilgrims were themselves aware that there was no escaping the sinfulness of human nature. The New England minister Thomas Shepard, in his *The Sincere Convert* (1641), demonstrates the linkages that existed in the Puritan mind between homosexual acts and other sins/crimes: "Thy heart is a foul sink of atheism, sodomy, blasphemy, murder, whoredom, adultery, buggery. . . . Although they break not out into thy life, they lie lurking in thy heart" (qtd. in Bray 40–41). It would not be until the end of the eighteenth century that there was a refining of what acts constituted sodomy, and so by the nineteenth century "sodomy" came to be understood as anal intercourse, between man and animal, man and woman, or man with man or boy (Eskridge 19–20). Although Eskridge identifies the seventeenth century as "the high point for the expansive interpretation and aggressive enforcement of sodomy and other sexual morality laws in America" (19), there were altogether fewer than ten executions for sodomy and almost all of these were instances of rape or bestiality (18). In the eighteenth century, even in puritanical New England, "there was less-aggressive monitoring of people's private activities by church and state," which meant that for the whole of the century there were "virtually no executions for sodomy" (19). D'Emilio and Freedman concur, but they add that other forms of chastisement were meted out, including seizure of property, "severe and repeated whipping, burning with a hot iron, or banishment"

(30). Beemyn points out that there was one known execution for sodomy in the British North American colonies during the eighteenth century, which "occurred in 1743 and involved an unnamed Irish doctor in Fort Frederica, Georgia. It was also the last use of the death penalty for sodomy in what became the United States" (152). After the revolution sodomy remained a criminal offense, but all of the original thirteen states repealed the death penalty for this crime (Eskridge 19).

In the nineteenth century, in most states, sodomy belonged to "crimes against public morals and decency" (21); an exception, though, was New York, which had a narrower definition of sodomy than most others. There it counted amongst "crimes against the person," which, Eskridge writes, "suggests that sodomy laws filled a regulatory gap as regards what we would today consider nonconsensual sex" (20). The testimony in such cases of a willing "accomplice" was inadmissible. Therefore, writes Eskridge, "In practice, police rarely enforced sodomy laws against anyone before 1880" (21). From the late eighteenth to the late nineteenth century, only twenty sodomy cases were prosecuted in New York (22). In the early and mid-nineteenth century, convictions of sodomy were uncommon anywhere in the United States. However, in the final decades of this century, as American society underwent radical change, the number of convictions of sex between men greatly increased. The 1880 Census records that 63 persons were incarcerated for "crimes against nature"; only five of these were in New York (Eskridge 22). In the span of ten years, by the time of the 1890 census, this number had risen to 224, which is, argues Eskridge, "an increase greatly exceeding growth in the general population" (50). Population growth was, though, a contributing factor. Immigration from Europe and urban migration caused the population of New York City to swell: in 1880 the city consisted of 1.9 million residents (Eskridge 22), by 1890 its population had reached over 2.5 million, and, over the next 30 years, it would surge to over 5.6 million (Eskridge 41). It was a similar story for other major US population centers. "The United States was transforming from a relatively homogenous, rural, farm-based society to an ethnically diverse, urban industrial one" (41). Eskridge writes that "America's population explosion" produced, among other things, "a subculture of Sodom," which, by 1890, "was dominated by self-consciously feminized men who called themselves 'fairies'" (45; see also D'Emilio and Freedman 226–29).

George Chauncey, in *Gay New York* (1994), tells the history of the development in the late nineteenth and early twentieth centuries of "a highly visible, remarkably complex, and continually changing gay male world," in which participants "forged a distinctive culture with its own language and customs, its own traditions and folk histories, its own heroes and heroines" (1). The contemporary observer Charles Gardener, in *The Doctor and the Devil; or, The Midnight Adventures of Dr. Parkhurst* (1894), recounts his visit to one of the sites of New York's male homosexual subculture, the "Golden Rule Pleasure Club": "The basement was fitted up into little rooms, by means of cheap partitions, which ran to the top of the ceiling from the floor. Each room contained a table and a couple of chairs, for the use of customers of the vile den. In each room sat a youth, whose face was painted, eye-brows blackened, and whose airs were those of a young girl. Each person talked in a high falsetto voice, and called the others by women's names" (qtd. in Katz 40). Contemporary commentators identified the European precedent of these New York homosexual subcultures. For instance, Colin Scott, writing in 1896, noted that "Coffee-clatches, where the members dress themselves with aprons, etc., and knit, gossip and crochet; balls, where men adopt the ladies' evening dress are well known in Europe. 'The Fairies' of New York are said to be a similar secret organization" (qtd. in Katz 44). In comparison to their European brethren though, their networks and communities were less established and less visible. Hirschfeld, in his *Die Homosexualität des Mannes und des Weibes* (*The Homosexuality of Men and Women*, 1914), based upon observations he made while traveling in the US in 1893, writes that "Homosexual life in the United States is more hidden to a greater extent than in the United Kingdom. For example, while visiting Philadelphia and Boston, I could hardly perceive any homosexuality, while visitors from those cities later assured me that in these centers of Quakers and Puritans, 'a great deal goes on' in intimate circles" (Hirschfeld, *Homosexuality* 523) ("Noch um einen Grad verstärkter als im United Kingdom spielt sich das homosexuelle Leben in den United States ab. So konnte ich bei einem Besuche von Philadelphia und Boston kaum etwas von Homosexualität wahrnehmen, während mir Besucher aus jenen Städten später versicherten, daß in diesen Zentren der Quäker und Puritaner in intimen Kreisen 'kolossal viel los' sei"; 550). Hirschfeld continues, however, pointing out in America's favor other differences between the US and Britain and Europe, particularly in regard to the publication of sexological research: "more than one manuscript has wandered from England over the Atlantic Ocean, in order to find a publisher and printer in America" (523) ("mehr als ein Manuskript wanderte von England über den Atlantischen Ozean, um in Amerika einen Verleger und Drucker zu finden"; 550). He is likely specifically alluding to John Addington Symonds and Havelock Ellis's *Sexual Inversion*, which, after being deemed indecent in England upon its publication in 1897, was published in Philadelphia (Crozier, "Introduction" 65–67). Legally, as well, the US contrasts favorably to Europe and especially to England. "It is true that so many urnish officers and government officials, for whom the European ground became too hot beneath their feet, so many business people and academics have begun a new life in the new world without the old persons changing, and who are exposed to the same temptations as in their native country directly after they arrive in Central Park in New York" (524) ("Hat doch so mancher urnische Offizier und Beamte, dem der europäische Boden zu heiß unter den Füßen wurde, so mancher Kaufmann und Akademiker in der neuen Welt ein neues Leben begonnen, ohne damit den alten Menschen zu ändern, an dessen Eigenart alsbald nach seiner Landung im Zentralpark von New York dieselbe Versuchung herantrat, wie in der Heimat"; 550).

  The United States that Hirschfeld visited, however, was a nation in the midst of great change. Growth and industrialization produced social upheaval and the nation's first visible same-sex subcultures, with scandals that garnered nationwide attention, like the case of Alice Mitchell (1873–1898) and Freda Ward (1875–1892).

Conservative backlash, a rising tide of neo-Puritanism, was responsible for "a revolutionary expansion of American sodomy law and its enforcement between 1881 and 1921" (Eskridge 50, see also D'Emilio and Freedman 171–221, especially Duggan, *Sapphic Slashers*). In the late nineteenth century, states that had no sodomy laws duly adopted them, and every state admitted to the Union after the Civil War, excepting Wyoming, had sodomy laws on the books. Additionally, writes Eskridge, "Existing sodomy laws were expanded, updated, and enforced more energetically" (49). The Oscar Wilde scandal contributed to this expansion, but, in most cases, "individual state statutes were introduced following local scandals in which the public learned that men were engaging in unnatural practices not covered by the traditional crime-against-nature laws" (51). One way in which these laws were expanded was by including oral sex within the scope of "sodomy," with the immediate result that "the number of sodomy arrests skyrocketed" (Eskridge 53, see table 57). It was this America in flux and its reactionary response through persecution of sex crimes that Edward Prime-Stevenson fled around the turn of the century. Although his viewpoint is clearly different to that of Hirschfeld, continental Europe may have seemed by comparison a far safer haven for "Uranian" men.

"Unnatural" sexuality came officially under the domain of temporal jurisprudence at about the same time in both England and Germany, being assigned the dual moniker of sin and crime. This was an era of great turmoil, as religious, state, and social norms in much of Europe were in numerous ways radically transformed. The anti-sodomy laws in England and Germany are an example of the shift in power from church to state, and in particular demonstrate that in these countries morality and sexual normativity became more and more the responsibility of secular authorities. In Britain, Germany, and the British colonies that would become the United States, the state adopted the definitions and penalties of the church: the range of forbidden sex acts, known as sodomy, was regarded as unnatural and demanded the death of the guilty. Until the end of the nineteenth century, though, this is where the similarities end. The decentralized political nature of the German Nation, until the foundation of the Kaiserreich in 1871, meant that regional legal standards varied more than in England. This political autonomy of the German states also made possible, in the early nineteenth century, movements that called for the abolition of these laws. But this progress was reversed with German unification. After the extension of Prussia's penal code to the entire German Empire, the legal situation pertaining to laws against sex acts between men were, on many significant points, quite similar to those in Britain. The expansion of and rise in enforcement of sodomy laws in the late nineteenth century in the United States reflect similar trends in the other two lands. If there is a commonality between the three nations, with regard to their legal statutes forbidding male same-sex intimacies, it is that nineteenth-century social change brought the rise of homosexual subcultures as well as the conservative response to this rise through increased persecution of male-male sex acts.

Organized emancipation and legal reform efforts began in Germany in earnest decades before Britain or America. And yet the Nazi takeover in January 1933 brought with it a reactionary backlash that effectively silenced the public discourse on sexuality and sexual reform. In the months after the Reichstag Fire, on 27 February 1933, most of the bars known as meeting places for homosexual men and women were closed in all major cities in Germany. Public libraries and bookshops were purged of all writings that were condemned as "indecent" (Grau 26). Although actual reform had come so close in 1929, Paragraph 175 was amended in 1935 to extend the definition of what constituted illegal homosexual acts. The term "unnatural sex act" ("widernatürliche Unzucht") was replaced by the more pliable term "sex offence" ("Unzucht") (Jellonek, *Homosexuelle unter dem Hakenkreuz* 113–14), which meant that "even the snuggling together of two naked male bodies came under this definition," writes Günter Grau (64). After the war, argues Robert Moeller, the "Federal Republic's break with the past was anything but clean" (Moeller, "Sex, Society, and the Law in Postwar West Germany" 427). Police reports indicate that between 1953 and 1965 there were 98,700 violators of Paragraph 175 of which nearly 38,000 were found guilty and sentenced. "The Federal Constitutional Court," writes Moeller, "did not view the expansive discriminatory laws against male homosexuals, introduced by the Nazis in 1935, to embody the abhorrent characteristics of National Socialism. Rather, a new West Germany explicitly endorsed this Nazi legacy as completely consistent with a 'democratic political order'" (428). The situation was considerably more favorable in Socialist East Germany: after 1957 the GDR stopped prosecuting men over the age of eighteen; and, in 1968, with the introduction of a new criminal code, Paragraph 175 was abolished (Beachy, "The German Invention of Homosexuality" 838). The following year the West German Bundestag lifted criminal sanctions against sexual activity between men over the age of twenty-one, but Paragraph 175 was not eliminated from the criminal code until 1994 (Herzer, "Communists, Social Democrats, and the Homosexual Movement in the Weimar Republic" 219; Moeller, "Sex, Society, and the Law in Postwar West Germany" 427; Beachy 838; see also Moeller, "Private Acts, Public Anxieties, and the Fight to Decriminalize Male Homosexuality in West Germany" 539–47).

Legal reform in the postwar era was slow in coming in England too. The scope of British homosexual activism was more modest by comparison, represented in writings such as the sexological studies of Havelock Ellis, particularly his multivolume *Studies in the Psychology of Sex*, and the diverse liberationist output of Edward Carpenter, including *Homogenic Love and its Place in a Free Society* (1894) and *The Intermediate Sex* (1908) (Hall, "Sexual Cultures in Britain" 37–38, 40–41). It was not until the Sexual Offences Act of 1967, ten years after the Wolfenden report made the recommendation, that sex acts between two men were partially decriminalized in England and Wales as long as they were in private and between two consenting partners above the age of twenty-one. Scotland and Northern Ireland lagged even farther behind, extending the provisions of the act in 1980 and 1982, respectively (Weeks, *Sex, Politics and Society* 263; Tatchell *Europe in the Pink* 84). In the United States, the repeal of laws regulating sex between men came to pass state by state during the course of the late twentieth and early twenty-first centuries. Illinois was the first state to decriminalize sex acts between men, doing so in 1961 (Eskridge 393), but other states were not quick in following. For instance, although New York reduced the punishment for sodomy between consenting adults from a felony to a misdemeanor in 1950, it did not repeal the law until 1980 (Eskridge 399). When the Supreme Court ruling in *Lawrence v. Texas* struck down all existing state statutes on 26 June 2003, fourteen states still had laws on the books, and in eight of those it was a felony (Eskridge 297, fig. 9.3, 325–30).

Religion, Law, and Homosexual Exile

The public discourse about homosexuality during the decades leading up to the publication of the works of fiction here under scrutiny was intense, owing to progress made in the field of sexology and in particular to public scandals, including the Cleveland Street Scandal, the Oscar Wilde trials, and the Eulenburg Affair. Writing and publishing fiction treating male-male love sympathetically would have been challenging in such a highly charged political environment. Prime-Stevenson circumvented restrictions at home in the United States by printing *Imre* privately in Naples, Italy, at a book press where the typesetters could not read English (Gifford, *Dayneford's Library* 8). In 1909 the publishers of Mackay's first two books of the nameless love, "Die namenlose Liebe: Ein Bekenntniss" ("The Nameless Love: A Creed") and "Wer sind wir? Eine Dichtung der namenlosen Liebe" ("Who are we? A Poem of the Nameless Love"), was fined 600 Marks for distributing writings deemed indecent by the courts, and consequently in 1913 the first edition of *Die Bücher der namenlosen Liebe* appeared with Paris as its place of publication and a Dutch address for its distributors (Fähnders, "Anarchism and Homosexuality" 144–45). Mann was an eminent author cautious, in particular at this point in his career, of reprisals from the guardians of bourgeois morality (Reed, "The Frustrated Poet" 132–34); he creates an ambivalent treatment of same-sex desire, one that permits divergent readings of the texts: simultaneously celebrating same-sex attraction while vilifying it, allowing the protagonist to free himself of the guilt and shame he associates with his homosexuality but disallowing the fruition of this liberation, and linking this desire to philosophy, beauty, and creativity while also associating it with the abyss, disease, and degeneration. And *Maurice* remained suppressed by Forster, who deemed that the novel was "unpublishable until my death and England's" (Moffat, *Forster* 115). Later in his life, in 1967, he readjusted this assessment, but only marginally. His biographer Wendy Moffat writes: "On the manuscript of *Maurice* he wrote— 'Publishable. But worth it?'" (319). But more than simply standing in the way of publication in the forms of censors and secularized religious strictures embodied in penal code statues and judicial rulings, religious and legal discursive formations are default discourses which are inexorably embedded in all four works of fiction. These discourses may not play a great role explicitly, but they are powerful in the implicit force they wield. One form this takes is in the travel motif. As men who loved men found opportunities to discover and express their sexuality in the role of foreigner—one might say "sex tourist"—in France, Greece, Italy, or North Africa, so too did homosexual fictional characters (Aldrich, *Seduction of the Mediterranean* 101–35; see also Aldrich, *Colonialism and Homosexuality*). For homophile literature of the era, travel and exile were key topoi. The theme recurrent in early gay writings is self-imposed exile, the escape from repression, and travel as the means towards sexual self-discovery and liberation; but, as I state above, without critical engagement with religion and law, travel and exile are little more than a coping mechanism, one only available to a small educated and leisure-class minority of homosexual subjects. Religious and legal discourses are present in the four works of fiction to differing degrees and with varying degrees of force. Of the texts, *Der Puppenjunge* demonstrates the most significant measure of direct engagement with these discursive formations, which are in large part a reflection in his fiction of the author's individual(istic) efforts at homosexual liberation.

His "feet are fixed!" Discovering a New Homeland

The confession is a structuring motif in the narrative of *Imre*. First, in the preface, Oswald and Imre offer their confession to the fictional editor Xavier Mayne (32–33). This preface sets the tone for the two confessions that make up the narrative that follows—first Oswald to Imre (81–103) and later Imre to Oswald (117–26). These are secularized acts of confession, influenced by sexological models of self-narration, as discussed in chapter 5. Religion, although not playing a direct role in the narrative, is still a force to be reckoned with, one which informs the opprobrium against love and desire between men that the central characters have internalized. As Oswald narrates his life story to Imre, he tells him that he had once thought of himself as "that anachronism from old—that incomprehensible incident in God's human creation" (85); this "anachronism" is likely the "sodomite," although the nomenclature of sin never enters the narrative. In turn, when Imre confesses his homosexuality to Oswald later in the narrative, he admits that from boyhood he understood that "a part of himself [ought] to be crushed out, if it could be crushed, because it was base and vile" (119). Again, sin is not explicitly named, but it no doubt informs the moralistic contempt he has internalized from a young age. Legal discourse is manifest more directly in the novel in the form of two minor characters who personify "popular ignorances" and "century-old and century-blind religious and ethical misconceptions" (120). When Oswald is confronted by conventional morality, this attack is not loaded with notions of the Sin of Sodom, but rather phrased in terms of disease and crime.

A mere ten days after visiting a specialist who prescribes marriage as a cure for his homosexuality, Oswald engages himself to "the daughter of a valued family friend," a young woman whom he "had always admired" (93). He breaks off this engagement after he meets and falls in love with another man. Oswald confesses his sexuality and love to this man, who answers his disclosure with scorn.

> He heard my confession through with ever more hostile eyes, with an astonished unsympathy, disgust curling his lips. Then, he spoke, slowly, piti-

lessly: "I have heard that such creatures as you describe yourself are to be found among mankind. I do not know, nor do I care to know, whether they are a sex by themselves, a justified, because helpless, play of Nature; or even a kind of *logically* essential link, a between-step, as you seem to have persuaded yourself. Let all that be as it may be. I am not a man of science nor keen to such new notions! From this moment, you and I are strangers! ... Farewell! If I served you as a man should serve such beings as you, this town should know your story tomorrow! Society needs more policemen than it has, to protect itself from such lepers as you!" (99)

Oswald, according to this character, is not a sinner, rather a "leper"; therefore, medical discourse has replaced religious discourse. He does not, however, insist that Oswald be carted off to an asylum; instead society's traditional mechanism for controlling this indecent form of passion, that is, "policemen," is called for. Imre recounts to Oswald that he has met with a similar figure in Karvaly Miklos, a senior officer for whom he secretly harbored "a fierce, despairing homosexual love" (120). When a conversation in the officers' club turns to the subject of homosexuality owing to a recent scandal, Karvaly tells Imre: "If I found that you cared for another man that way, youngster, I should give you my best revolver, and tell you to put a bullet through your brains within an hour! Why, if I found that you thought of me so, I should brand you in the Officers Casino tonight, and shoot you myself at ten paces tomorrow morning. Men are not to live when they turn beasts. Oh, damn your doctors and scientists! A man's a man, and a woman's a woman!" (121). Karvaly's opinion is telling as a reflection of popular male fear of same-sex desire and acts. It is an infringement upon male honor, and thus the military code dictates that one whose honor is compromised must seek satisfaction or, barring that, commit suicide. Merely possessing this sexual desire compromises male honor, so if Imre were homosexual, he would have "to put a bullet through [his] brains within an hour." Additionally, even being desired by another man is compromising. This may have been a recurrent problem for Karvaly who, Imre describes, "looks so astonishingly like that statue, you know—the one by that Greek—Praxiteles" (42). Thus, Karvaly would challenge Imre to duel with pistols if he discovered that the younger man felt sexual desire for him. In regard to desire between men, the military code of honor is a system of values which is inspired by religious and legal injunctions against "unnatural" vice, "Men are not to live when they turn beasts," but it supersedes these structures as well. Regarding the similarity between the two men whom Oswald and Imre had loved, although they are products of different countries, the former the representative of England and the latter of Austria-Hungary, they share the "true conviction of the dionistic [i.e., heterosexual] temperament" (121) in that they both reject liberal, liberationist science and cling to older, more conservative notions, their societies' default discourses.

The first line of defense that Oswald and Imre have against the attitudes expressed by these characters is the "Mask." "The Mask—the eternal social Mask for the homosexual!—worn before our nearest and dearest, or we are ruined and cast out!'" (101). The mask is a central, organizing trope in the novel. The first part is titled "Masks" (35); the second is "Masks and—a Face" (69); and the third is "Faces—Hearts—Souls" (106)—indicating the gradual laying aside of masks and dissimulation, the progression towards forthrightness, which directs the progression of the plot. Early in the narrative, Oswald notes Imre's "nervous habit of personal reserve" (39) which is so out of place amongst the "demonstrativeness, never unmanly, which is almost as racial to many *Magyarak* as to the Italians and Austrians" (39). His reserve is comparable to that of "the average English gentleman," which is something that Oswald actually admires, "certainly not wishing it less" (59). "Imre might have been an Englishman, if it came to outward signs of his innermost feelings" (61). The physical signs of intimacy between men, common in Hungarian culture, Imre finds "so hideously womanish" (62). His mask conceals "the deeply buried mystery of a heart's uranistic impulses" (64), which he seems to fear will at any moment spring forth and betray him, but he overplays his reserve, he protests too much. "I have had to learn the way to keep myself so, to study it till it is a second nature to me! I am not easy to know! But, Oswald, Oswald, *ich kann nicht anders, nein, nein, ich kann nicht anders*!" (80). After he drops his mask in the third part, he admits that it was after Karvaly had commented inadvertently that men like him should "put a bullet through your brains within an hour" (121) that Imre was worked up "into a sort of panic" and had "sworn to make no intimate friendship again" (121). He adopts an "exaggerated, artificial bearing" which necessitated "shrinking from commonplace social demonstrativeness" (122). Oswald explains to him that "You wore your masks so closely—gave me no inch of ground to come nearer to you, to understand you, to expect anything except scorn" (123).

Religion and law also impact the text in terms of the travel and exile motifs. Oswald relates to Imre that after he had confessed himself to the man he loved, he left England for continental Europe. "I started quietly on a long travel-route on the Continent, under excuse of ill-health. I was far from being a stranger to life in at least half a dozen countries of Europe, east or west. But now, now, I knew that it was to be a refuge, an exile!" (99). Initially, he is a reluctant exile from his former life, but he comes to accept his banishment. Oswald searches for a "new identity" (100); he becomes estranged from his "birth-land": "Little by little, my birth-land, my people, became strange to me. I grew wholly indifferent to them. I turned my back fuller on them, evermore" (100). He also uses this expression, "birth-land," as opposed to "homeland," earlier in the narrative to relate to Britain (37), which seems to indicate the character's sense of detachment and may well be a reflection of Prime-Stevenson's feelings toward America. From Europe, Oswald can pass judgment upon "Anglo-Saxon civilization": "where is still met, at every side, so dense a blending of popular ignorances; of century-old and century-blind religious and ethical misconceptions, of unscientific professional conservatism in psychiatric circles, and of juristic barbarism; all, of course, accompanied with the full measure of British or Yankee social hypocrisy toward the daily actualities of homosexualism" (120).

In this passage the character identifies a triad: religion, law, and medicine—further consideration is granted the third in chapter 5. So difficult is the life of the homosexual man or woman in America and Britain that the nations of Europe, "even those yet hesitant in their social toleration or legal protection of the Uranian," seem by comparison "educative and kindly," characterized by "national common-sense and humanity" (120). That Oswald includes the United States in his invective would suggest that the author is railing against his own "birth-land" as much as his character is against his. Oswald has traveled widely and, especially in this aspect, shares commonality with the fin-de-siècle "invert" discussed by Yvonne Ivory. "The invert is a figure that is literally mobile, who moves unnoticed from culture to culture and finds like kind in foreign cities" ("The Urning and His Own" 339). Many of these detached and rootless homosexual subjects drew upon discourses of individualism and superiority to establish identities which "counteracted many of the prevailing prejudices of the medico-juridical system" (Ivory 346). Ivory argues, "For the turn-of-the-century European invert, under pressure to self-identify as a criminal type, there is no more comforting thought than that laws are the contrivances of a despotic state, that duty is not an eternal truth, that obedience to oneself is superior to obedience to a system" (339). Oswald's mobility as well as the "Uranian" superiority he cultivates for his identity (which is explored in chapter 3) have distinct affinities with the invert Ivory describes. But *Imre* presents important variations on the travel and exile motif of early twentieth-century homosexual writings.

The destination of Oswald's travel, Hungary, contrasts to other works where France, Greece, Italy, and North Africa are recurrent locales. In contrast to the usual haunts, in Austria-Hungary homosexual sex was illegal. Budapest might not have been a haven and destination for homosexual men in the same way that at this time Venice and Capri were. An encounter early in the narrative between Imre and a former captain of his regiment suggests this. The man, whom Oswald describes as "a man of perhaps forty years, with the unmistakable suggestion of a soldier about him, and of much distinction of person along with it, but in civilian's dress" (65), "was requested privately to give up his charge," owing to hints that he was engaged in a "little love-affair with a . . . cadet" (65). "You know, or perhaps you do not know, how specially sensitive—indeed implacable—the Service is on *that* topic," Imre explains to Oswald. "Anything but a hint of *it*! There mustn't be a suspicion, a breath! One is simply ruined!" (65). Alone, this is relatively minor in itself. What Imre narrates would have been the case in practically any army in any country in Europe at the time. This incident simply indicates that Oswald and Imre do not extract themselves entirely from the "real" world where homophobia is a fact and part of life. They do not escape to an Arcadian idyll of homosexual fantasy. Instead, Oswald finds a new homeland in Hungary. He is no longer the perpetual outsider like Ivory's itinerant invert. "Imre, I will never go away from thee. Thy people shall be mine. Thy King shall be mine. Thy country shall be mine—thy city mine: My feet are fixed! We belong together" (201; see also Tobin, "Kertbeny's 'Homosexuality'" 3–18). Escape comes to an end; unlike Ivory's inverts, in *Imre* he puts down roots. It is difficult to say whether this also applied to Prime-Stevenson, who lived out his life mostly in Switzerland, or if he had more in common with the inverts of Ivory's essay than his protagonist did.

Italian Travel and Ambivalent Liberation

The language of religion and law plays an important, but subtle, role in the narrative of *Der Tod in Venedig*, which reveals the influence of this discourse in the text. The word "sin" is used only once in the narrative, by Aschenbach, during his final Socratic monologue. He discourses that the artist must follow where Eros leads, along the path of Beauty, which is an "errant and sinful path" (264) ("ein Irr- und Sündenweg"; 153). Thus, the protagonist does not condemn same-sex desire per se, but rather rejects the utilitarian imperative that art be morally instructive. The language of law, on the other hand, occurs with greater frequency in the text. It is used with regard to the artist's pursuit of Beauty, which "may lead a noble mind into terrible *criminal* emotions" (265; emphasis added) ("führ[t] den Edlen vielleicht zu grauenhaftem Gefühlsfrevel"; 154). Owing to this fact, Aschenbach concludes that "the use of art to educate the nation and its youth is a reprehensible undertaking which should be *forbidden by law*" (265; emphasis added) ("[dass] Volks- und Jugenderziehung durch die Kunst ein gewagtes, zu verbietendes Unternehmen [sei]"; 153). Again, this evocation of law is not a specific condemnation of homosexuality; instead it is a statement with implications that are akin to the aestheticist creed: art for art's sake (see chapter 7).

Legal language, though, does cast a shadow across Aschenbach's desire for Tadzio in a manner parallel to the metaphor made between Aschenbach's desublimating homosexuality and the cholera that spreads through the canals of Venice (see chapter 4). In the fifth chapter of the novella, once the cholera outbreak becomes evident, despite the authorities' efforts to cover it up, the narrator links Aschenbach's passion, his "innermost secret" ("eigenst[es] Geheimnis"), with the "guilty secret of the city" ("schlimme[n] Geheimnis der Stadt") (246; 128). Not only is his desire associated with disease, but also with crime. "For to passion, as to crime, the assured everyday order and stability of things is not opportune, and any weakening of the civil structure, any chaos and disaster afflicting the world, must be welcome to it, as offering a vague hope of turning such circumstances to its advantage" (246) ("Denn der Leidenschaft ist, wie dem Verbrechen, die gesicherte Ordnung und Wohlfahrt des Alltags nicht gemäß, und jede Lockerung des bürgerlichen Gefüges, jede Verwirrung und Heimsuchung der Welt muß ihr willkommen sein, weil sie ihren Vorteil dabei zu finden unbestimmt hoffen kann"; 128). Somewhat later in the narrative, the link between Venice's cholera outbreak and Aschenbach's homosexual passion is reiterated again, associating criminality and lawlessness with desire: the "adventure of the outside world which darkly mingled with the adventure of his heart, and which nourished his passion with vague and *lawless* hopes" (250; emphasis added) ("jenem Abenteuer der Außenwelt, das mit dem seines Herzens dunkel zusammenfloß und seine Leidenschaft mit unbestimmten, gesetzlosen Hoffnungen nährte"; 133). The cholera has created the social chaos, the English travel clerk tells Aschenbach, the lawless state of affairs for which the protagonist had secretly hoped: the cholera has led "to a certain breakdown of moral standards, to an activation of the dark and antisocial forces, which manifested itself in intemperance, shameless licence and growing criminality" (259) ("brachte eine gewisse Entsittlichung . . . hervor, eine Ermutigung lichtscheuer und antisozialer Triebe, die sich in Unmäßigkeit, Schamlosigkeit und wachsender Kriminalität bekundete"; 144).

The police are also a recurrent motif in the narrative, not by their physical presence, but in that they are invoked by several characters. Trying to discover the truth about the disease, Aschenbach questions various Venetians about the "sweetish, medicinal smell that suggested squalor and wounds and suspect cleanliness" (245) ("süßlich-offizinellen Geruch, der an Elend und Wunden und verdächtige Reinlichkeit erinnerte"; 127), which is the telltale sign that all is not well in Venice. Until asking the Englishman, he receives a common refrain: "The police have laid down regulations" (246) ("Eine Verfügung der Polizei"; 127); "It is merely a police measure" (250) ("eine Maßnahme der Polizei"; 133–34); "Because of the police! It's the regulations" (253) ("Von wegen der Polizei! Das ist Vorschrift"; 138); "a police precaution" (254) ("Eine polizeiliche Anordnung"; 138). The police, though, are ineffective in controlling the spread of the cholera, which overtakes the city. As the disease and homosexuality are inexorably linked in the narrative, this might be a subtle commentary on police surveillance of sex between men. The scene of the action, though, is Italy, which had not penalized homosexual acts since the introduction of a new penal code in 1889 (Wanrooij, "Italy" 123), and so the "police" regulating Aschenbach's desire is he himself. He proves to be as ineffective at keeping himself in check as the Venetian authorities are in containing the infection. This need the protagonist feels for this "self-policing" stems from religious discourse. The opprobrium attached to same-sex desire by the ethos of Judeo-Christian teachings manifests itself surreptitiously in the text, taking the form of the guilt and shame that Aschenbach experiences for the life he has led in devotion to art and for not meeting the high standards of austere manliness which his forbears—men who devotedly served king, country, and God—represent to him. The roots of this shame spring from the mores of a culture saturated in notions of morality and immorality which find their sources in religion.

In addition, as in *Imre*, legal injunctions against homosexuality are suggested in the travel and exile motifs. Travel to Italy by this time was a well-established topos for sexual, especially homosexual, exploration and liberation, writes Robert Tobin, "at least since Goethe made his erotic discoveries there and Winckelmann moved there to lead his life more freely. In particular, Venice had become by the late nineteenth century a vacation center for homosexuals with means" ("Why is Tadzio a Boy" 224–25). James Jones agrees: "Certainly there are many artistic reasons for locating the story in Venice—e.g. its attraction for German homosexuals such as Platen because of its acceptance of homosexual relationships, its function in German literature as a source of inspiration and rejuvenation, and its links to antiquity" (*Third Sex* 282). The lure of Italy, as well as that of Greece and the Mediterranean basin in general, writes Robert Aldrich in his study, *The Seduction of the Mediterranean* (1993), affected not just German writers—although, he writes, they did form "the largest contingent of writers on the Mediterranean and homosexual visitors to the South" (101)—but British and French writers and artists as well. To list but a few examples of men who had blazed the trail for Aschenbach's fictional sojourn: the classicist Johann Joachim Winckelmann, Goethe, the poet August von Platen, Lord Byron, John Addington Symonds, Bosie and Oscar Wilde, Prime-Stevenson, Mann himself, and others sought and found sexual freedom in Italy (see Aldrich 101–35). The attraction to the Mediterranean, argues Aldrich, certainly had much to do with interest in the great ancient civilizations, their toleration, acceptance, and even praise of male-male love, and the point of reference these served for homosexual subcultures. Moreover, the financial disparity between traveler and native equated to a nearly inexhaustible supply of willing partners (Aldrich, *Seduction of the Mediterranean* 181–84). These are, perhaps, the "present charms" ("gegenwärtig[e] Reize") that the "goat-bearded man" ("ziegenbärtig[e] Mann") is hinting at as Aschenbach purchases his ticket: "Ah, Venice! A splendid city! A city irresistibly attractive to the man of culture, by its history no less than by its present charms!" (210) ("Ah, Venedig! Eine herrliche Stadt! Eine Stadt von unwiderstehlicher Anziehungskraft für den Gebildeten, ihrer Geschichte sowohl wie ihrer gegenwärtigen Reize wegen!"; 78). For Aldrich, Aschenbach is emblematic of the lure of the South on the northern European; he discusses the "Aschenbach Phenomenon" in the introduction to his study (9–11). "Whether Apollonian fable or Dionysian song, *Death in Venice* comprises a revolutionary breakthrough in the expression of gay desire," writes Mann's biographer Anthony Heilbut. "*Death in Venice* does more than evoke a pederastic episode; it constitutes a virtual Baedeker's guide to homosexual love" (*Eros and Literature* 261).

Of course, it is not an unproblematic portrayal of liberation of same-sex Eros; instead *Der Tod in Venedig* problematizes the literary motif of Italian travel and exile. While working with this motif—allowing Venice and its environs to free the protagonist from the exhausting discipline and dry, formal intellectualism which have ruled his life—the novella works against this motif at the same time. Aschenbach's journey is not one of necessity, like Oswald's, an escape from certain social ostracism and disgrace. Rather, he is led and finally entrapped by a series of male figures. The first of these is the stranger near the park in Munich, whose stare awakens in him "a young man's longing to rove to far-off and strange places" (259) ("[eine] schweifende Jünglingssehnsucht ins Weite und Fremde"; 145) and who spurs him toward "the charming south" (202) ("[den] liebenswürdigen Süden"; 67). Another is the unlicensed gondolier who ferries Aschenbach in his coffin-like boat to the Lido, the location of his fateful meeting with the beloved boy. And there is the leader of the troupe of musicians, who provides the nervous stimulation that will help in pushing Aschenbach over the edge. Venice is a meeting place, a bridge between the East and the West; at times it is Hades, the city is "extremely injurious to him" (228) ("ihm höchst schädlich"; 104), "an impossible and forbidden place" (231) ("[ein] ihm unmögliche[r] und verbotene[r] Aufenthalt"; 107–08), and at other times it is "the Elysian land . . . where lightest of living is granted to mortals" (235) ("[das] elysische Land, . . . wo leichtestes Leben den Menschen beschert ist"; 113). The narrator comments upon the dual nature of Venice: "this city, half fairy-tale and half tourist trap" (248) ("diese Stadt, halb Märchen, halb Fremdenfalle"; 131). Aschenbach achieves liberty from the tyranny of intellectualism, from the reason which insists that his same-sex desire be repressed or at least sublimated into Platonism, only to fall victim to a maniacal excess of emotion and desire.

The novella is not Mann's first treatment of the Italian travel motif. Ilsedore Jonas writes that in the short story "Tonio Kröger" (1903), the eponymous protagonist "had succumbed to the temptations of Italy for some time; but then he had come to his senses, and precisely on account of his erotic adventures in the south and their ultimate conquest, had matured into an artist" (*Thomas Mann and Italy* 39). Contrastingly, Kröger is a young man at the outset of his career, whereas Aschenbach is not: "in his exhaustion and susceptibility he lacks the strength to resist the temptation of the total abandonment" (Jonas 41). It is an ambivalent treatment of this literary motif. Later works, including *Maurice* and *Der Puppenjunge*, for instance, demonstrate much less reliance upon travel and exile. *Der Tod in Venedig* works within as well as against the motif of sexual liberation through travel, thereby questioning the literary convention of how to deal with the moralistic and legalistic condemnation of love between men.

The Outlaws of the Greenwood

Religion and law infringe upon the narrative at various points in Forster's novel. Instances of the former include Clive Durham's early struggles with his desire. "Deeply religious, with a living desire to reach God and to please Him, he found himself crossed at an early age by this other desire, obviously from Sodom. . . . He had in him the impulse that destroyed the City of the Plain. It should not ever become carnal, but why had he out of all Christians been punished with it?" (55). When Clive discovers the classics, "the horrors the Bible evoked for him were to be laid by Plato" (55), he is able "to throw over Christianity" (56); however, I wonder how effectively he was able to accomplish this as the motif of sin recurs later in the narrative, for instance, after Maurice's initial rejection of Clive's advances. "Great was the pain, great the mortification, but worse followed. So deeply had Clive become one with the beloved that he began to loathe himself. His whole philosophy of life broke down, and *the sense of sin was reborn in its ruins*, and crawled along corridors. Hall had said he was a criminal, and must know. He was damned. He dare never be friends with a young man again, for fear of corrupting him. Had he not lost Hall his faith in Christianity and attempted his purity besides?" (58; emphasis added). Maurice too is haunted by "the sense of sin" associated with desire for another man, for instance, after his consultation with Dr. Barry, who invokes the language of religion: "never let that evil hallucination, that temptation from the devil, occur to you again" (134). Afterward Maurice resolves to "keep away from young men," but he soon realizes that "he could not keep away from their images, and hourly committed sin in his heart" (131). Mark Lily writes that Christianity "is taken up extensively in the novel through the general discussion of belief, and specifically through the character of Penge's vicar, Mr Borenius" who "personifies the anti-life spirit of Christianity" (*Gay Men's Literature* 57). His exaggerated concern for the spiritual wellbeing of Mrs. Durham's domestic staff makes him appear ridiculous, even to Mrs. Durham. He is, certainly by design, a figure that cannot be taken entirely seriously: "If the parson hadn't looked so damned ugly [Maurice] wouldn't have bothered, but he couldn't stand that squinny face sneering at youth" (163). Borenius views himself as a combatant against "all sexual irregularities" in the church's struggle to "reconquer England" (206). Borenius and his fight might be portrayed in caricature, but this treatment masks the seriousness of what was at stake. Writing in March 1915 to Forrest Reid, who was one of the early readers of *Maurice* and himself a gay author, Forster states: "The man in my book is, roughly speaking, good, but Society nearly destroys him, he nearly slinks through his life furtive and afraid, and burdened with a sense of sin" (Furbank, *Forster* 2: 14). The misguided machinations of agents like the absurd village parson, who "assumed that love between two men must be ignoble" (207), the bigoted college don, the well-meaning but clueless school master, and the hypocritical suburban doctor nearly crush the development of the gay protagonist.

In *Maurice*, law, like religion, is society's default discourse, society's buttress, and a threat to the homosexual man. "So they proceeded outwardly like other men. Society received them, as she receives thousands like them. Behind Society slumbered the Law" (80–81). And like religion, the language of law crops up at various points in the narrative, such as when Clive admits his love for Maurice early in the novel. Maurice tells him: "it's the worst crime in the calendar, and you must never mention it again" (44). Legal discourse receives sustained attention in the narrative through the recurrent trope of the homosexual "outlaw" and in a reversal of the motif of travel and exile. The association between crime and homosexuality recurs in the narrative in the outlaw living outside of or against societal strictures. From early in the novel, a will to rebel exists with its earliest instance being when Clive admits to Maurice: "I'm a bit of an outlaw, I grant, but it serves these people right. As long as they talk of the unspeakable vice of the Greeks they can't expect fair play. It served my mother right when I slipped up to kiss you before dinner. She would have no mercy if she knew" (72–73). Clive subverts familial and university power structures. The family and the university each are microcosms of society at large, and Clive's actions, in general, are an affront to the hypocrisy that informs sanctions against love between men. In particular, they are willful defiance of Mr. Cornwallis, the college authority figure, who instructs his students to omit "a reference to the unspeakable vice of the Greeks" from their translations (37–38), and his mother, the head of the family, for whom appearances and decorum are more important than truth or conviction. Maurice echoes this sentiment: "'You and I are outlaws. All this'—he pointed to the middle-class comfort of the room—'would be taken from us if people knew'" (108).

There is an excitement, a certain sexiness associated with living dangerously, even if it is secret subversion as in the case of Clive and Maurice's relationship. However, the risk of exposure, blackmail, social ostracism, and prison were undeniably genuine threats. Although Forster portrays Clive's hetero-conversion in mystical terms, I argue that it would be a justifiable reading of the text to assume societal pressures play no mean role in Clive's transformation. This seems to be Maurice's first reaction when Clive informs him that he has "changed" and now loves women. Maurice's responds: "Clive, you're in a muddle" (107). The mystical conversion did not play on the big screen. In James Ivory's 1987 film adaptation of *Maurice*, the criminalization of sex acts between men takes a more prominent position in the narrative. Clive's turn to a "normal" life is prompted by Risley's conviction for gross indecency; he recognizes that a relationship with Maurice is too high a liability for a man with social standing and ambition.

In the post-Platonic relationship period of the narrative, Maurice fully comprehends what is at stake as a sexual misfit. "At first he was proud of his self-control: did not he hold Clive's reputation in the hollow of his hand? But he grew more bitter, he wished that he had shouted while he had the strength and smashed down this front of lies. What if he too were involved? His family, his position in society . . . He was an outlaw in disguise" (114). The will to rebel is no longer boyish unruliness, rather, in this later phase it takes on a darker, more serious hue. Escape from the mandatory sexual homogeneity of Edwardian England, to flee the pressures of social class, to embrace the outlaw identity fully, is posited as the protagonist's only avenue. During his second consultation with the hypnotist Lasker Jones, who fails to cure Maurice's aberrant sexuality, Jones recommends that Maurice relocate to a country in which same-sex acts are not criminalized, such as France or Italy. "'You mean that a Frenchman could share with a friend and yet not go to prison?' 'Share? Do you mean unite? If both are of age and avoid public indecency, certainly.' 'Will the law ever be that in England?' 'I doubt it. England has always been disinclined to accept human nature'" (183).

Exile in a foreign country is not an option for Maurice though. The novel refuses to operate within this convention of early gay literature. Before the episode with the hypnotist, Maurice and Clive travel in Italy. In light of the author's other works, the reader might reasonably expect travel in the south to beget sexual awakening, which could lift Platonic constraints upon their relationship. This is not the case though. Although their sojourn through Italy receives little description in the narrative, it becomes clear that Maurice is more the type of middle-class English tourist that Forster lampoons in his other writings, such as *A Room with a View* (1908) or even *A Passage to India* (1924). "He liked [Italy] well enough in spite of the food and the frescoes" (91), finding the country "very jolly—as much as one wants in the way of sight-seeing" (92). Though, "Maurice had no use for Greece" (91), and so when Clive is determined to extend his pilgrimage "to the yet holier land beyond the Adriatic," Maurice refuses to go. Greece, for him, begins to carry with it a taint of "morbidity and death" (92). The theme of the Mediterranean as liberator is then fully turned on its head when travel in Greece brings about not liberation, but further repression and the end to Clive and Maurice's relationship. There Clive sees "only a dying light and a dead land," concluding that "the past was devoid of meaning like the present, and a refuge for cowards." In the Theater of Dionysus, Clive converts to heterosexuality (97). This site, the Theater of Dionysus, is of importance. In *Der Tod in Venedig*, Dionysian forces lead Aschenbach to the south and unleash his repressed and sublimated desires. In two of Forster's short stories, "The Story of a Panic" (1904) and "The Curate's Friend" (1911), Dionysian spirits—Pan in the former and a faun in the latter—liberate the central characters. One could reasonably expect something similar for Clive, a moment of catharsis at which point he abandons thwarting Platonic restraint. However, nothing of the sort occurs. Instead this literary motif appears to be reversed. Perhaps Clive looked for liberation in the wrong place? Or maybe he found it, but turned his back on it, like Mr. Lucas in the short story "The Road from Colonus" (1911)? Perhaps, in his cold connubial bed with Anne, Clive, like Mr. Lucas, is haunted by "the noise of running water" (*Selected Short Stories* 90). In the tale, the sound of running water is a memento of Mr. Lucas's encounter with a shrine, a spring gushing from a hollow tree, in the Greek countryside. He is offered the possibility of fulfilling his desire "to die fighting" (80), but he returns to England to be haunted by the sound of the spring and the lost opportunity. Clive too may be haunted by lost opportunities for happiness. This is suggested in Clive and Maurice's final dialogue toward the end of the narrative. When Maurice refers to the time when Clive kissed his hand, Clive rejoins, "'Don't allude to that,' . . . not for the first and last time, and for a moment causing the outlaw to love him" (211). Although he might have secured himself socially by marrying, Clive is still an outlaw and still loves Maurice.

The literary motif of travel in the Mediterranean is reversed. The forces of nature that liberate Maurice are English and unite him with Alec, the gamekeeper. During the second session with Jones, Maurice realizes that "Men of my sort could take to the greenwood" (183). And so he and Alec do. "Maurice finally loses his virginity in the arms of an English working man," writes Aldrich, "Forster's view of homosexuality is that it allows men to cross social barriers, not recreate an ancient culture" (99). Social forces like religion and law are "too incompetent to catch them," writes Forster in the novel's "Terminal Note," which was written and appended to the manuscript in 1960, "the only penalty society exacts is an exile they gladly embrace" (216). The trope of the outlaw is a leitmotif in the novel which comes to fruition at the conclusion of the narrative. Maurice goes into exile with Alec, but it is an English exile of Forster's own fashioning, which was modeled on Millthrope, the home and commune of Edward Carpenter and his partner George Merrill. Jeff Bush argues that Maurice and Alec's "escape to the greenwood does not merely represent escapist gay wish-fulfilment," rather, "The novel becomes a pastoral unlike any other, a modern pastoral infused with queer sexual politics" ("The Queering of the Greenwood" 11). This "queer pastoral becomes truly liberatory," Bush concludes. "In the final scene of the novel, Forster appeals to the greenwood to formulate his own philosophy of sexuality which is indebted to, and extends, Carpenter" (11). They are not robbed of their homelands, forced to take refuge abroad or in an Arcadian idyll; instead "England belonged to them" (207).

Proving Who Is the Stronger

Der Puppenjunge, as well as the first six *Die Bücher der namenlosen Liebe*, feature direct confrontation, more direct than what one sees in the other three works of fiction, with church and state stigmatization and persecution of love and sex between men. Mackay's writing program strives to grant a voice to and rally support for the "nameless love," which denotes specifically intergenerational same-sex liaisons—the texts treat love between adult men and boys between fourteen and seventeen years of age—rather than homosexual relations in general. For this mode of desire, he opts to avoid the term "pederasty" ("Päderastie") or its synonym in German, "Knabenliebe" (literally, "lad-love"). By doing so, he evades existing nomenclatures. In the introduction to *Die Bücher der namenlosen Liebe*, titled "Die Geschichte eines Kampfes um die namenlose Liebe" ("The History of a Fight for the Nameless Love"), Mackay writes that this "love I call 'nameless,' since no name yet correctly names it today" (15) ("die Liebe, die ich die 'namenlose' nannte, da kein Name sie heute recht noch nennt"; 13). In the first book, "Die namenlose Liebe: Ein Bekenntniss," he addresses this love, explaining that "Each name that has named you until now has become a term of abuse in the dirty mouths of the vulgar, a misunderstanding in dull minds, which is worse than all insults" (57) ("Jeder Name, der Dich genannt bisher, ist ein Schimpfwort geworden in dem schmutzigen Maule der Gemeinheit, ein Mißverständniß in trüben Gehirnen, das schlimmer ist als alle Beschimpfung"; 79). Mackay is not the only writer of the era to take up his pen in support of same-sex desire only to be confronted with the discursive baggage with which existing naming structures were laden. John Addington Symonds begins his essay on homosexuality, "A Problem in Modern Ethics" (1891), stating that he can "hardly find a name" for discussing same-sex love "which will not seem to soil this paper" (*Symonds and Homosexuality* 128); Oscar Wilde cites Alfred Douglas's poem, calling it "the love that dare not speak its name"; and Edward Carpenter and Elisar von Kupffer invent their own terminology for same-sex love in their writings. Mackay was engaging in a deft strategy. Instead of creating yet another new name, as Carpenter had with "homogenic love" and Kupffer had with "Lieblingminne," he avoids names altogether. In this way, not only has he avoided, like Symonds, Carpenter, and Kupffer, terms with connotations loaded with moralistic derision, but passes judgment upon sexological terminology, which, for Mackay, carries with it associations of illness and gender inversion. "In these books I have not used one of those technical terms taken from foreign and dead languages, not once even one of those ambiguous words that appear to have become the most indispensable aids and the most effective tricks of science" (43) ("Ich habe in diesen Büchern nicht einen jener fremden und toten Sprachen entlehnten Fachausdrücke, nicht einmal auch nur eines der vieldeutigen Worte gebraucht, die zu den unentbehrlichsten Hülfsmitteln und den wirkungsvollsten Allüren der Wissenschaft geworden zu sein scheinen"; 59). Thus his strategy is closest to Wilde's use of Douglas's poem in that it refuses to name this love at the same time that it refuses to remain silent about it.

Of the seven nameless love writings, this study focuses primarily on the full-length novel and supports its analysis with reference to the earlier texts, especially the novella, *Fenny Skaller: Ein Leben der namenlosen Liebe* (Fenny Skaller: A Life of the Nameless Love), which was written in 1906 and published in 1913 as the third book in the *namenlosen* collection. In *Der Puppenjunge*, religion and law are hand in glove. This theme is communicated too in the earlier writings. "Cursed by parsons of all religions and all sects as an unmentionable sin; persecuted by judges" (*Books* 148) ("Von den Pfaffen aller Religionen und aller Art als unnennbare Sünde verflucht; von den Richtern . . . als Verbrechen verfolgt"; *Bücher* 264); religion and law are the social forces which for centuries have discredited and persecuted love between men (see J. Bauer, "On the Nameless Love and Infinite Sexualities" 7). In the novel, religious structures play a secondary role to that of legal forces. Indeed, notions of the sinfulness of same-sex desire and same-sex acts exert little force over either protagonist. In the narrative, Graff does not struggle with guilt and shame in the way that Oswald, Imre, Aschenbach, Clive, and Maurice do; there is no indication that Günther is even aware that his profession is considered a vice or is illegal.

In the first six books of the nameless love, religion and notions of sin play a greater role than in the novel. In "Die namenlose Liebe: Ein Bekenntniss," Mackay equates the coming of Christianity with "night" falling upon Europe: "For centuries this love, which the Greeks set in its beauty and nobility in the bright sunshine and before the eyes of the world, was buried: its name was debased and outlawed, it was itself dishonored, persecuted and despised" (53) ("Auf Jahrtausende hinaus wurde die Liebe, die die Hellenen in ihrer Schönheit und ihrem Adel unter das heitere Licht der Sonne und vor die Augen der Welt gestellt, begraben: ihr Name entehrt und verfemt, sie selbst geschändet, verfolgt, verachtet"; 73). Religion and Christian morality are personified twice in *Der Puppenjunge*. The first instance takes the form of a village pastor whom Günther compares with his first john. "The pastor in his village had also done that with them, only he had not been friendly, but clumsy and rough, and had only given them a couple of apples from his garden" (41) ("Das hatte der Pfarrer auf ihrem Dorfe auch mit ihnen gemacht, nur war der nicht freundlich, sondern grob und roh gewesen und hatte ihnen nur ein paar Äpfel aus seinem Garten gegeben"; 43). Unlike Borenius in *Maurice*, this parson cannot be said to represent any particular aspect of religious doctrine or teaching; instead he serves to highlight social hypocrisy in general. Second, this discourse is personified in Graff's landlady. She strikes an ominous chord from her first appearance, "a woman dressed entirely in black, with scrawny features and strikingly dark, sharp eyes" (34) ("Eine ganz in Schwarz gekleidete Frau mit hageren Zügen und auffallend dunklen, scharfen Augen"; 35). She could be a frustrated spinster or a mourning war widow, and, along with the obvious association of death, the color of her clothing could hint at religion through an association with the robes of a religious order. She is a personification of "the night" that Mackay likens Christianity to in the "Bekenntniss." Unbeknownst to Graff, nothing would escape the notice of these "dark, sharp eyes," and eventually an unspoken hate wells between the two. "Her entire appearance was strange and unpleasant to him: the black, staring eyes, the stern mouth, the hard, cold face, even the invariably black dress, and the whole attitude of her gaunt bony figure" (157) ("Ihre ganze Erscheinung schon war ihm fremd und unsympathisch: die schwarzen, starren Augen; der strenge Mund; das harte, kalte Gesicht; selbst das unabänderlich-schwarze Kleid, wie die ganze Haltung der hageren, knochigen Gestalt"; 183). This hate culminates in her denunciation of Graff to the authorities as a corrupter of youth. At his trial she is a key witness for the prosecution. "She stood there in her dark dress, the very bones of morality. Her black eyes sparkled in her pale and haggard face" (278) ("Sie stand da, in ihrem dunklen Kleide, ganz knochengewordene Moral. Die schwarzen Augen funkelten in dem blassen und hageren Gesicht"; 321). Her physical characterization mirrors her deeds: she is a caricature of religion's antilife spirit working with the state out of a twisted sense of Christian and civic duty.

Legal discourse is more central in the plot as the force that tears the two lovers apart. As complications arise, Graff contemplates leaving his life behind and escaping with Günther. The south lures him, over the Alps to Italy, "in safety, in peace and happiness. Yes, Italy, there it's cheap and lovely—nice and warm" (237) ("in Sicherheit, in Frieden und Glück . . . Ja, Italien, dort ist es billig und schön . . . warm und schön"; 272–73). He does not act in time and Günther is taken into custody by the police and interned at a juvenile detention center. The lawyer Graff consults evokes a Dickensian image of the legal profession. "Everything about the small, misshapen man was yellow: his hair, his skin, his eyes, his teeth, the nails of his greedy hands" (256) ("An dem kleinen, schlechtgewachsenen Manne war Alles gelb: die Haare, die Haut, die Augen, die Zähne, die Nägel der gierigen Hände"; 296–97). He advises Graff not to become involved in petitioning for Günther's release from the center. Disregarding this advice leads to Graff's arrest for indecent assault against a minor and a member of his own sex. At his trial, although the color trope black is repeated in the "black figures" ("schwarze[n] Gestalten"), these judges are different to the landlady, who derives a sadistic satisfaction from upholding morality. They, on the other hand, seem to fulfill their function in the legal structure without any great conviction. They ask insulting and shameful questions to which the protagonist is unable to reply. "Questions . . . questions—more shameless than anything he had ever heard in the Adonis Lounge from the boy prostitutes there—struck his ear. He did not understand them. He only felt: they were shameless—shameless and absurd" (278) ("Fragen . . . Fragen—schamloser als Alles, was er je in der Adonis-Diele von den prostituierten Jungens dort gehört, schlugen an sein Ohr. Er verstand sie nicht. Er empfand nur: sie waren schamlos . . . schamlos und widersinnig"; 321). Günther, his will broken by the institution, also testifies against his former lover and friend. Graff is convicted and sentenced to two months in prison for "indecent assault" (289) ("Sittlichkeitsverbrecher"; 333). When a court official, as if excusing himself, tells Graff "I don't make the laws, I carry them out" (289) ("ich mache die Gesetze nicht, ich führe sie aus"; 334), Graff is scandalized that "He carries out laws . . . which he considers unjust and convicts innocent people—daily and hourly. And can sleep peacefully" (289) ("Er führt Gesetze aus . . . die er für ungerecht hält und verurteilt Unschuldige—täglich und stündlich. Und kann ruhig schlafen"; 334).

Upon his release, he declares: "Either I am a criminal or the others are, who made this law and carry it out" (289) ("Entweder bin ich ein Verbrecher oder die Anderen sind es, die diese Gesetze gemacht haben und sie ausführen!"; 333). The eponymous protagonist of *Fenny Skaller* also comes to realize that "human laws" ("Menschengebot[e]"), which "forbade what nature ordered" ("verboten, was die Natur gebot"), lack any sort of justification or foundation. Skaller is resolved that "From now on he intended to obey only the laws of his nature" (*Books* 157–58) ("Von jetzt an wollte er nur noch den Gesetzen seiner Natur gehorchen"; *Bücher* 280). Mackay overturns notions of crime and criminality. The men "who made this law and carry it out" are "petty and stupid bureaucrats" (*Hustler* 276) ("klein[e] und dumm[e] Amtsmenschen"; *Puppenjunge* 319), unthinking, unfeeling cogs in the machine of state oppression; theirs is the true crime, the infringement upon the civil liberty of the individual. "What are all the crimes in the world compared with the ones committed by those in gowns and vestments, robes and uniforms" (289) ("Was sind alle Verbrechen der Welt gegen die, begangen von Denen in Talaren und Ornaten, Roben und Uniformen!"; 334). These scenes in *Der Puppenjunge* are informed by the author's philosophy of individualist anarchism. "Mackay regarded himself as an anarchist," writes Ruth Kinna. "Anarchy, he argued, meant the abolition of the state, of artificial boundaries, the bureaucracy, the military and the judiciary; it meant the freedom of individuals to determine and pursue their own interests, consistent with the equal liberty of all. In anarchy, individuals would be free to live their private lives as they saw fit and to experiment without limit" ("The Mirror of Anarchy" 47). His struggle for the nameless love fits within this struggle for individual freedom. He writes in "Die Geschichte eines Kampfes um die namenlose Liebe" that "the question of this love also is in its deepest basis a social question: the fight of the individual for his freedom against whatever kind of oppression" (44) ("auch die Frage dieser Liebe ist in ihrem tiefsten Grunde eine sociale Frage: der Kampf des Individuums um seine Freiheit gegen jede wie immer geartete Unterdrückung"; 61). It is not only "those in gowns and vestments, robes and uniforms" who are guilty of curtailing the liberty of the individual; it also applies to anyone who can witness the liberty of their fellow man be trampled. "There are few human beings who have not become criminals against their fellow humans—not directly, but rather indirectly, in that they tolerate and advocate laws such as this one for example" (289) ("Es gibt wenig Menschen, die an ihren Mitmenschen noch nicht zu Verbrechern geworden sind—nicht direkt, sondern indirekt, indem sie Gesetze, wie dieses zum Beispiel, dulden und befürworten"; 333).

After his release, Graff resists the lure of escape and exile: "He did not travel toward the south. He traveled back to Berlin" (292) ("Er fuhr nicht nach dem Süden. Er fuhr zurück nach Berlin"; 336). He returns to Berlin in order to prove that the unjust law has not "won" and succeeded in robbing him of his dignity and homeland. "As a young man who knew almost nothing of life and little about himself, Hermann Graff had come to the metropolis a year ago. As a man who wanted to know and master life as it was, he returned again. He had to show himself who was the stronger" (292) ("Als ein junger Mensch, der fast Nichts vom Leben wußte und Wenig von sich, war Hermann Graff vor nun einem Jahre in die große Stadt gekommen. Als ein Mann, der das Leben erkennen und es meistern wollte, wie es war, kehrte er wieder. Es mußte sich zeigen, wer der Stärkere war"; 336). Graff returns to Berlin in a contest of wills against a repressive, homophobic society. Like Fenny Skaller in the autobiographical novella, Graff's life has purpose: "His life had meaning. It had become a fight. A fight for his love!" (*Books* 153) ("Sein Leben erhielt einen Sinn. Es war ein Kampf geworden. Ein Kampf um diese Liebe!"; *Bücher* 272).

The exile theme is rejected in *Der Puppenjunge*. Whereas the other works of fiction demonstrate new variations on the travel and exile motif in homosexual literature—Oswald's exile ends when he finds a new homeland, *Der Tod in Venedig* operates within the bounds of the convention of Italian travel as sexual liberator while subverting it as well, and Maurice and Alec create their own refuge from societal condemnation by escaping into folklore—Mackay's novel breaks new ground. In his earlier texts, travel and exile are still central motifs. In "Wer sind wir? Eine Dichtung der namenlosen Liebe" ("Who are We? A Poem of the Nameless Love"), the second book of the volume, the speaker is in exile from his homeland: "Homeless, I chose for myself a freer land for my home" (82) ("Heimathlos wählte ich selbst mir / zur Heimath ein freieres Land"; 150). And, as a young man, Skaller discovers himself and his love through travel, through "roving through the world" ("die Welt durchstreifen"): "A restless wandering form place to place. A flight from himself. A fleeing from people" (117) ("Ein ruheloses Schweifen von Ort zu Ort. Eine Flucht vor sich selbst. Ein Fliehen auch vor den Menschen"; 208). In particular, Paris is mentioned in both of these works. "Mackay visited Paris many times and it may well be that his first sexual adventures were in that city," writes Hubert Kennedy in the introduction to his translation of *Die Bücher der namenlosen Liebe*. "He also gives Paris as the place of the sexual awakening of his alter ego Fenny Skaller in the third book" (6). Although travel is crucial to his process of self-discovery, he returns to Germany to be an agent of change. After "Years of travel, passed in foreign lands" (137) ("Jahre auf Reisen, in fremden Ländern verbracht"; 243), he returns home to Berlin. "He has only one place left in the world where he can set his foot: thus he will claim it with all his power and no one shall drive him from this little place. No one!" (133) ("Er hat nur noch einen Platz auf der Welt, auf dem er Fuß fassen kann: so will er ihn behaupten mit aller Macht und Niemand soll ihn von diesem kleinen Platze verdrängen. Niemand!"; 235–36).

Graff's and Maurice's refusals to exile themselves in France or Italy share a good deal of commonality. Both texts assert the validity of the fight for individual freedom against moralistic and legal condemnation and lead the reader to imagine the ultimate success of this fight. The protagonists refuse to be banished. Where these two portrayals differ is from where the struggle is fought. Maurice recreates for himself an English myth of the outlaws in the greenwood, a fantasy of an England more true to itself; but in doing so the novel takes a negative view of the possibility that society can be changed. It is a fantasy and an anachronism. On the other hand, Graff accepts the world for what it is, and chooses to live in that world in order to subvert its power structures from within. While Maurice rejects the Mediterranean exile discourse for an exile of his own fashioning, Graff strives to win understanding and acceptance for his nameless love. *Der Puppenjunge* counters the yearning for escape and the desire to recover an Arcadian idyll that characterizes much homosexual literature of the era, whether this escape and recovery was in the conventional destinations like Italy or France, or more surprising locales like Hungary or the English greenwood. Instead it situates the protagonist in the very midst of a hostile society.

Conclusion: Speaking Its Name

The works of fiction were written in and reflect societal contexts that were not, as I argue above, dissimilar. In England and Germany, same-sex acts came under temporal jurisdiction around the same time and, by the end of the nineteenth century, laws were firmly ensconced in the penal codes of both nations which punished "gross indecency" and "widernatürliche Unzucht," respectively. American laws were, in most colonies, extensions of English law. By the 1890s, rapid social change in the United States gave rise to expansive use of sodomy laws to combat what must have seemed to be a rising tide of "the crime against nature." Consequently, all four texts respond and react to religious and legal discourses, if in different ways. *Imre*, in addition to recounting the protagonists' reckonings with the alleged sinfulness/criminality of their sexualities, depicts an important variation of the travel and exile motif. In *Der Tod in Venedig*, Aschenbach struggles with the shame he associates with emotion, sensuality, his artistic temperament, and his homosexual desire. The south liberates this desire and frees him of his shame, but the ambivalence of this freedom means that the novella subverts the theme of sexual liberation through travel and exile. *Maurice* challenges this motif as well, to a greater extent. In Forster's novel, homosexuality is at odds with the Edwardian social order, and rather than flee to Italy, Maurice and Alec find a home in "an England where it was still possible to get lost" (219). And, in *Der Puppenjunge*, after he is jailed for his love for another male, Hermann Graff returns to Berlin to effect change in society, in order to win tolerance and understanding for the nameless love.

What becomes clear is the subversive potential of all four works of fiction. These texts not only take on society's default discourses, but draw on alternative conceptual and taxonomical structures—challenging and expanding these discourses, negating stereotypes, and broadening the range of images and motifs with and through which to fictionalize love and desire between men. Over the course of the following chapters this will become increasingly evident, as I approach the literary texts by way of the three distinct counterdiscourses to the religio-legal formation—Greek love, sexology, and Oscar Wilde—in order to demonstrate how the texts respond to each. Fiction was (and still is) a crucial means for affirming this desire, and the works of this era, in demanding to speak the name of same-sex love, set in motion literary and cultural revolutions. This love has refused to be silenced.

Part 2

Greek Love

Chapter 2

Transcending Greek Love

Although it was not the nineteenth century's first Greek love apologia, or defense of love between men, Oscar Wilde's testimony during his second trial deployed classical philosophy in perhaps the most public invocation of this discursive strategy. He refuted that "the love that dare not speak its name" was base sensuality or unnatural vice; he elevated it rather to a higher, purer plane:

> "The love that dare not speak its name" in this century is such a great affection of an elder for a younger man as there was between David and Jonathan, such as Plato made the very basis of his philosophy, and such as you find in the sonnets of Michelangelo and Shakespeare. It is that deep, spiritual affection that is as pure as it is perfect. It dictates and pervades great works of art like those of Shakespeare and Michelangelo, and those two letters of mine, such as they are. It is in this century misunderstood, so much misunderstood that it may be described as the "Love that dare not speak its name," and on account of it I am placed where I am now. It is beautiful, it is fine, it is the noblest form of affection. There is nothing unnatural about it. It is intellectual, and it repeatedly exists between an elder and a younger man, when the elder has intellect, and the younger man has all the joy, hope, and glamour of life before him. That it should be so, the world does not understand. The world mocks at it and sometimes puts one in the pillory for it. (Hyde, *Trials* 201)

Noble and high minded, chaste, pure, and solely intellectual, this love is elevated and sanitized, thereby differentiating it from the Sin of Sodom. Wilde establishes the historicity of same-sex desire through the biblical love of David and Jonathan, through Plato's philosophy, and the verse of two cultural titans like Michelangelo and Shakespeare. It is this effort which is the central pillar of Greek love justification. In this defense is a statement of identity. Against the older language of sin and crime, writes Linda Dowling, Wilde deployed "a new and powerful vocabulary of personal identity, a language of mind, sensibility, and emotion, of inward and intellectual relations" (*Hellenism and Homosexuality* 2) which saw same-sex desires as "belong[ing] to human experience in its fullest historicity and cultural density" (134). Wilde constructed an identity for himself, drawing upon history and philosophy, employing models from the past to structure his relations.

The courtroom defense speech gives an idea of the core beliefs about love between men inherent in nineteenth-century Hellenism. The ideals come directly from Plato's writings, from the *Phaedrus* and especially from the *Symposium*, in particular the speech of Pausanias. First, this love "is intellectual, and it repeatedly exists between an elder and a younger man, where the elder has intellect and the younger man has all the joy, hope, and glamor of life before him" (Hyde, *Trials* 201). In other words, it is intellectual or pedagogic. This is the "gratification" in exchange for being made "wise and good" described by Pausanias in the *Symposium* (Plato 19). Often these relationships were conducted between men of disparate ages, between adult men and teenage boys, but in some cases the age difference was negligible. Greek love could justify romances between upper- and lower-year students, as the relationship between Clive and Maurice in E. M. Forster's *Maurice* demonstrates. Second, "It is that deep, spiritual affection that is as pure as it is perfect. . . . It is beautiful, it is fine, it is the noblest form of affection" (201). It was believed that love between males is a higher form of love, surpassing the love between a man and a woman: "heavenly" love opposed to "common" love (Plato, *Symposium* 13–14). And third, "There is nothing unnatural about it [love between men]" (201). Because the Socrates that Plato presents in the *Symposium* and *Phaedrus* believes that love is most likely to remain "heavenly" if sublimated and channeled toward philosophic ends, in the nineteenth century Greek love apologists often endorsed relations between males that valued the spiritual dimensions of love, while disavowing the sensual. At best, this conception of Greek love had to remain an unattainable ideal toward which its followers could strive; but at its worst it was merely a sham, a way of clothing sex with male prostitutes in the garb of intellectual mentorship.

This chapter examines the ways in which Thomas Mann's novella *Der Tod in Venedig* and John Henry Mackay's *Die Bücher der namenlosen Liebe* (in particular the novella *Fenny Skaller: Ein Leben der namenlosen Liebe* and the novel *Der Puppenjunge*) question and challenge the notions which form the justificatory and defensive backbone of much late nineteenth- and early twentieth-century Greek love apologia. Writing on Mann's novella, Robert Tobin discusses the influence of contemporary discourses of Greek love in his essay "Queering Thomas Mann's *Tod in Venedig*" (2012). Tobin argues that a medico-psychiatric understanding of same-sex subjectivity comes into conflict with a "masculinist," Greek-inspired concept like that envisioned by Hans Blüher, Benedict Friedländer, Adolf Brand, and other writers and theorists associated with the homophile association the *Gemeinschaft der Eigenen* (Community of the Exceptional). This tension plays out between the protagonist and narrator: "Aschenbach sides with the masculinist approach, while the narrator is a liberal emancipationist" (69). Below, I argue that Aschenbach does not voice the masculinist understanding expounded in the writings of these contemporary German writers, but rather the older transnational discourses of Greek love, similar to that which Wilde invokes in his courtroom defense. The issue that shows that Aschenbach is meant to be part of this tradition, that which differentiates him from the German masculinist movement, is the anxiety about sex. This angst, which features in the ancient sources and which is compounded in the writings of many of the nineteenth-century inheritors of this philosophy, assumes pride of place in the novella.

Like *Der Tod in Venedig*, Mackay's books of the nameless love depict intergenerational same-sex desire and love. The former work of fiction portrays a man's struggle to reconcile his desire for a beautiful youth with his respectable, bourgeois identity. He calls upon Greek love to justify this desire to himself, but Platonic philosophy proves to be insufficient. Mackay's fiction appears to partake of a similar vision of love. J. Edgar Bauer writes that, in his nameless love writings, Mackay "basically pleaded for a renaissance of pederastic Eros under the auspices of past Greek ideals," finding there "the needed paradigms for reinventing the future" ("On the Nameless Love and Infinite Sexualities" 6). However, I argue here that Mackay's fiction unambiguously rejects invoking Greek love to defend or justify intergenerational same-sex desire and relationships, which also distinguishes his writings from "masculinist" approaches. Thus a factor which differentiates Mackay's writings from Mann's is Mackay's further-reaching rejection of Greek justificatory strategies. This chapter investigates the responses to Greek love incorporated into the two German works of fiction, in particular their depiction of intergenerational same-sex love. This chapter considers aspects of Plato's *Symposium*, especially the anxiety surrounding the issue of sexual relations between men and then discusses the revived form of Greek love which developed in Germany before it engages in a literary analyses of the responses to Greek love ideals in Mann's *Der Tod in Venedig* and Mackay's in *Der Puppenjunge*.

Plato's Anxieties

The contemporary sources for information on homosexual relations in the Greek world are diverse: literary references, historical narratives, philosophical writings, and visual arts all feature age-structured relations between males. One of the single most important figures for the inheritors of this legacy was Plato (428–348 BCE), and one of the most important texts was his *Symposium* (c. 385–380 BCE) (see Evangelista, "Lovers and Philosophers at Once" 231). In this philosophic text, each of seven speakers at a symposium, or drinking party, hosted by the poet Agathon, must give an encomium in praise of love. Pausanias, the second speaker, in his speech distinguishes between two loves: "we've been told simply to praise Love. If Love were a single thing, this would be fine, but in fact it isn't. . . . Since there are two kinds of Aphrodite, there must also be two Loves" (Plato 13). The older goddess, and by extension form of love, is the daughter of Uranus and has no mother, she is Uranian or Heavenly Aphrodite; whereas the younger is born of Zeus and Dione and is called

Pandemic or Common (13). Common love "is the kind of love that inferior people feel," and men led by this love "are attracted to women as much as boys, and to bodies rather than minds" (14). In contrast to this wanton and purely physical attraction, there is Heavenly love, which springs from Uranian Aphrodite, "who has nothing of the female in her but only maleness" (14). Men who are inspired by Heavenly love "are drawn toward the male, feeling affection for what is naturally more vigorous and intelligent" and are "attracted to boys only when they start to have developed intelligence, and this happens around the time that they begin to grow a beard" (14). For the ancient Greeks, who kept no record of age in years, the appearance of facial hair indicated when a boy transitioned from childhood to manhood and thus became a citizen (see Davidson, *The Greeks and Greek Love* 71–82). James Davidson writes that the customs structuring pederastic relations differed from city-state to city-state, and in Athens were particularly complex (*The Greeks and Greek Love* 68–98).

The lover precariously treads a fine line between the noble and disgraceful. Pausanias attempts to clear up the ambiguity between proper and vile love by laying out in his speech exactly under which circumstances a relationship could be consummated without bringing dishonor upon the lover or the beloved: "the lover is justified in any service he performs for the boyfriend who gratifies him, and . . . the boyfriend is justified in any favor he does for someone who is making him wise and good. Also the lover must be able to develop the boyfriend's understanding and virtue in general, and the boyfriend must want to acquire education and wisdom in general. When all these conditions are met, then and then alone it is right for a boyfriend to gratify his lover, but not otherwise" (19). The exchange of teaching for "gratification" is characterized as heavenly love, which "is a source of great value to the city and to individuals, because it forces the lover to pay attention to his own virtue and the boyfriend to do the same" (20). These relationships were, in the younger of the two men, intended to cultivate *aretē*, which Thorkil Vanggaard describes as an embodiment of all manly virtues (*Phallós* 34–35) and Beert C. Verstraete and Vernon Provencal translate as "human excellence" (Introduction 10–11). James Davidson notes that particularly the passage quoted above "is the main basis for the popular notion that Greek love was all about education, the lovers acting like adult volunteers in a youth club, helping teenagers to develop useful skills and knowledge of the world" (115–16). In his "reappraisal" of Greek love, Davidson is notably skeptical of this interpretation, suggesting that while this may have been an ideal or goal, it is doubtful that the Greeks lived up to it.

Further complicating the model of same-sex relations which the Victorian readers could derive from the *Symposium* is that, according to Plato's Socrates, relations between an older and a younger man are most likely to be uplifting, to be heavenly love, if they remain unconsummated. In his speech, the philosopher recounts his dialogue with a woman named Diotima who introduces the concept of spiritual begetting to the text. This is a refinement of Pausanias's distinction between "heavenly" and "common" love described above. Rather than education in exchange for sexual gratification, for her, heavenly love is based on the exchange of ideas.

Whereas common love between men and women can bring forth children, heavenly love between men produces offspring of a more undying nature: ideas. "People like that have a much closer partnership with each other and a stronger bond of friendship than parents have, because the children of their partnership are more beautiful and more immortal" (*Symposium* 58). Diotima removes the sexual element from these relations. This is why she argues that "he should regard the beauty of minds as more valuable than that of the body, so that, if someone has goodness of mind even if he has little of the bloom of beauty, he will be content with him, and will love and care for him, and give birth to the kinds of discourse that help young men to become better" (60). Regardless whether the Greeks or they themselves could achieve heavenly love, this ideal represented for the inheritors of this text an invaluable counter to church teaching in the Christian era. It is in this speech that the intellectual and pedagogic character of pederastic relations is founded, the notion that Greek love is a higher and purer form of love.

Plato's mistrust of the body would spell the end of the usefulness of his erotic philosophy toward the end of the nineteenth century. He goes to great lengths to differentiate heavenly love, which is good, noble, and benefits the practitioners as well as the polis, from common love, which seeks merely satiation of its appetite. This painstaking care with which "beneficial" desire is demarcated from "destructive" betrays the anxiety the Greeks felt about love and sex between males. Michel Foucault regards the large amount of Greek literature about loving boys as proof that this desire was a problem for the Greeks. "Because if there were no problem, they would speak of this kind of love in the same terms as love between men and women. The problem was that they couldn't accept that a young boy who was supposed to become a free citizen could be dominated and used as an object of someone's pleasure" ("On the Genealogy of Ethics" 344–45). For the Greeks, the woman or slave could be used as an object of pleasure. In Plato, physical pleasure and the reciprocity of friendship were seen as mutually exclusive. "The Greek ethics of pleasure is linked to a virile society, to dissymmetry, the exclusion of the other" (346). The views Plato puts forth in his dialogues regarding love between males not only is marked by angst but is often contradictory. Robert Allen argues that there are two Platos: "the homosexuality-friendly Plato of the *Symposium*, who values same-sex love as the bottom rung on the great ladder that leads up to God, and the homophobic Plato of the *Laws*, who forbade homosexuality for the first time in the history of Greek thought" (*The Classical Origins of Modern Homophobia* 33). Theodore Jennings, on the other hand, draws three categories into which Plato's texts fall. First are those dialogues that take love between men for granted, such as *Charmides*, *Lysis*, and many of the speeches in the *Symposium*. Second are those that understand that a man might fall in love with a beautiful youth but insist that this love be sublimated toward some philosophic end, the contemplation of beauty, education, or spiritual begetting, for instance. This group includes Socrates's speeches in the *Symposium* and *Phaedrus*. And the third is the *Laws*, which rejects love between men (*Plato or Paul?* 15). Thomas Hubbard writes that in the *Laws*, his final work, Plato "drops all pretence of defending pederasty as chaste love or as a metaphor for union with ideal Beauty: instead it is dismissed as an unnecessary and 'unnatural' pleasure" ("Pederasty and Democracy" 10).

The anxiety and contradictions present in the source texts are compounded in their later invocations, namely, whether or not these relations could be intellectual as well as physical was a site of struggle for the inheritors of this legacy. Men who drew on this discourse were presented with one of two options: either sublimation of physical desire, which often resulted in a consuming struggle, or hypocrisy. A literary example of the former, of the disavowal or repression of the physical aspects of love between men, can be found in Leopold von Sacher-Masoch's *Die Liebe des Plato* (The Love of Plato, 1870) which draws on Pausanias's distinction between heavenly and common love and Diotima's concept of spiritual begetting. Oscar Wilde's speech could be considered an example of the latter, of hypocrisy. His speech before the court in the Old Bailey "was a theatrical *tour de force*, but did not stand up to the testimony of boy prostitutes," writes Rictor Norton. "Wilde of course lied throughout much of his trials, and this particular line of defence was perhaps hypocritical and well rehearsed" (*The Myth of the Modern Homosexual* 222). This point of contention would be the impetus for movements that departed from Greek love.

The Love of the "Eigenen"

A new strand of Greek love took shape in Germany around the turn of the twentieth century, which is often termed the "masculinist" movement and which, for the purposes of this study, I refer to as "Eigene" love. This term was a neologism which Adolf Brand (1874–1945) coined for the title of his homosexual journal, *Der Eigene: Ein Blatt für männliche Kultur*, whose first edition appeared in 1896 and which was published intermittently until 1932. The publication spawned an organization, founded in 1902 by Brand and Benedict Friedländer (1866–1908), the *Gemeinschaft der Eigenen* (GdE) (Keilson-Lauritz, *Die Geschichte der eigenen Geschichte* 61–142). The term "Eigene" loses something when translated into English as "exceptional," or sometimes "self-owner." Marita Keilson-Lauritz explains that these options are one-sided; the advantage of the nomenclature lies in the equivocal nature of this unconventional German term (74). The German movement justified and defended same-sex desire by historicizing and deploying Greek love to map out relations between males. They did not disavow the physical manifestations of this love, but cautioned against excesses. Friedländer writes in *Renaissance des Eros Uranios* that the goal of their movement was "the revival of Hellenic *Lieblingminne* and its social recognition; however with the greatest possible avoidance of all sexual excesses" ("die Wiederbelebung der hellenischen Lieblingminne und deren sociale Anerkennung; jedoch mit möglichster Vermeidung aller sexueller Ausschreitungen"; *Renaissance des Eros Uranios* 259). Unlike English-speaking writers and theorists, who were reinventing Greek love at nearly the same time (which is explored further in the following chapter), Brand, Friedländer, and Kupffer remained true to the Greeks particularly in one aspect: they wrote of not intragenerational male same-sex love, but intergenerational love, or pederasty. The German *Eigenen* conceived of relations between males as between an older and a younger one. To describe these relations, however, they did not employ the term "pederasty" (*Päderastie*)—or its synonym in German "Knabenliebe." Friedländer instead uses the term "Lieblingminne" to describe the "courtly love" (*Minne*) of a man for a male favorite. This term was coined by Elisar von Kupffer (1872–1942) in his essay "Die Ethisch-politische Bedeutung der Lieblingminne" ("The Ethical-Political Significance of *Liebingminne*," 1899), which became the introduction to his literary anthology dedicated to the love of friends and love of a man for a youth that appeared the following year. Friedländer writes: "Under *Lieblingminne* is understood in particular close friendships between youths and still more the relations between men of unequal ages" ("Unter Lieblingminne sind insbesondere die engen Jugendfreundschaften und noch mehr die Bündnisse zwischen Männern ungleichen Alters zu verstehen"; *Renaissance des Eros Uranios* 259). Although there are two types of love described here, the one on which special emphasis is placed is that "between men of unequal ages."

The *Eigenen* viewed the ability to love homosexually as not confined to a particular species of human, but rather as a universal drive. Friedländer insists that this natural instinct forms the cement of sociability. "So-called homosexuality is only an extreme special case of a fully normal and necessary, psychological and biological characteristic of the human" ("Die sogenannte Homosexualität [ist] nur ein extremer Specialfall einer an sich völlig normalen und nothwendigen, physiologischen und biologischen Eigenschaft des Menschen"; *Renaissance des Eros Uranios* xiii). This understanding of male-male desire is also the foundation of the writings of Hans Blüher (1888–1955), in particular the third of his three-volume of his history of the *Wandervogelbewegung* (youth movement), *Die deutsche Wandervogelbewegung als erotisches Phänomen* (The German Youth Movement as an Erotic Phenomenon, 1912), and his most famous work, the two-volume *Die Erotik der männlichen Gesellschaft* (The Erotic in Manly Society), published in 1917 and 1919 (see Bruns, *Politik des Eros* 107–66). Friedländer contends that denying these normal and necessary drives is at the root of much modern social degeneration. This renaissance of Uranian Eros was imagined to be a panacea for social problems plaguing Wilhelmine German society. James Steakley, in his seminal history of the German homosexual liberation movements, posits that many social and community initiatives in Germany that formed during the late nineteenth century were responses to the rapid and turbulent industrialization and urbanization which followed the foundation of the German Empire in 1871. This rebirth of pederasty was part of this larger societal phenomenon, the *Lebensreformbewegungen* (life-reform movements), which promised to reverse a perceived decline of modern German culture. Steakley cites examples of other social movements, like the *Wandervogelbewegung*, *Freikörperkultur* (nudist movement), and various nutritional movements, such as vegetarianism (*The Homosexual Emancipation Movement in Germany* 26–27, 44). Using ancient practices and conceptions of love as a model, Germany could return to what Friedländer and other leading figures of the *Eigenen* argue would be more authentic love relations and thereby could undo the damage done to society by shoring up the social order.

Mentorship, Spiritual Begetting, and Mania

Greek love serves a dual purpose in *Der Tod in Venedig*. On the one hand, as Ignace Feuerlicht argues, it makes same-sex desire distant, impersonal, and inoffensive. On the other hand, it is an important tool which enables Aschenbach to conceptualize and to give voice to his desire and to imagine a path that a relationship between him and his beloved boy might follow. Ultimately, though, Greek love disintegrates. Its models are shown to constrain and thwart same-sex desire rather than liberate it. Reconciling pedagogy and Eros becomes a Sisyphean effort. Its intellectual conceits prove to be baseless. Thus, what results is that while Greek love operates on the one level, serving to distance the reader from material deemed morally objectionable, on the other level, these discourses and values fail. With regard to the latter, the novella challenges Greek love, positing the insufficiency of this philosophy in the modern world.

On the first of these levels, "For the reader, who otherwise might have been shocked by the 'perversion,'" writes Feuerlicht, the utilization of Greek love discourse meant that the novella's action was "unfolding in a time and place where 'such things' were 'beautiful'" ("Thomas Mann and Homoeroticism" 93). The "Greek backdrop" was "a help and refuge for Mann" as he transformed his experience of being captivated by the beauty of a Polish youth into fiction "and as the author who had to think of the public's reaction to that experience" (94). Feuerlicht suggests that Mann's use of Hellenism is indirectly explained in his essay on the poet August von Platen (1796–1835). In the essay, which was published in 1930, eighteen years after *Der Tod in Venedig*, Mann writes that Platen's homosexuality was evident in his verse even to his contemporaries: "His only disguise lay in his choice of the traditional forms in which he poured himself out; they gave a frame of tradition to his kind of passion. The Persian ghazal, the Renaissance sonnet, the Pindaric ode, all of them knew the youth-cult and gave it literary legitimacy" (*Essays of Three Decades* 264–65) ("Seine einzige Maskerade lag in der Wahl der überlieferten lyrischen Formen, in denen er sich ausströmte und die auch seiner Gefühlsart eine Überlieferung boten: Das persische Ghasel, das Renaissancesonnett, die Pindar'sche Ode kannten den Knabenkult und verliehen ihm literarische Legitimität"; *Gesammelte Werke* 9: 275). The poet channeled depictions of love between males into established poetic motifs, thereby granting it "literary legitimacy," allowing the subject matter to evade censure. "Thus the erotic feelings in Platen's works could be viewed by his readers as traditional, impersonal, and inoffensive" (Feuerlicht 94). But Greek love in Mann's novella is not limited to this role. Additionally, Greek love facilitates the protagonist's conceptualization of his desire, how he gives voice to his attraction, and the models through which he can imagine love relations between two males.

After he is first confronted with his object of desire, Aschenbach deploys his storehouse of art-historical knowledge to give voice to his appreciation of the boy's beauty. Tadzio is a living work of art: "With astonishment Aschenbach noticed that the boy was entirely beautiful. His countenance, pale and gracefully reserved, was surrounded by ringlets of honey-colored hair, and with its straight nose, its enchanting mouth, its expression of sweet and divine gravity, it recalled Greek sculpture of the noblest period" (219) ("Mit Erstaunen bemerkte Aschenbach, daß der Knabe vollkommen schön war. Sein Antlitz, bleich und anmutig verschlossen, von honigfarbenem Haar umringelt, mit der gerade abfallenden Nase, dem lieblichen Munde, dem Ausdruck von holdem und göttlichem Ernst, erinnerte an griechische Bildwerke aus edelster Zeit"; 91). Greek art is Aschenbach's first port of call: he sees Tadzio's beauty in artistic terms, feigning an impersonal interest, cloaking his "ecstasy" ("Entzücken") and "rapture" ("Hingerissenheit") in the "cool professional approval" ("fachmännisch kühlen Billigung") of an artist confronted with a masterpiece (223; 96). Ritchie Robertson describes how in general *Der Tod in Venedig* "continues and comments on the long-standing German fascination with Greece and Greek sculpture" and in particular explores the unstable relation between art and desire ("Classicism and Its Pitfalls" 96–97). Regarding Aschenbach's unconscious decision to conceptualize physical desire in terms of appreciation for artistic beauty, Robertson asks, "Does art sublimate desire, or release it?" (97). This strategy of channeling his attraction through these concepts depersonalizes the desire, thereby rendering homoeroticism unthreatening to his persona as the revered, dignified *Dichter*. As the narrative progresses, his culture not only gives him the vocabulary with which he can voice his attraction, but it provides him with models through which he can imagine a relationship with the boy.

In the mind of the protagonist, a mentorship develops between him and Tadzio. The first instance of these imagined dialogues occurs after he watches another boy named Jaschu kiss Tadzio. Quoting Xenophon's *Memorabilia of Socrates* (c. 371 BCE), Aschenbach jestingly contemplates giving Jaschu the same advice that Socrates gives to Critobulus after he had kissed Alcibiades's son (Deuse, "Griechisches in *Der Tod in Venedig*" 44). "Aschenbach was tempted to shake his finger at him. 'But I counsel you, Critobulus,' he thought with a smile, 'to go travelling for a year! You will need that much time at least before you are cured'" (226) ("Aschenbach war versucht, ihm mit dem Finger zu drohen. 'Dir aber rat ich, Kritobulos,' dachte er lächelnd, 'geh ein Jahr auf Reisen! Denn soviel brauchst du mindestens Zeit zur Genesung'"; 100–01). Over the ensuing days he follows and watches the boy, and the more he watches, the more his Socratic fantasy grows. "And a delightful vision came to him, spun from the sea's murmur and the glittering sunlight. It was the old plane tree not far from the walls of Athens. . . . But on the grass . . . there reclined two men . . . one elderly and one young, one ugly and one beautiful, the wise beside the desirable. And Socrates, wooing him with witty compliments and jests, was instructing Phaedrus on desire and virtue" (238) ("Und aus Meerrausch und Sonnenglast spann sich ihm ein reizendes Bild. Es war die alte

Platane unfern den Mauern Athens. . . . Auf dem Rasen aber . . . lagerten zwei . . . ein Ältlicher und ein Junger, ein Häßlicher und ein Schöner, der Weise beim Liebenswürdigen. Und unter Artigkeiten und geistreich werbenden Scherzen belehrte Sokrates den Phaidros über Sehnsucht und Tugend"; 117). Within the Platonic paradigm, Tadzio promises to be a source of rejuvenation for Aschenbach's art. "The boy's beauty is the writer's inspiration," writes T. J. Reed (*Making and Unmaking a Master* 56). "The *Phaedrus* talks of 'spiritual begetting' as something analogous to, but higher than, the production of physical offspring. Homosexual love might lead men to write poetry, to pursue philosophy, or to act bravely in a common cause" (55). The rejuvenating effect attributed to the boy's beauty is particularly appealing to Aschenbach who, as the reader learns in the first chapter, takes no pleasure in his writing and fears that the emotion he enslaved to reach the heights of honor and respectability is now avenging itself. "Could it be that the enslaved emotion was now avenging itself by deserting him, by refusing from now on to bear up his art on its wings, by taking with it all his joy in words, all his appetite for the beauty of form?" (201) ("Rächte sich nun also die geknechtete Empfindung, indem sie ihn verließ, indem sie seine Kunst fürder zu tragen und zu beflügeln sich weigerte und alle Lust, alles Entzücken an der Form und am Ausdruck mit sich hinwegnahm?"; 67). He longs to work in the presence of his beloved boy whose beauty he sees as an embodiment of the divine and a medium to divine inspiration, and Aschenbach does have this opportunity. "Never had he felt the joy of the word more sweetly, never had he known so clearly that Eros dwells in language, as during those periously precious hours in which, seated at his rough table under the awning, in full view of his idol and with the music of his voice in his ears, he shaped upon Tadzio's beauty his brief essay—that page and a half of exquisite prose which with its limpid nobility and vibrant controlled passion was soon to win the admiration of many" (239) ("Nie hatte er die Lust des Wortes süßer empfunden, nie so gewußt, daß Eros im Worte sei, wie während der gefährlich köstlichen Stunden, in denen er, an seinem rohen Tische unter dem Schattentuch, im Angesicht des Idols und die Musik seiner Stimme im Ohr, nach Tadzios Schönheit seine kleine Abhandlung,—jene anderthalb Seiten erlesener Prosa formte, deren Lauterkeit, Adel und schwingende Gefühlsspannung binnen kurzem die Bewunderung vieler erregen sollte"; 118–19). This page-and-a-half essay is an "act of intercourse and begetting between a mind and a body" (240) ("zeugender Verkehr des Geistes mit einem Körper"; 119), but it is the only artistic fruit Aschenbach's love bears, and the writing thereof seems nearly indecent to the author after the intoxication wears off. "It is as well that the world knows only a fine piece of work and not also its origins" (239) ("Es ist sicher gut, daß die Welt nur das schöne Werk, nicht auch seine Ursprünge"; 119). Once his reserve reasserts itself, Aschenbach is ashamed of his dalliance, as if he had been involved in "some kind of debauch" (240) ("einer Ausschweifung"; 119). His passion for the beloved boy does not ultimately lead to "spiritual begetting"; instead it leads him to stalk the lad and his family maniacally through Venice (see R. Robertson, "Classicism and Its Pitfalls" 102).

As his obsession grows ever more intense, Aschenbach pauses and asks: "Where is this leading me! he would reflect in consternation" (249) ("Auf welchen Wegen! dachte er dann mit Bestürzung"; 131). He justifies his love and his actions to himself through Greek love discourse. "Had it not been highly honoured by the most valiant of peoples, indeed had he not read that in their cities it had flourished by inspiring valorous deeds? Numerous warrior-heroes of olden times had willingly borne its yoke, for there was no kind of abasement that could be reckoned as such if the god had imposed it; and actions that would have been castigated as signs of cowardice had their motives been different, such as falling to the ground in supplication, desperate pleas and slavish demeanour—these were accounted no disgrace to a lover, but rather won him still greater praise" (249–50) ("Hatte er nicht bei den tapfersten Völkern vorzüglich in Ansehen gestanden, ja, hieß es nicht, daß er durch Tapferkeit in ihren Städten geblüht habe? Zahlreiche Kriegshelden der Vorzeit hatten willig sein Joch getragen, denn gar keine Erniedrigung galt, die der Gott verhängte, und Taten, die als Merkmale der Feigheit wären gescholten worden, wenn sie um anderer Zwecke willen geschehen wären: Fußfälle, Schwüre, inständige Bitten und sklavisches Wesen, solche gereichten dem Liebenden nicht zur Schande, sondern er erntete vielmehr noch Lob dafür"; 132). There we have a case of Mannian irony directed at Greek love justification. Potentially any undignified action, any exotic extravagance of feeling, can be justified as manly in this paradigm that the protagonist has set up for himself. "Signs of cowardice" ("Merkmale der Feigheit")—such as refusing to inform Tadzio's mother that a quarantine of the city is imminent—as well as "falling to the ground in supplication, desperate pleas and slavish demeanour" ("Fußfälle, Schwüre, inständige Bitten und sklavisches Wesen") are accorded honor, indeed they are praiseworthy, because they are performed out of love. Any otherwise unsavory act or behavior can be vindicated via the Greeks. Aschenbach's love reveals itself to be common love, base sensuality which one feels for boys or women, according to Pausanias, and not sexless, intellectual heavenly love. The portrayal is ironic in that it brings into question the overwrought nature of this distinction. As the narrative progresses, the philosophic justification for his attraction assumes an ever diminishing importance until the final monologue, where the protagonist repudiates the assumed mentor role.

The intellectual and pedagogic aims of the intergenerational liaison were seen as crucial to the apologia of Greek love, and for Aschenbach his attraction to Tadzio, and the relationship that he fantasizes exists between the two, are rooted in this tradition. And yet, in the final Platonic monologue, Aschenbach gives up pretentions to reconciling Eros with philosophic mentorship. After stalking Tadzio through the dark and dirty alleyways of Venice, he collapses in a rubbish-strewn square and eats overripe strawberries to quench his "no longer endurable thirst" (264) ("nicht mehr erträgliche[n] Durst"; 152). This thirst is for sexual gratification rather than for water because he chooses strawberries, which, as Ellis Shookman points out, was an established literary trope for succumbing to the temptation of sexual pleasure (*A Reference Guide* 114). Symbolically Aschenbach consummates his love for Tadzio, and as these forbidden fruit are overripe and most likely tainted, this act may also indicate an intentional self-infection with cholera (see Binion, *Sounding the Classics* 139; see also Kitcher, *Deaths in Venice* 125–29 for an alternate interpretation). As he sits in the square, his intellect warped by the "strange dream-logic" ("seltsam[e] Traumlogik") of his degraded mental and physical condition, he imagines for the last time that he converses with his beloved Phaedrus/Tadzio. At this point in the narrative, Aschenbach rejects the pedagogic aims and ideals of Greek love *paiderastia* first in his specific case and then in general. He admits defeat in mentoring his beloved: "For Beauty, Phaedrus, mark well! only Beauty is at one and the same time divine and visible, and so it is indeed the sensuous lover's path, little Phaedrus, it is the artist's path to the spirit.... For I must tell you that we artists cannot tread the path of Beauty without Eros keeping company with us and appointing himself as our guide .... Do you see now perhaps why we writers can be neither wise nor dignified? That we necessarily go astray, necessarily remain dissolute emotional adventurers?" (265) ("Denn die Schönheit, Phaidros, merke das wohl, nur die Schönheit ist göttlich und sichtbar zugleich, und so ist sie denn also des Sinnlichen Weg, ist, kleiner Phaidros, der Weg des Künstlers zum Geiste.... Denn du mußt wissen, daß wir Dichter den Weg der Schönheit nicht gehen können, ohne daß Eros sich zugesellt und sich zum Führer aufwirft.... Siehst du nun wohl, daß wir Dichter nicht weise noch würdig sein können? Daß wir notwendig in die Irre gehen, notwendig liederlich und Abenteurer des Gefühles bleiben?"; 153). And then he continues, calling into question whether any artist could assume the role of educator: he spurns "the use of art to educate the nation and its youth" ("Volks- und Jugenderziehung durch die Kunst"), characterizing it as "a reprehensible undertaking which should be forbidden by law" ("ein gewagtes, zu verbietendes Unternehmen"). "For how can one be fit to be an educator when one has been born with an incorrigible and natural tendency toward the abyss?" (265) ("Denn wie sollte wohl der zum Erzieher taugen, dem eine unverbesserliche und natürliche Richtung zum Abgrunde eingeboren ist?"; 153). The artist, in particular love-drunk Aschenbach, is unworthy of acting as a mentor because his artistic temperament and the nature of artistic production prevent him from being a wise and suitable educator. Caroline Picart explains that "The artist is the slave of desire and passion—such is his calling, his craving, and his shame, which renders him unfit to become a worthy citizen" (*Thomas Mann and Friedrich Nietzsche* 28). Reed writes that the final dialogue "draws the conclusion that there simply was no right path for [Aschenbach]. Whatever he did—and, more generally, whatever any artist does—must be tragically wrong in one direction or another" (*Making and Unmaking a Master* 66). The only lesson Aschenbach can teach is the impossibility of mentoring even an imagined pupil (70). Tobin points out that "While Socrates becomes more idealistic about love in the *Phaedrus*, Aschenbach becomes less so in *Der Tod in Venedig*. The narration presents Aschenbach's arguments in a way that rejects the Grecophilic understanding of male-male desire" ("Queering Thomas Mann's *Der Tod in Venedig*" 76–77). What Tobin considers, but neither Picart nor Reed do, is that by condemning mentorship and by extension the pedagogic defense of intergenerational same-sex love, the novella is toppling the central buttress to the Greek love apologia, thereby indicating a major rupture with contemporary discourses of Greek love. The novella works simultaneously within and against the legacy of Hellenism applied to love between men. Aschenbach reasons that he, and the artist in general, is an unfit educator, owing to his incorrigible, inborn "sympathy with the abyss" (207) ("Sympathie mit dem Abgrund"; 74); on the other hand, the text intimates that the artist should follow the path of Eros to love and create art, to be an adventurer of emotions, free from the moral imperatives to educate, to be a guardian of values and morals, and to be a wise and worthy citizen. That the text is willing to call this discourse into question signals a significant shift in thinking toward Greek love; as a conduit for the expression of same-sex love in the modern era it is insufficient, constraining, and ends in tragic disappointment.

Dramatizing the shortcomings of Greek love ideals and models is the chief means through which the novella breaks with literary Hellenism. Absent from the text's incorporation of Greek love discourses is the justification that same-sex love is a higher and purer form of love because of its educative and intellectual components. Later in his career, Mann would address this issue again in his essay "August von Platen," in which he states unequivocally that same-sex passion is a love like any other. Platen was a key figure whom Mann referenced in the creation of Aschenbach (Feuerlicht, "Thomas Mann and Homoeroticism" 93–94; R. Robertson, "Classicism and Its Pitfalls" 96; Tobin, "Queering" 77–78; see also Henry, "August Graf von Platen und *Der Tod in Venedig*" 27–50; and Kitcher, *Deaths in Venice* 75–82). Mann was fascinated by the relationship between Platen's poetry and his sexuality, and the poet's death inspired events in the novella. When a cholera epidemic hit Italy, Platen fled Naples, but he had already contracted the disease and he died a few days later in Sicily (Aldrich, *Seduction of the Mediterranean* 62). In the essay, Mann considers the role the poet's homosexuality played in his artistic production: "Platen realized that his homosexual constitution was his profoundest impulse, and then again did not realize it. He suggests it, in the sense of a sacred subjection to the beautiful, as the purity and consecration of the poet to the highest he knows, in love as well" (*Essays of Three Decades* 264) ("Platen selbst hat diesen seinen tiefsten Impuls [seine exklusiv homoerotische Anlage] gekannt und auch wieder nicht gekannt: er deutet ihn als heilige Unterjochung durch das Schöne, als Dichterreinheit, Dichterweihe zum Höheren auch in der Liebe"; *Gesammelte Werke* 9: 274). Mann asserts that Platen was correct in recognizing his homosexuality as his deepest impulse in the creation of his art. But his belief that same-sex love is a higher form of love is only a "half-understanding" ("halbe[s] Verständnis"). Mann writes that Platen believed that "his love was in some sense higher, instead of a love like anybody else's, only—at least in his time—with smaller prospects of happiness" (264) ("seine Liebe durchaus keine höhere, sondern eine Liebe war wie jede andere, nur—wenigstens zu seiner Zeit—mit selteneren Glücksmöglichkeiten"; 274).

It is problematic to read the novella in light of a later essay, nonetheless there is a certain affinity here deserves to be mentioned. Aschenbach's love for Tadzio, although not a higher form of love, as many nineteenth-century and contemporary Greek love enthusiasts were wont to claim, possesses the power to bear his art upon its wings. In this way, Mann juxtaposes Platen and Aschenbach significantly. Platen's recognition of his Eros, despite it being a half-understanding, enriches his poetry and imbues it with beauty and vitality. Platen merges classicism with "softness, soaringness, lyric enchantment, music, that magic breath and bloom, those accents of inspiration" ("Weichheit, Beschwingtheit, Liedzauber, Musik, jener Hauch und Farbenstaub, jener Tonfall magischer Innigkeit"; 260) to craft poetry which is "truly lyric" ("eigentlich lyrisch"; 269). Aschenbach's art has brought him national acclaim and a title of nobility, but it brings him neither joy nor pleasure. His art is an exhausting struggle, a battle which in the course of the narrative he loses. Thus, a half-understanding is better than none at all. By the time Aschenbach begins to delight in sensuality, he lacks the ability to regulate his pleasure and it consumes him. The novella does not condemn this desire, as Hannelore Mundt argues, only the extremes to which it leads (*Understanding Thomas Mann* 93). The novella partakes of the understanding of same-sex love that, because it is a love like any other, is a wellspring of artistic inspiration. This claim is lent credence by the fact that same-sex desire was a source of inspiration in the production of the novella. Like his protagonist, Mann encountered and was captivated by the beauty of a Polish youth while on holiday in Venice in 1911. Although the fictional author is unable to utilize his desire toward significant creative production, the novella proves that Mann was able to do so (see Heilbut, *Thomas Mann: Eros and Literature* 247; Kurzke, *Thomas Mann: Das Leben als Kunstwerk* 194). While utilizing the literary legacy of Greek love to grant the novella's portrayal of intergenerational same-sex love legitimacy, *Der Tod in Venedig* undermines the foundations upon which this legacy is set. The novella achieves this by thematizing the shortcomings of *paiderastia*, especially the intellectual and pedagogic basis of these relations.

Intergenerational, but Not Greek, Love

The first book of the nameless love, "Die namenlose Liebe: Ein Bekenntniss," begins with an evocation of ancient Greece: "Once, more than two thousand years ago, it was one of the roots from which the in so many ways unrivalled culture of a people, the most thirsty for beauty and drunk on beauty that the world has ever known, drew its best nourishment. Health, strength and greatness blossomed for the Greeks from the love of a man for a youth, of a youth for a man, a love prized by its thinkers and sung by its poets" (53) ("Einst, vor mehr als zweimal Tausend Jahren, war sie eine der Wurzeln, aus denen die in so Vielem unerreichte Kultur des schönheitsdurstigsten und schönheitstrunkensten Volkes, das die Erde bisher getragen, ihre beste Nahrung sog. Gesundheit, Kraft und Größe erblühte den Grichen aus ihrer, von ihren Denkern gepriesenen, von ihren Dichtern besungenen Liebe des Mannes zum Jüngling, des Jünglings zum Manne"; 73). Despite the contemporary moral and legal persecution of this love, writes Mackay, "a Greek inheritance ineradicably lives on" (56) ("ein hellenisches Erbteil . . . unausrottbar weiterlebt"; 78). Yet, ironically, it does not live on in *Die Bücher der namenlosen Liebe*. Mackay's fiction confronts some aspects of the Greek love legacy, but then moves beyond these concerns to depict the joys and sufferings involved in actual love relationships between men and teenage boys in the modern world. There are three key aspects of Mackay's fiction which challenge nineteenth- and early twentieth-century Greek love discourses—the texts reject (1) the ideal that sexual desire should be repressed or sublimated, (2) that these relations are pedagogic, and (3) that, because they are conducted between men and are intellectual, they are higher and purer than love between men and women.

The one aspect of the nameless love which does bears a great deal of similarity to ancient erotic practices, as well as some nineteenth-century interpretations of them, is that the nameless love is between men and youths. Mackay's fiction fits into an ephebeophilic tradition, operating within the established Greek love literary conventions by depicting intergenerational love with its associated celebration of adolescent beauty. In the books of the nameless love, all the same-sex love relations portrayed are intergenerational: "always an older man and a younger" (*Hustler* 49) ("immer ein Älterer und ein Jüngerer"; *Puppenjunge* 53). In *Fenny Skaller*, none of the boys are "under fourteen, none over seventeen" (*Books* 180) ("unter vierzehn, keines über siebzehn"; *Bücher* 316); they belong to "the sweet and mysterious, the inexplicable ripening age" (180) ("dem süßen und geheimnißvollen, dem unerklärlichen Alter des Reifens"; 316). This applies to Günther as well, and his beauty is indeed celebrated. The two central characters share a bedroom in a hotel and, while the lad slumbers, Graff has his first opportunity to take his beauty in fully. "How beautiful he was! How divinely beautiful! Never had he believed that a human being, that he could be so beautiful" (122) ("Wie schön er war!—Wie göttlich schön!—Nie hatte [Graff] geglaubt, daß ein Mensch, daß er so schön sein könne!"; 142). The narration of the youth's physical beauty, channeled, as it is, though Graff's perception, rhapsodically catalogs his attributes. "How beautiful were his legs! How tender his knees and hips! How well-proportioned his still-so-childlike breast! How undeveloped still his slim shoulders, those still-so-thin arms! And how beautiful were those hands, those slender hands, the only part of this body he had come to know, those hands that he had held in his own and which he loved almost more than that face!" (122) ("Wie schön waren diese Beine!—Wie zart ihre Gelenke und Hüften!—Wie ebenmäßig die noch so kindliche Brust!—Wie unentwickelt noch die schmalen Schultern, diese noch so dünnen Arme!—Und wie schön waren diese Hände, diese schlanken Hände, die allein von diesem Körper er erst kannte, diese Hände, die er in den seinen gehalten und die er liebte, wie kaum das Gesicht!"; 142). The adjective "tender" ("zart") appears here and recurs in other descriptions of Günther. As an object of desire, he is described by Graff in terms of his immature characteristics: his tender knees and hips, his childlike chest, undeveloped shoulders, and thin arms. The most striking fact about Günther's physical characterization is that there is nothing particularly masculine about him. Such characterizations are also found in the writings of contemporaries, such as André Gide, Stefan George, and Constantine Cavafy, as well as

Mann. Günther and Tadzio contrast interestingly. The adjective "zart" is often used to describe both, although Günther's tenderness differs from that of Tadzio's. The latter is tender in terms of fragility, weakness, decline, and death (central themes to Mann's novella), whereas the former's tenderness represents amelioration; Günther is like a blossoming rose. Both lads are possessors of divine beauty, but Tadzio's beauty communicates an eternal quality as opposed to the transience of Günther's "short springtime of his life" (295) ("kurze Frühling seines Lebens"; 340). Like his youthful beauty, desire of an "ephebe" is transitory by nature. "For this love was appointed only a modest span, and eternal it was not. It swore no oath and they did not bind themselves in a bond for life. They came and they went, and if friendship developed and the friendship remained, that was good" (*Books* 199) ("Denn dieser seiner Liebe war nur eine Spanne beschieden, und ewig war sie nicht. Sie schwor keine Treue und sie band sich nicht zu einem Bunde für das Leben. Sie kam und sie ging, und wenn Freundschaft blieb, so war es gut"; *Bücher* 347). It is the age, not the individual young man, which Skaller and Graff love. "It is the age which you love, Hermann. . . . Would you love him if he had a mustache?" (290) ("Es ist das Alter, welches Du liebst, Hermann. . . . Würdest Du ihn lieben, wenn er einen Schnurrbart hätte?"; 334–45). Graff's spiritual "mother," the only other character in the book to understand him fully, makes it clear to him that although he might have remained friends with Günther, he could love him or find him sexually attractive only as an adolescent. For the Greeks, explains James Davidson, facial hair marks entry into manhood, it is nature's signal that passivity in a homosexual relationship is no longer acceptable (*The Greeks and Greek Love* 80–81). The mustache fulfills a comparable function in the novel. Hence, in terms of the desire the nameless love fiction depicts, there are marked similarities with Greek love and contemporary interpretations of it.

However, the nameless love books reject the philosophical framework of the Hellenism. The first and foremost of the ideals which Mackay's fiction rejects is the one that insists that so-called "heavenly love" between men and youths must remain chaste. In *Der Puppenjunge* especially, male-male sexuality is freed from many of the complications entailed in the sublimation of physical desire. Unlike Aschenbach or Clive, Graff consummates his relationship with his beloved. Mackay's fiction takes the physical manifestations of love for granted in a way that other works of fiction of the era do not. Under the relatively liberal Weimar Republic, greater openness in depictions of homosexual love in fiction was possible, and thus *Der Puppenjunge* was not subject to the strict censorship that even the earlier nameless love writings faced. Graff, unaware that the boy he has fallen in love with is a *Strichjunge* (hustler or renter), initially resists making an amorous advance. Fighting his urge causes him no mean amount of internal conflict. This behavior, inexplicable to Günther, drives the boy away. Eventually Graff comes to the conclusion that his efforts at chastity are nothing but "self-torture" ("Selbstquälereien") and he spurns the notion that love can or ought to remain unconsummated, the "love of souls": "Why did people talk and twaddle about the love of souls! It did not exist. It was the sentiment of weak, eccentric, sick people! The healthy person wanted and had to possess what he loved, not in unstable dreams of longing, but in the warm reality of life. Everything ... that he felt for him had been nothing other than this one burning wish: to possess him!" (171–72) ("Was redeten und faselten die Menschen von einer Liebe der Seelen? Es gab sie nicht. Es war das Empfinden schwacher, überspannter, kranker Menschen!—Der gesunde wollte und mußte besitzen, was er liebte: nicht in haltlosen Träumen der Sehnsucht, sondern in der warmen Wirklichkeit des Lebens. Alles ... was er für ihn gefühlt, war Nichts Anderes gewesen, als dieser eine glühende Wunsch: ihn zu besitzen!"; 200). Graff voices a concept that is intimated in *Der Tod in Venedig* with Aschenbach and is communicated in *Maurice* through the decline of Clive's appearance and his estate, Penge: the association between suppression of physical desire and illness, and consequently between sexual fulfillment and health. This challenges the moralistic position that thwarting sexual desire is an admirable undertaking. Even before Freud challenged conventions by asserting that sex was a healthy and necessary basic drive, the Austrian psychiatrist Richard von Krafft-Ebing in his magnum opus, *Psychopathia Sexualis* (first edition, 1886), writes that pederasts "who sometimes satisfy themselves with platonic love" do so at "the risk however, of becoming nervous (neurasthenic) and insane as a result of this enforced abstinence" (231) ("Es gibt feinfühlige und willensstarke Individuen, die ihre Triebe zu beherrschen im Stande sind, freilich mit der Gefahr, durch diese erzwungene Abstinenz nervensiech (neutasthenisch) und gemüthskrank zu werden"; 249). Mackay's characters are reunited and they have intercourse; afterward Günther tells him: "You could have had that long ago, if—you had not been so dumb!" (179) ("Das hättest Du längst haben können, wenn—Du nicht so dumm gewesen wärest!"; 208).

The pedagogic aims and justification of the intergenerational liaison are negated in *Puppenjunge* in the same forthright manner. Earlier in the narrative, after Graff has seen Günther in the street, but not yet met him, he imagines a friend whom he could love and who would love him in return: "A young friend, a quite young friend, still impressionable, before whom the world lay as a closed book full of suspense and mystery, whose title only was known, whose first pages he wanted to turn and read with him, explaining to him what he still did not yet understand and was not yet able to understand" (58) ("Ein junger Freund, ein ganz junger, empfänglicher noch, vor dem die Welt noch lag wie ein verschlossenes, geheimnisvoll-spannendes Buch; wie ein Buch, von dem er erst das Titelblatt kannte; dessen erste Blätter er mit ihm zusammen wenden und lesen wollte, ihm deutend, was er noch nicht verstand und noch nicht verstehen konnte"; 64). Thus at the outset at least, he intends to mentor the boy he loves, to assist him in gaining *Bildung* (education and socialization) and transition from boyhood to manhood. Graff at this point in the narrative imagines that he would reject the idea of a relationship based upon goods for services rendered (58; 64). As the relationship between Graff and Günther develops in the narrative, this proves not to be the case. Theirs is less about the education and socialization of the young man than it is about the emotional and sexual needs of the older partner. Günther may appreciate his friendship, this can be assumed but is never made explicit, but it is clear that the sexual encounters are not mutually satisfying. "Disgust?

No, he felt no disgust really, but also no pleasure—he simply went along. In the end, the main thing in all this was only the money" (51) ("Ekel?—Nein, er empfand eigentlich keinen Ekel. Aber auch kein Vergnügen. Er machte eben mit. Schließlich war bei dem Allen doch nur das Geld die Hauptsache"; 55). In this regard Günther is typical of interwar male prostitutes in Berlin. Frank Rector explains that "Many of the boys and young men of post-World War I Germany were not *homo*sexual, they were simply *sexual*" (*The Nazi Extermination of Homosexuals* 22). And Graff's efforts to better the lad's lot appear half-hearted at best, while class differences and their disparate educational levels act as an insurmountable barrier to any pretence at mentorship. This is not only true for this particular case, but the text demonstrates this in regard to any attempt at educating the *Strichjungen*. "If a decent man came among them, one with good intentions toward one of them . . . that opportunity too was wasted until the gentleman, discouraged by his lethargy, dropped him again. They all returned back here again . . . semiconscious by day, living it up at night" (252) ("War einmal ein anständiger Mensch darunter, der es gut mit einem von ihnen [den Strichjungen] meinte . . . so ließ man sich auch Das gefallen, bis 'der Herr' ihn, entmutigt durch diese Lethargie, wieder fallen ließ. Alle kehrten sie . . . zurück, verdämmernd die Tage, durchjubelnd die Nächte"; 291). Thus, according to the novel's portrayal, blame lies with the boys, their dissolute behavior, their lack of ambition. *Fenny Skaller* goes so far as to characterize love for adolescent boys as a curse because of the lack of empathy of adolescent boys: "It was a horrible age, and a curse to love it" (*Books* 184) ("Es war ein schreckliches Alter, und ein Fluch, es zu lieben"; *Bücher* 322). For this reason pedagogy is not merely unnecessary, but impossible. "This age was confused and uncertain, impulsive and lacking in insight. They say it must be taught. But there was nothing of the teacher in him. He could only be its friend, no more, no less. He could only understand it" (*Books* 183) ("Verworren und schwankend war es, dies Alter, triebhaft und einsichtslos. Sie sagten, man müsse es erziehen. Aber in ihm war Nichts von einem Erzieher. Er konnte nur sein Freund sein, nicht mehr, nicht weniger. Er konnte es nur verstehen"; 321). Skaller can offer his young friends understanding and love, but not mentorship, not education. The reader can infer that the same is true in Graff's case. The rejection of pedagogy in *Der Puppenjunge* and *Fenny Skaller* is twofold: overtly mentorship is impossible because adolescence simply will not have it, and implicitly this justification and defense of this love is superfluous. The implication is that love does not need pedagogy to justify it, playing no more of a role in these relations than it would play in heterosexual love or any other form of love.

From the beginning of the narrative, Graff understands that his love needs no explanation: "It was a love just like any other love" (158) ("Es war eine Liebe wie jede andere Liebe"; 184) And toward the novel's climax, after Graff has been released from prison for violating Paragraph 175, this is reiterated to him by his "mother" who assures him: "It is a love, like every other" (289) ("Es ist eine Liebe, wie jede andere"; 333). This is the novel's only defense of same-sex love, which recurs throughout the Sagitta writings. Same-sex love needs no justification, explanation, or excuse any more than cross-sex love does. Owing to this bold stance, Mackay's fiction differs from that of many of his contemporaries, including writers associated with Adolf Brand's journal, *Der Eigene*, and the homophile association *Gemeinschaft der Eigenen*. Mackay was in some respects sympathetic to this movement, but not a part of it. His writings regularly appeared in *Der Eigene*, and he materially contributed to the philosophy of individual anarchism which was central to the *Eigenen* movement by rediscovering and circulating Max Stirner's *Der Einzige und sein Eigentum* (*The Ego and His Own*, 1844) (Keilson-Lauritz, *Die Geschichte der eigenen Geschichte* 66–67; Ivory, "The Urning and His Own" 338). At the same time, Mackay charts his own course toward the liberation of male-male love in his writings. He never formally joined the GdE and rejected the association's right-wing nationalistic leanings and anti-Semitism (J. Bauer, "On the Nameless Love and Infinite Sexualities" 8), and, crucially, he avoids turning to the past for answers for love between males in the modern era. Although the love he depicts in his fiction is intergenerational, it is distinct from the understanding of love between a man and a youth, "hellenische Lieblingminne," theorized by Friedländer in *Renaissance des Eros Uranios* and by Kupffer in the introduction to his anthology. Indeed, Mackay is critical of key aspects of their path toward liberation. In the introduction to *Die Bücher der namenlosen Liebe*, Mackay criticizes Greek love apologia, and thereby subtly distinguishes his vision of same-sex love from that of the GdE. He identifies the positioning of love between males as a higher, purer form of love as one of the failings of homosexual liberation efforts up to that point: "In reaction to a persecution that had increased until it was unbearable, it has been sought to represent this love as special, as 'nobler and better.' It is not. This love is a love like any other love, not better, but also not worse" (44–45) ("Man hat, im Umschlag gegen eine bis zur Unerträglichkeit gesteigerte Verfolgung, versucht, diese Liebe als eine besondere hinzustellen, als eine 'edlere und bessere.' Das ist sie nicht. Diese Liebe ist eine Liebe, wie jede andere Liebe, nicht besser, aber auch nicht schlechter"; 62). In elevating love between men, one must necessarily denigrate love between man and woman; Mackay rejects this strategy. "The fight *for* [same-sex love] should never degenerate into a fight *against* another" (45) ("Der Kampf für [gleichgeschlechtliche Liebe] sollte nie ausarten in einen Kampf gegen eine andere"; 62). He opposes an effort that "sought to promote the freedom of the love of a man at women's expense" ("versucht, die Freiheit der Liebe des Mannes zu fordern auf Kosten der Frau"). Mackay cautions against emancipation efforts that alienate the heterosexual mainstream and could make the enemies of today into the irreconcilable enemies of tomorrow (45; 62). The introduction does not openly name the *Gemeinschaft der Eigenen*, but by censuring the misogynist and retrogressive movement toward liberation, it leaves little doubt from which stances Mackay distances himself. Mackay's fiction implicitly opposes the masculinist movement by rejecting their retrogressive vision of universal same-sex desire structured as Hellenic *Lieblingminne*. Instead, love between an older and a younger man is a love like any other, it is not nobler or better than the love shared between a man and a woman, it is not educative, and certainly is not the key to the renewal of German culture.

Mackay's Sagitta texts develop and advocate an alternate vision of love between men: one that neither surrenders itself to the hands of the scientists, immersing itself in their taxonomy and thought structures, nor indulges in an anachronistic fantasy of a rebirth of pre- and early modern conceptions of love, the renaissance of Hellenic *Lieblingminne*. Greek love is briefly invoked in *Fenny Skaller*: the nameless love is identified as "that between the masculine man, whose masculine inclination was for the masculine youth—the ancient love of the Greeks" (*Books* 148) ("den zwischen dem männlichen Manne, dessen männliche Neigung der männlichen Jugend galt—die alte Liebe der Hellenen"; *Bücher* 263); but this serves another purpose. The key word in that passage is "manly," which indicates the importance of tropes of masculinity in the nameless love vision and identity (which is discussed in greater depth in chapter 7). Greek love does not provide in *Der Puppenjunge*, or the other books of the nameless love, the historical validation or the philosophical justification of love between men that it had effected in earlier texts; instead Mackay's fiction validates same-sex desire and love through its insistence that it is a love like any other, and thus requires no defense or justification outside itself.

Conclusion

Greek love had been in the nineteenth century an indispensable counter to church teachings and state persecution. But the repudiation of the body which is found in the source texts, such as in particular speeches of Plato's *Symposium* and in the *Phaedrus* (and which is communicated directly in the *Laws*), spelled the end of the primacy of this discourse in homosexual identity formation, in homosexual politics, and in homosexual literature. Mann's *Der Tod in Venedig* dramatizes the Western European legacy of Hellenism and specifically calls into question many of the conceits of this philosophy. The novella discounts many of the cornerstones of the Greek love defense: that this desire is educative and intellectual, that physical desire should be sublimated, and that this love consequently is higher and purer than so-called "common" love. Mackay's *Der Puppenjunge* too responds to legacies of Hellenism as well as "Eigene love," the revived Greek love particular to the German cultural context, but progresses further than the former literary texts in throwing off Greek loves. And one way that it does this is by fully affirming the sexual component to intergenerational love. The anxiety about sexual consummation of same-sex love embedded in Plato, which is problematized in *Der Tod in Venedig* as a longing for sexual relations that unhinges the protagonist, Gustav von Aschenbach, is cast off in *Der Puppenjunge* when Hermann Graff sleeps with Günther.

Chapter 3

The "manly love of comrades"

The classicist and poet John Addington Symonds (1840–1893) in his *Memoirs*, which were written between 1889 and 1893, recalls his sexual awakening through the writings of Plato, by "stumbl[ing] on the *Phaedrus*": "I read on and on, till I reached the end. Then I began the *Symposium*; and the sun was shining on the shrubs outside the ground-floor room in which I slept, before I shut the book up . . . Here in the *Phaedrus* and the *Symposium*—in the myth of the Soul and the speeches of Pausanias, Agathon, and Diotima—I discovered the true *liber amoris* at last, the revelation I had been waiting for, the consecration of a long-cherished idealism. It was just as though the voice of my own soul spoke to me through Plato, as though in some antenatal experience I had lived the life of a philosophical Greek lover" (*Memoirs* 99). He would go on from this point to become one of the nineteenth century's most influential Greek love theorists. It seemed to him that through the *Symposium* he "had obtained the sanction of the love which had been ruling [him] from childhood" (*Memoirs* 99). And yet, Plato did not offer young Symonds the means of expressing the physical dimensions of his love. In his case history in *Sexual Inversion* (1897), Symonds recounts to Havelock Ellis that even after his encounter with Plato he suffered under society's mandate to repress and sublimate his same-sex desire, experiencing physical manifestations of this unrest in "insomnia, obscure cerebral discomfort, stammering, chronic conjunctivitis, inability to concentrate his attention, and dejection." Only once he "began freely to follow his homosexual inclinations" did Symonds's health improve (Ellis and Symonds, *Sexual Inversion* 145). In the verse of Walt Whitman, Symonds eventually found a new means for situating male same-sex sexuality into an affirmative context. Comparable confrontations with Plato, aspects of Platonic philosophy, and the classics take place in both novels *Imre* and *Maurice*. This chapter explores these confrontations and the ways in which the authors reworked Greek love in their fiction.

Edward Prime-Stevenson's *Imre: A Memorandum* invokes the Greeks, Walt Whitman's verse, and other sources to assist in formulating a modern homosexual identity and model for homosexual relations. Although the vision of homosexual identity and relations depicted in Prime-Stevenson's writings is in many ways similar to that theorized in England in the writings of Symonds and Edward Carpenter (1844–1929), as I explain below, there was little or no interaction between the American émigré living on the Continent and the British theorists. On the other hand, in *Maurice*'s "Terminal Note," Forster acknowledges the debt he owed to Carpenter and his partner George Merrill, especially the gentle inspirational pat Merrill gave him just above the backside, in envisioning an enduring love relationship between two men (*Maurice* 215). Carpenter and Merrill's partnership is the archetype for a vision of cross-class comrade love central to the novel. Robert Martin considers this vision of love between men and contrasts it to the novel's other mode of homosexuality, charting the shift between the two types. "The novel opposes two kinds of homosexuality—one that is identified with Cambridge and Clive, and one that is identified with Alec and the open air—and uses the opinions on homosexual love expressed by Clive to indicate a stage in Maurice's development, but one that does not represent the author's concept of the final stage of development: this Maurice can achieve only through the encounter with Alec" ("Edward Carpenter and the Double Structure of *Maurice*" 35). Martin argues that the former variant of homosexuality "is dominated by Plato and, indirectly, by John Addington Symonds and the apologists for 'Greek love,'" whereas the latter "is dominated by Edward Carpenter and his translation of the ideas of Walt Whitman" and thus is a vision that represents a reorientation of conceptualizing same-sex passion (36). Martin's discussion of the double structure of the novel is an important reference point for this chapter of my study. But, despite this fact, I take issue with his identification of Symonds as merely a Greek love apologist rather than giving him credit for the role he played in developing comrade love. Rainer Guldin too, in his study of Symonds, Carpenter, and Forster, draws this line between Symonds and Carpenter. "In his novel *Maurice* of 1913–1914, Forster confronts both approaches: Symonds's idealizing, sex-negative aestheticism is repudiated in favor of Carpenter's social-critical and sex-affirmative standpoint." ("In seinem 1913–1914 geschriebenen Roman 'Maurice' [*sic*] konfrontiert er [Forster] die beiden Ansätze: Symonds' idealisierender, körperfeindlicher Ästhetizismus wird zugunsten von Carpenters sozialkritischem und körperbejahendem Standpunkt abgelehnt"; Guldin, *Verbrüderung* 15). Both viewpoints, I argue, undervalue Symonds and his writings and construct an artificial opposition between Symonds and Carpenter. That they do not recognize the link between Oxbridge Hellenism and Uranian love, embodied both literally and figuratively in Symonds, is my critique of Martin's seminal essay as well as Guldin's study. Martin concludes that Carpenter "brought an end to Forster's search for a homosexual tradition because he seemed to create his own tradition, to offer a world where the homosexual could build a new social order" (44). I certainly agree that Carpenter seemed to offer a vision for building a new social order, but this new homosexual tradition was established firmly with reference to the legacies from the ancient world. Both novels, *Imre* and *Maurice* deploy the past in order to create something new. This chapter first explores Symonds's and Carpenter's efforts at reviving Greek love, then analyzes Prime-Stevenson's novel and the comparable uses and misuses of history and Whitman's poetry which the author worked into the text, and finally examines Forster's novel and the influence of Symonds and Carpenter in the triumph of "the manly love of comrades" over Oxbridge Hellenism.

The English Comrades

Toward the end of the nineteenth century, Symonds and Carpenter revived Greek love in their writings by drawing on Walt Whitman's "love of comrades" (*The Complete Poems* 150), which is found in his verse, especially in *Leaves of Grass* (first edition 1855). What they envision I designate in this study as "Uranian comrade love." Hellenism proved to thwart Symonds as much as it had liberated him. Whitman's "Calamus" cluster from *Leaves of Grass* offered another, for him more authentic, vision of same-sex love. "The book became for me," writes Symonds in his *Memoirs*, "a sort of Bible" (189). At the close of his book-length treatment of Whitman's verse, *Walt Whitman: A Study* (1893), he describes a transformation in himself triggered by comrade love—without explicitly broaching what he saw as its homosexual aspects. Symonds confesses how, in 1865, *Leaves of Grass* saved him body and soul. He writes that the poem that begins "Long I thought that knowledge alone would suffice me" sent "electric thrills through the very marrow of my mind" (*Walt Whitman* 158). In a letter Symonds wrote to Whitman in 1872, he explained the shift in his understanding of his attraction to other men (again, without at this point explicitly broaching homosexuality) which the poetry had catalyzed. Prior to this he had labored under "a delusion of distorted passions, a dream of the Past, a scholar's fancy," but *Leaves of Grass* allowed him to conceptualize his desire as a "strong and vital bond of man to man," a comradeship which Symonds places "on a par with the Sexual feeling for depth and strength and purity and capability of all good" (*Letters* 2: 201–02). Whitman supplants Plato: "I have pored for continuous hours over the pages of *Calamus* (as I used to pore over the pages of Plato), longing to hear you speak, *burning* for a revelation of your more developed meaning . . . Someday, perhaps—in some form, I know not what, but in your own chosen form—you will tell me more about the Love of Friends!" (201–02). Whitman's vision of comradely love surpasses Platonic philosophy. Symonds was "struggling to free himself and the English Uranians from one half of the inheritance of Oxford Hellenism while retaining the other half of its powerful ideological support" writes Linda Dowling. "Attempting to discard the crippling sexual sublimation of the Platonic eros, Symonds fights at the same time to preserve the ideal of Dorian comradeship" with "its tremendous force as a counterweight" to contemporary religious, legal, and medical discourses (*Hellenism and Homosexuality* 130). *Leaves of Grass* empowered Symonds to reconcile spiritual and physical aspects of love between men.

Edward Carpenter recounts a similar response to the writings of Whitman in his autobiography *My Days and Dreams* (1916). As was the case with Symonds,

Whitman supplanted the place reserved for Plato: "in Plato and the Greek authors there had been something wanting" (64–65). The American bard "sent shock-waves through the furtive gentility of Britain's Uranian community," writes Gregory Woods. "He transformed their nostalgia for pastoral Greece into yearning for a utopian New World of open frontiers and open-necked shirts" (*A History of Gay Literature* 177). Yet, it would be wrong to characterize this shift as an abandonment of Hellenism in favor of this interpretation of Whitman's manly "adhesiveness." Ancient Greek comrades-in-arms—Achilles and Patroclus, Harmodius and Aristogeiton, and the Sacred Band of Thebes—remained powerful images and models in the imaginations of the Uranians. Whitman was, especially for Symonds, a torchbearer in the legacy of male love. "The language of 'Calamus' . . . has a passionate glow, a warmth of emotional tone, beyond anything to which the modern world is used in the celebration of the love of friends," he writes in the essay "A Problem in Modern Ethics" (1891). "It recalls to our mind the early Greek enthusiasm—that fellowship in arms which flourished among Dorian tribes, and made a chivalry for prehistoric Hellas" (*Symonds and Homosexuality* 195). Whitman served to revitalize this heritage by stripping it of the intellectualism, effete learning, and over-refinement with which it had become encumbered in the nineteenth century (see M. Robertson, *Worshipping Walt* 140–88; Herrero-Brasas, *Walt Whitman's Mystical Ethics of Comradeship* 83–116).

There are three recurrent issues raised in these Uranian writings: (1) they do not deny the physical aspects of love between men; (2) they stress the health and manliness of Uranian men; and (3) they discuss the "democratic" nature of this love. First, an affirmation of physical love between men is a central tenet of their writings. Symonds, in "A Problem in Greek Ethics" (1873) defines Greek love as "a passionate and enthusiastic attachment subsisting between man and youth, recognized by society and protected by opinion, which, though it was not wholly free from sensuality, did not degenerate into mere licentiousness" (*Symonds and Homosexuality* 50). He is careful to emphasize the validity of the emotional bonds between two males—in the case of the Greeks "between man and youth"—while affirming, although in cautious wording, that sexuality did indeed play a potent role in these relations. Carpenter too is careful to emphasize the emotional over the physical aspects of same-sex love without completely disavowing the latter dimension. He writes in *The Intermediate Sex* that "the Uranian temperament, especially in regard to its affectional side, is not without faults," but these so-called faults are hardly what early twentieth-century guardians of morality would have leveled against them. "I think one may safely say that the defect of the male Uranian, or Urning, is not sensuality—but rather sentimentality" (13). It would be hard to fault Uranians for such a virtuous "defect." "It would be a great mistake to suppose that their attachments are necessarily sexual, or connected with sexual acts. On the contrary (as abundant evidence shows), they are often purely emotional in their character; and to confuse Uranians (as is so often done) with libertines having no law but curiosity in self-indulgence is to do them a great wrong" (26). It is with some reservations that they acknowledge physical Eros; but they deserve credit where it is due. In their writings,

Symonds and Carpenter do not deny sexual desire or argue that it should be sublimated and channeled toward supposedly purer aims.

Second, both writers stress the health, vitality, and manliness of homosexual men. In the 1891 essay, Symonds argues against "the common belief that all subjects of inverted instinct carry their lusts written in their faces; that they are pale, languid, scented, effeminate, painted, timid, oblique in expression." Symonds admits that although "A certain class of such people are undoubtedly feminine," the majority of homosexual men do not differ from "normal" men (*Symonds and Homosexuality* 134). "They are athletic, masculine in habit, frank in manner, passing through society year after year without arousing a suspicion of their inner temperament" (135). This claim was not only of importance in arguing against the stereotype of homosexual effeminacy (which would become highly visible after the Wilde trials), but in particular it countered medical discourses that hypothesized that homosexuality was a product of physical and mental degeneration. Symonds's and Carpenter's visions of homosexuality and homosexual love were that of manly men, *intra*generational partners, bonding in a society that not only tolerates their form of affection, but values it for its contribution to the progress of civilization as a whole.

Third, a facet of this contribution to progress would take the form of the breaking down of inequitable power structures of social hierarchy. Symonds writes that "the blending of Social Strata in masculine love seems to me one of its most pronounced and socially hopeful features" (*Letters* 3: 808), and Carpenter posits that Eros can bridge "the most estranged ranks of society." "Eros is a great leveler. Perhaps the true Democracy rests, more firmly than anywhere else, on a sentiment which easily passes the bounds of class and caste, and unites in the closest affection the most estranged ranks of society. It is noticeable how often Uranians of good position and breeding are drawn to rougher types, as of manual workers, and frequently very permanent alliances grow up in this way, which although not publicly acknowledged have a decided influence on social institutions, customs and political tendencies" (*The Intermediate Sex* 114–15). The Uranians drew their conclusions about future society from the ancient world, but seem to ignore the aspects of Greek society that conflicted with their visions. Matt Cook highlights that "Athenian life was neither so stable nor so democratic as many in the later nineteenth century chose to believe" (*London and the Culture of Homosexuality* 126). James Davidson concurs, writing that same-sex relations in ancient Greece represented a reinforcement of social hierarchies, not a challenge to them (*The Greeks and Greek Love* 96–98).

It is also important to notice that this form of comradeship, as D. H. Mader notes, "was not defined in terms of sameness" ("The Greek Mirror" 378); instead, Uranian love theorizes sexual difference in terms of class difference. In these relations both partners are adult, if not coevals; thus sexual difference was not determined by age, as it had been for the Greeks and was the case for the *Gemeinschaft der Eigenen* in Germany. Carpenter and Symonds searched for a philosophic underpinning for their attraction to "rougher types" and they find it in Whitman's democratic and egalitarian love of comrades (M. Robertson, *Worshipping Walt* 151–58,

175–81). For the Uranians, this difference took the form of cross-class liaisons and alliances. Symonds, on the one hand, always maintained the position of benefactor in his relations. Cook describes how, for Symonds, any shame incurred by a visit to a London male brothel could be alleviated by becoming acquainted with and befriending his bedfellows. Comradeship, even the barest pretence at such, would allow him to reframe the liaison as "a more laudable and 'respectable' fraternity" within the philosophy of comrade love (131). Carpenter, on the other hand, went to greater lengths to realize his ideals. The longest-lasting of his relationships was with George Merrill, a young working-class man whom Carpenter met in 1891. The two began living together at Millthorpe, Carpenter's farm/commune in rural Derbyshire, in 1898 and remained together until Merrill's death in 1928 (Rowbotham, *Edward Carpenter* 179, 242, 435–36).

Whitman's verse enabled Symonds and Carpenter to formulate a vision of love between men that was egalitarian, masculine, and enduring, but making this vision work in reality proved to be a challenge. They were undoubtedly aware that their cross-class comradeships could be viewed as sexual exploitation of members of the working class. There may have been tension between the stated aims of the Uranian comrades and the relations which many conducted in actuality. Jeffrey Weeks writes that there were "complex patterns recurring": "On the one hand was a form of sexual colonialism, a view of the lower classes as a source of 'trade.' On the other were an often sentimental rejection of one's own class values and a belief in reconciliation through sexual contact. . . . In the rarefied atmosphere of the 'Uranian' poets, money would change hands but ideology minimized its significance" ("Inverts, Perverts, and Mary-Annes" 203–04; see also Sedgwick, *Between Men* 210; Weeks, *Coming Out* 44; Cook 129–33; M. Robertson 153). Be that as it may, Symonds and Carpenter went beyond the bounds of Greek love, thereby catalyzing a departure from dependence on this discourse for their imitators and inheritors. They salvaged some core values and ideals from the past, revived these images with Whitman's love of comrades, drew upon liberationist theories of same-sex sexuality from the leading German researchers in the field, and incorporated their efforts into larger social reform movements.

The (Mis)uses of History

In Prime-Stevenson's *Imre: A Memorandum*, in contrast to Forster's *Maurice*, there was undoubtedly little or no influence from John Addington Symonds or Edward Carpenter. If both writers had been influenced by the British Uranians, this would provide a convenient explanation for the many similarities between the two novels in terms of the homosexual identities and relations depicted. But as no such influence can be substantiated, the similarities are all the more remarkable for this fact. There is little evidence to connect the US-American, who lived on the Continent from around 1900 until his death in 1942, to Symonds and Carpenter. It is likely that Prime-Stevenson had read Symonds's essay "A Problem in Greek Ethics," which was included, as the first appendix, to *Sexual Inversion* (1897), the medical textbook on homosexuality produced in collaboration between Symonds and the physician Havelock Ellis. In a letter to his friend and literary executor, Paul Elmer More, which was written in 1906, Prime-Stevenson mentions Ellis and Symonds's work ("Letter to Paul Elmer More" 135). Considering that in the letter Prime-Stevenson regarded *Sexual Inversion* as "dealing with pathologic conditions, with only limited 'typic' aspects, and [is] too much from and for exclusively a professional-psychiatric standpoint" (135), I doubt that he had read the German translation of the book which appeared in 1896, although he was especially well versed in German sexological writings (as is discussed in greater depth in chapter 5). Titled *Das konträre Geschlechtsgefühl*, the German translation was closer to Symonds's conception than the English edition published the following year (Crozier, "Introduction" 57–58).

Particularly interesting are the similarities between Prime-Stevenson's and Carpenter's writings, especially between the former's *The Intersexes: A History of Similisexualism as Problem in Social Life* and the latter's *The Intermediate Sex*, both of which were published in 1908. It would seem then that Prime-Stevenson had read Carpenter's *Homogenic Love and Its Place in a Free Society*, the forerunner to the 1908 work, which was first published privately in 1894. This is perhaps why James Gifford writes that the novel's defense of masculine homosexuality is "inspired both by antiquity and by the philosophy of Edward Carpenter" (*Dayneford's Library* 113). Yet, Carpenter's explicitly homosexual writings would have been difficult to come by. *Homogenic Love* was not available to those outside Carpenter's circle until its publication as a chapter in *Love's Coming of Age* in 1906 (Brady, *Masculinity and Male Homosexuality in Britain* 202). Thus, although Carpenter had read *Imre* and quotes it in the appendix of his study (*The Intermediate Sex* 167–69), it is unlikely that Prime-Stevenson had read Carpenter. Perhaps, then, it was the other way around; perhaps Prime-Stevenson influenced Carpenter. More likely, though, is that any similarity between the visions of homosexual love and relations theorized by the two writers is due to them drawing from the same well of inspiration—German sexology, Greek love, Walt Whitman's verse—and coming to comparable conclusions. Prime-Stevenson depicts in his work of fiction homosexual identities and love relations which seem to mirror those theorized at the same time in England. Similar to the writings of Symonds and Carpenter and Forster's novel, Greek love discourse and Whitman's poetry play decisive roles in shaping the visions of homosexual identities and love relations. The novel draws upon the past, but ultimately utilizes it to create something new. Oswald fashions a cultural-historical narrative of love between men which speaks of this impulse in association with creative accomplishments, philosophy, bravery, and martial valor, thereby challenging contemporary society's condemnation of him as sinful, criminal, diseased, and effeminate.

The centrality of Greek love is flagged early in the narrative by the epigraph attributed to "Magyarbol": "Is there really now, as ages ago, a sexual aristocracy of the male? A mystic and Hellenic Brotherhood, a sort of super-virile man? A race with hearts never to be kindled by any woman; though, if once aglow, their strange fires can burn not less ardently and purer than ours? An élite passion, conscious of a superior knowledge of Love, initiated into the finer joys and pains than ours?—that looks down with pity and contempt on the millions of men wandering in the valleys of the sexual commonplace?" (34). "Magyarbol," Gifford writes, is one of Prime-Stevenson's personae, a name which translates as "from the Hungarian" (34, note 1). This epigraph would seem to suggest that the standard nineteenth century Greek love apologia, comparable to the one Clive voices to Maurice (*Maurice* 73), holds sway in the novel. The fact that these are not the words of another person, but of the author himself, would reinforce this assumption. Theirs is "An élite passion, conscious of a superior knowledge of Love." When Oswald describes to Imre the means through which he forged his identity, the first discourse he accesses is Greek love, which allows him to develop an understanding of his desire as "the Love-Friendship of Hellas" (84). The sources Oswald invokes do not stop with ancient Greece, which would seem to indicate that this work draws on a broader range of sources in shaping the identities depicted. "Between man and man could exist the sexual-psychic love. That was still possible! I knew that now! I had read it in the verses or the prose of the Greek and Latin and Oriental authors who have written out every shade of its beauty or unloveliness, its worth or debasements—from Theokritos to Martial, or Abu-Nuwas, to Platen, Michelangelo, Shakespeare. I had learned it from the statues of sculptors . . . [and] had half-divined it in the music of a Beethoven and a Tchaikovsky" (84). He identifies an affinity between himself and great men from diverse epochs and civilizations: this affinity that spans time, place, and culture is same-sex desire. "Tens of thousands of men, in all epochs, of noblest natures, of most brilliant minds and gifts, of intensest energies . . . scores of pure spirits, deep philosophers, bravest soldiers, highest poets and artists, had been such as myself" (86). Counter to the taboos and moral strictures of his day, he recognizes that among many of history's greats, love and desire between men was a vital force in their philosophies, works, and lives. He confidently asserts to Imre "that they belonged to Us" (88).

Despite the essential role played by history, the novel makes significant departures from these classical and postclassical sources and models. *Imre* depicts love between adult men, not love for a teenage boy. Tariq Rahman draws a useful distinction between androphilia, attraction to "manly as opposed to boyish physical features," and ephebophilia, attraction to beautiful pubescent boys and youths ("Ephebophilia" 126). Thus the manly Uranian love depicted in Prime-Stevenson's novel, although a mode of same-sex desire, is fundamentally different to the "ephebophilia" celebrated in the works of many of the writers Oswald invokes (for instance Plato, the Greek and Roman poets, Shakespeare, Marlowe, and Platen). Indeed, the protagonist repudiates the desire described and depicted in Greek philosophic dialogues and poetry as well as in Roman, Arabian, and Renaissance writings. These men are "the cynical debauchers of little boys; the pederastic perverters of clean-minded lads in their teens" (87). Prime-Stevenson's study *The Intersexes* provides insight into the author's understanding of male same-sex relations in history. He writes that there were "three distinctions in Hellenic love" (49). The first was "merely spiritual passion and bond, untouched by physical desires" and thus "was not love, but friendship, at its highest throb." The second was "the similisexual physical love" which included "high idealism, intellectual companionship ... along with the physical passion for him, and its natural satisfaction." This mode of same-sex passion is not boy-love, but is intragenerational. "This is a sort of similisexual passion and love-sentiment in which the friends are relatively of equal and fairly matures ages." And the third, which he credits for sapping the "Greek military spirit," is the "mere physical possession of a youth" which "we know today under the phases of Pederasty, or boy-love" (49). It is a fast-and-loose reading of history as well as of the literary sources, but one from which Oswald derives a sense of homosexual selfhood. Against the fierce opprobrium of his day, it is an incredibly potent resource to tap.

When he shares this discourse with Imre, it may be that he projects his understanding of his sexuality, a product of cultural forces specific to his own era, to figures from the past, assigning an early-twentieth century conception of homosexual subjectivity onto earlier generations who understood and expressed their sexual drives differently. This is an endeavor which is now recognized as anachronistic. And yet, this possible misuse of history represents a positive force for the characters as well as for readers of the novel, having the potential to open avenues toward self-awareness. Such "list[s] of great queens of history," writes Rictor Norton, are "compiled by queers in order to find a place for themselves in a historical tradition, to celebrate that they are part of a cultural unity." A narrative like the one Oswald weaves "celebrates the fact not so much that queers are great, or even that they are creative, or even that they are good, but that queers are part of history" (*The Myth of the Modern Homosexual* 223). Oswald asserts that his love does exist, contrary to charges of its unnaturalness. He is not mistaken in recognizing that love between men transcends its contemporary condemnation; thus his endeavor is less about applying terms and notions anachronistically onto figures from the past, and more about deploying a historical narrative to turn the tables on the argument made by moral, legal, and some medical authorities, to contend that it is the condemnation of love between men which in fact is unnatural. Oswald sees the possibility the past offers for forging identities in the present and constructs a narrative of queer history, finding a place for himself within this cultural legacy (see also Wilper, "Sexology, Homosexual History, and Walt Whitman" 52–68).

It is clear that this effort is twofold in its purpose. On the one hand, this is the means through which the protagonist builds his identity. On the other, it incorporates a defensive and justificatory strategy (somewhat awkwardly from an artistic standpoint) into the novel. I am inclined to agree with James Levin that "the use of such lists in fiction is awkward" (*The Gay Novel* 18–19). The stratagem he mobilizes was by no means new or untested. By 1906, the year of the novel's first publication, Oscar Wilde had defended himself, his writings, and "the Love that dare not speak its name"; Symonds had penned two essays that were influential in developing Uranian love; Elisar von Kupffer, in *Lieblingminne und Freundesliebe in der Weltliteratur*, and Carpenter, in *Ioläus: An Anthology of Friendship* (1902), had anthologized many of the same authors referenced by Oswald in their respective literary compilations; and Friedländer had argued in *Renaissance des Eros Uranios* that the persecution of same-sex desire was unnatural and harmful to society. Wilde's speech and these texts historicize love between men, arguing for its cultural legitimacy, insisting that this impulse is natural and healthy, and that its recognition would benefit society. *Imre: A Memorandum* is a voice in a movement of Greek love apologia which defended same-sex love. It demanded that the existence of this form of love be acknowledged and that its worth be recognized and valued.

Oswald draws upon the past, the Greek, Roman, Arabian, and postclassical Western authors and artists whose diverse works celebrate male beauty and love between men, thus enabling him to conceptualize his sexuality and himself positively (84–88). But these works of art do not seem, in and of themselves, to possess the discursive authority to challenge Judeo-Christian condemnation of the sex act between men directly. "And I had recognized what it all meant to most people today, from the disgust, scorn and laughter of my fellow-men when such an emotion was hinted at! I understood perfectly that a man must wear the Mask. . . . Love between two men, however absorbing, however passionate, must not be . . . a sexual love, a physical impulse and bond" (84). Crossing this line between spiritual love and the physical act makes this noble desire "a nameless horror—a thing against all civilization, sanity, sex, Nature, God!" (84). Oswald in time learns with the assistance of progressive sexology that this notion was a fallacy, eventually rejecting a conception of love that demands the sublimation of its physical expression. He casts off many of the anxieties about relations between males embedded in the source texts and their later invocations, specifically rejecting the ideals that insist love between men must remain a chaste "romantic friendship" (46). Nevertheless, in the narrative he must learn this lesson again.

While he still believes that Imre is heterosexual, he is willing to sublimate his desire in order to remain close to the man he loves. He resigns himself to forming a Platonic bond with him. The relationship model that the text seems to develop for the two is one of nonsexual love between comrades. Oswald's confession takes place under a monument "To the Unforgettable Memory of Z. Lorand, and Z. Egon," a memorial to brotherly love and self-sacrifice, which James Gifford notes is a Hungarian recasting of the Greek story of Damon and Pythias (Introduction 18). Lorand and Egon appear to figure as the patron saints of Oswald and Imre's passion, but later in the narrative when the two share a moment of intimate physical contact—Imre buries his head in Oswald's chest while he searches for the words to confess his homosexuality and the love he reciprocates—Oswald becomes visibly sexually aroused, or as he puts it, "the Sex-Demon brought his storm upon my traitorous nature, in fire and lava" (115). "Oh, this cursed outbreak and revelation of my sensual weakness! this inevitable physical appeal of Imre to me! This damned and inextricable ingredient in the chemistry of what ought to be wholly a spiritual drawing toward him, but which meant that I desired my friend for his gracious, virile beauty—as well as loved him for his fair soul! Oh, the shame of it all, the uselessness of my newest resolve to be more as the normal man, not so utterly the Uranian" (115). The scientific language Oswald employs emphasizes the essential nature of homosexual passion: physical desire is an "inextricable ingredient in the chemistry" of their relationship. Sexual desire is like a law of nature, an "inevitable physical appeal." Oswald laments to Imre that "I have tried to change myself, to care for you only with my soul. But I cannot change" (116). The imagery employed in this passage suggests more than a mere obvious erection; "in fire and lava" is certainly a metaphor for orgasm. *Der Puppenjunge* also employs nature as a metaphor for sex—in that case it is a release of atmospheric tension in a sudden summer storm (*Hustler* 178; *Puppenjunge* 208). These images communicate a sense that sexual desire is a force that transcends human efforts to rein it in, a force of nature that is eventually victorious. Imre then confesses that he too is "wholly homosexual" and that he loves Oswald (117). After Imre narrates his life story to Oswald, which Oswald, as the narrator, summarizes for the reader (119–26), the novel winds down with a speedy denouement, concluding with the suggestion that the two finally consummate their love: "Come then, O friend! O brother, to our rest! Thy heart on mine, thy soul with mine!" (127). Thus the novel deploys history to build affirmative identities and structure relationships between men, but it does so in a way that avoids being constrained by these discourses. The novel invokes the past and evokes its ideals and virtues, but, like the English comrades, does not see emotional and physical love as mutually exclusive. And, like the comrades, the novel takes cues, particularly for how to structure relations between males, from a more modern source, interpreting them from the verse of Walt Whitman.

The cultural-historical narrative which the novel draws upon and consequently promotes emphasizes the sterling qualities of homosexual men and thus fosters a vision of love between men colored in shades of superiority; Oswald rhetorically asks Imre: "Are we not the extreme of the male? its supreme phase, its outermost phalanx—its climax of the aristocratic, the All-Man?" (86). The novel stresses the manliness of homosexual men to counter charges of enfeeblement and effeminacy, derangement and disease, and a key influence in this discourse of Uranian manliness is Whitman. Although his name is listed with other writers, such as Shakespeare, Marlowe, Byron, and Platen (87), his full impact upon the novel only becomes explicit when read in light of the author's treatment of the poet in *The Intersexes*. Prime-Stevenson deems Whitman "one of the prophets and priests of homosexuality" whose verse is pervaded with a homoerotic atmosphere springing from "the neo-hellenic, platonic democracy of Whitman's philosophic muse" (377). In many of "Whitman's philosophico-political poems," writes Prime-Stevenson, "he accents the idea of the importance of masculine ties on lines of the old hellenic sort—the Sacred Band—as vital to the State, in the restoration of the true democracy" (380). *The Intersexes* constructs a homosexual literary heritage which situates Whitman's poetry as the most recent apotheosis of a cultural legacy of male love traceable from Plato, through Shakespeare, Marlowe, and Platen: in Whitman's verse "is to be heard a new voice, if with an accent classically old, in its philosophic message of conviction as to the purity, the naturalness of true uranian love and its high mission to the individual and toward nations" (381). The study's glowing account of Whitman's place within the homosexual literary canon indicates the role played in the novel by the American poet's paeans to manly comrade "adhesiveness," which, I posit, is the basis of the relationship between Oswald and Imre.

An interpretation of the homoerotic aesthetic of Whitman's verse, which especially marks the "Calamus" poems, is an essential point of reference for the Uranian subjectivity portrayed in the novel and provides the essential model for love relations between men. The manly "lifelong love of comrades" embodies an ideal, a model, and a vision of masculine, egalitarian, and enduring love between men (see Herrero-Brasas, *Walt Whitman's Mystical Ethics of Comradeship* 83–116). The author's emancipatory and didactic undertaking with the novel is parallel to the program formed by the writings of Symonds and Carpenter. Like the English comrades, in Prime-Stevenson's interpretation, comrade love is primarily a minority affair and denotes love between adult men rather than that of an adult man for an adolescent boy—androphilia instead of ephebophilia, in Rahman's terms ("Ephebophilia" 126). This is in distinct contrast to the ways which the American poet's ideals were understood in Germany by writers associated with Adolf Brand's journal *Der Eigene* or by André Gide in France. *Imre* is a meditation in novel form upon a vision of homosexuality and homosexual relations which owes an immense debt to Whitman.

Imre: A Memorandum draws upon the past in order to create something new. The greatest difference between *Imre*, on the one hand, and Forster's novel, on the other, is how sexual difference is theorized. In both novels, the partners are adult, and high value is placed upon their manliness. Whereas Forster formulates difference around cross-class outreach, difference takes shape in terms of "race," or rather nationality, in *Imre*. Both Imre and Oswald are aristocrats; the former belongs to an ancient, yet impoverished, noble family (37), and the latter is a leisure-class English gentleman who commands the pecuniary resources to live comfortably in exile in Europe. Both are educated, both are interested in art and music. Whereas neither Maurice nor Alec cares for art and culture, for the characters of *Imre*, it is their shared interests in art and music which initially draw them together. Through Oswald's exposition of Imre, in the first part of the novel, it becomes evident that Imre's "race" is a source of keen attraction, situating him as the "other." Oswald romanticizes the "Oriental quality, ever in the Magyar" to the point of fetishization. He admits to Imre that interest in his nationality plays a significant role in his attraction to him: "the mysterious affinity between myself and your race and nation; of my sensitiveness, ever since I was a child, to the chord which Magyarország and the Magyar sound in my heart. . . . Thy land, thy people, Imre, are they not almost my land, my people?" (103). Thus theirs is not a relationship based upon sameness; instead it is one based upon difference too, but in the form of nationality.

Comrade Love over Hellenism

In *Maurice*, Hellenism is represented by Clive Durham and the relationship he frames for himself and Maurice. In this portion of the novel, conflict is cast in terms of opposition between Judeo-Christian doctrine and Hellenism. For Clive, study of the classics opens new avenues toward self-awareness. In his youth, he believed that he was "damned," in possession of a "tainted soul," and "punished" with the desire of Sodom (55)—classical philosophy liberates him from the constraining forces of religion. Clive swaps the Bible for Plato. "Never could he forget his emotion at first reading the *Phaedrus*. He saw there his malady described exquisitely, calmly, as a passion which we can direct, like any other, toward good or bad" (55–56). The church's interpretation of same-sex desire being at odds with his nature, Clive throws off Christianity: "he could not find any rest for his soul in [the church] without crippling it, and withdrew higher into the classics yearly" (56). Clive initiates Maurice into this discourse. Plato's *Symposium* provides a conduit through which Clive can broach the subject of homosexuality with Maurice. "The Greeks, or most of them," Clive assures him, "were that way inclined, and to omit it is to omit the mainstay of Athenian society" (38). It is not that at this point Maurice does not understand what Clive drives at—he has read an unexpurgated edition of the poetry of Martial—but "He hadn't known it could be mentioned, and when Durham did so in the middle of the sunlit court a breath of liberty touched him" (38). Nevertheless, religion still presents an obstacle to their coming together. Maurice does not read the *Symposium* during the vacation, and so when Clive confesses his love, Maurice is "scandalized," "horrified," and shocked to the "bottom of his suburban soul": "it's the only subject absolutely beyond limit as you know, it's the worst crime in the calendar, and you must never mention it again" (44). Maurice's slow nature eventually senses his blunder. He sees that from boyhood he has "been fed upon lies," meaning conventional morality, Judeo-Christian norms, values, and strictures. "He loved men and always had loved them," he finally realizes. "He longed to embrace them and mingle his being with theirs" (47). He adopts Hellenism to understand and voice his sexual nature: "I have always been like the Greeks and didn't know" (50).

Through the means of classical philosophy, the two build a relationship: "by linking their love to the past [Clive] linked it to the present" (58). Maurice and Clive shared the "love that Socrates bore Phaedo," a love both passionate and temperate. Clive "led the beloved up a narrow and beautiful path, high above either abyss . . . He educated Maurice, or rather his spirit educated Maurice's spirit, for they themselves became equal" (80). Their relationship is structured along similar philosophical lines to the one Aschenbach imagines between himself and Tadzio. The same models, Socrates and Phaedrus, are referenced. Furthermore, the relations are justified by way of their intellectual and pedagogic basis. A notable difference is that whereas Greek love is a shared discourse in the case of Clive and Maurice, which helps them mutually to understand and structure their relationship, in *Der Tod in Venedig* only Aschenbach has access to this discourse. And the most evident difference is that whereas approximately thirty-nine years separate Aschenbach and Tadzio, only one year separates Clive and Maurice. The former relationship is (or rather would be) intergenerational, and thus nearer to Greek practices in this sense, and the latter relationship is intragenerational. Nevertheless, despite the nearness of their ages, Clive is very much the active partner—perhaps not in the sexual sense, as their relationship is never consummated, but definitely in "carv[ing] a channel for" their love, setting boundaries, in leading and "educat[ing] Maurice," in spite of the assertion that "they themselves became equal" (80). Owing to the intellectual and pedagogic bent and the fact that these relations are conducted between men, who allegedly experience emotion more deeply, Clive characterizes this love as higher and purer: "I feel to you as Pippa to her fiancé, only far more nobly, far more deeply, body and soul, no starved medievalism of course, only a—a particular harmony of body and soul that I don't think women have even guessed" (73). Theirs is a textbook example of Oxford or Cambridge Greek love.

Forster was certainly treating familiar material because, by the time he arrived at Cambridge in 1897, this manner of Platonic love was well established among undergraduates (Halperin, *One Hundred Years of Homosexuality* 3). It was a means to conceptualize and express love and desire between men as a form of "sexless devotion" (Jenkyns, *The Victorians and Ancient Greece* 280–97; see also Richards, "Passing the Love of Women" 92–121; Bowden, "Education, Ideology, and the Ruling Class" 161–86). Thus despite the challenge Hellenism offers Christianity, the latter is not entirely vanquished. Sex between men in this form of Hellenism is disavowed while the purity and nobility of the sentiment is touted in order to prove that the practitioners are not breaking the Christian prohibition against "lying" with another man as well as legal sanctions against acts of "gross indecency." Clive's Hellenism at first appears to free Maurice, but as the narrative wears on it proves to trap him in another cage. Forster writes in the terminal note that Clive "believed in platonic restraint and induced Maurice to acquiesce, which does not seem to me at all unlikely. Maurice at this stage is humble and inexperienced and adoring, he is the soul released from prison, and if asked by his deliverer to remain chaste he obeys. Consequently, the relationship lasts for three years—precarious, idealistic, and peculiarly English, what Italian boy could have put up with it?" (217). In some ways this relationship is "peculiarly English," and in other ways not. In contrast to the German-language works of fiction, *Maurice* presents a Greek love relationship between two characters of similar ages. In this regard the relationship can be regarded as somewhat particular to the British context, especially to the elite universities of Cambridge and Oxford. But, as for invoking the ancients to justify and structure male-male relations, Clive's Platonism is not unique. At points in both German works of fiction (more so in Mann's novella), as well as to some extent in Prime-Stevenson's *Imre*, Greece is invoked not only to justify love between males, but also to offer a philosophic framework for these relations. And comparable to both German texts, as well as to *Imre*, reliance on discourses of nineteenth-century Hellenism, with the accompanying ideal that these relations must be chaste, impedes Clive and Maurice's love. "Classical studies may awaken a person's homosexuality," writes Robert Aldrich, "but too much book-learning can stifle sex" (*Seduction of the Mediterranean* 99). Debrah Raschke explains that a paradox exists in Clive's philosophy: "Platonism gives voice to homoerotic expression, but because it situates truth away from the body, it thwarts the physical fulfillment of this alternative expression; it, in effect, becomes a site of struggle for characters who fall under its influence" ("Breaking the Engagement with Philosophy" 153). *Maurice* shows the deficiencies of a relationship that supposedly enriches the spirit but makes no provision for bodily manifestations of love. Maurice begins to understand the shortcomings of this mode of expression in the course of the narrative. "His interest in the classics had been slight and obscene, and had vanished when he loved Clive. The stories of Harmodius and Aristogeiton, of Phaedrus, of the Theban Band were well enough for those whose hearts were empty, but no substitute for life. That Clive should occasionally prefer them puzzled him" (91). Clive's insistence on Hellenic philosophy set the boundaries of the relationship which Maurice eventually recognizes as entirely contrived. He bitterly recalls that "The less you had the more it was supposed to be—that was Clive's teaching" (159). And, at the close of the novel, Maurice confronts Clive and his philosophy that places the sprit above the body: "I'm not here to get advice, nor to talk about thoughts and ideas either. I'm flesh and blood, if you'll condescend to such low things—" (212). The novel shows the dangers inherent in the sublimation of the needs of the body not only with the relationship's dead end, but also in rendering the decline of Clive's physical appearance and the impending dereliction of his estate: "both house and estate were marked, not indeed with decay, but with the immobility that precedes it" (69). These represent vivid metaphors of what one risks in ignoring the body's needs and unambiguously symbolize the author's rejection of the Platonic sublimation of physical Eros ingrained in Cambridge or Oxford Hellenism.

The alternative vision of homosexual relations, which also springs from the Greek love tradition, is embodied in Alec Scudder. Although Maurice is older than Alec, the relationship is intragenerational. This is, writes Tariq Rahman, certainly the influence of Carpenter, who "was among the pioneering poets of adult homosexuality—Walt Whitman and John Addington Symonds were others—defined as a phenomenon distinct both from love of pretty boys and youths (paedophilia and ephebophilia) and platonic friendship." In contrast to other contemporary Victorian writers, Carpenter's "distinction was to have articulated the desire of men for young men with *manly* rather than *boyish* good-looks and vice versa" ("Edward Carpenter and E. M. Forster" 51). This novel, as well as *Imre: A Memorandum*, were among the first to depict relations that would become the norm in modern gay novels.

In *Maurice*, the basis of this form of Carpenter-inspired comrade love appears early in the narrative, long before Maurice and Alec meet. Young Maurice first feels this manner of bond for the garden boy, George. After he left the Hall's employ, his memory "stirred [something] in the unfathomable depths of [Maurice's] heart" (10). And later, in a dream, young Maurice is confronted with "his friend," an encounter that "filled him with beauty and taught him tenderness. He could die for such a friend, he would allow such a friend to die for him; they would make any sacrifice for each other, and count the world nothing, neither death nor distance nor crossness could part them" (12). Maurice attempts to understand this image of his "friend" in religious as well as Hellenic terms, but neither notion fits. Maurice "tried to persuade himself that the friend must be Christ. But Christ has a mangy beard. Was he a Greek god, such as illustrates the classical dictionary? More probable, but most probably he was just a man" (12). Forster wrote to an early reader of the novel that he believed he had "created something absolutely new, even to the Greeks" (qtd. in Furbank, *E. M. Forster* 2: 14). That it is asserted that Maurice's friend was neither Christ nor a Greek god suggests this intent.

Nonetheless, the ancient world still has a strong bearing on Carpenter's new tradition, social order, and consequently Forster's novel. For the Uranian comrades, Doric virtues and manliness were highly prized and emulated, and the examples of ancient heroes and fighting forces, such as the Sacred Band of Thebes, provided powerful images. Young Maurice's dream of his friend which would evolve into the outlaws-of-the-greenwood vision has its basis in ancient Greece, as is reflected in the *Symposium*, where Phaedrus envisions a state or army consisting entirely of lovers and their beloveds: "If there was any mechanism for producing a city or army consisting of lovers and boyfriends, there could be no better form of social organization than this: they would hold back from anything disgraceful and compete for honour in each other's eyes. If even small numbers of such men fought side by side, they could defeat virtually the whole human race" (Plato 11). This cohesive bond described by Phaedrus also lay behind the valor of the Theban Band, which greatly influenced Carpenter's ideals of homosexual relations and the future role of the Uranian in society. *Maurice* fuses the Theban Band with English folklore to recreate this type of union but in a native setting. The result is a homosexual Robin Hood fantasy for which Maurice eventually sacrifices his career and position in society. "He was an outlaw in disguise. Perhaps among those who took to the greenwood in old times there had been two men like himself—two. At times he entertained the dream. Two men can defy the world" (114). Maurice's vision is a clear reference to Phaedrus's assertion, but the character does not invoke the *Symposium* to justify this belief. This would prove cumbersome, like the artificial restrictions that complicated Clive's Hellenism. Instead, Maurice's outlaw vision develops organically. Later in the narrative, he speaks of the fantasy to the hypnotist. "On the other hand, they could get away. England wasn't all built over and policed. Men of my sort could take to the greenwood. . . . It strikes me there may have been more about the Greeks—Theban Band—and the rest of it. Well, this wasn't unlike. I don't see how they could have kept together otherwise—especially when they came from such different classes" (183). The situations are not "unlike," but neither are they exactly the same. Maurice and Alec's greenwood is an English haven, different to a classically inspired exile in Italy or Greece.

The issue of social class arises as a concern. Maurice is a middle-class stockbroker and Alec is a gamekeeper and the son of a butcher. At first class differences present a boundary to their relationship. Their first sexual encounter was impetuous, a force of nature that refused to be denied, but in the morning social division drove a wedge between them, "Class was calling, the crack in the floor must open at sunrise" (171). The "primitive abandonment" of their coming together gave rise to suspicion and fear. Alec "held out his hand. Maurice took it, and they knew at that moment the greatest triumph ordinary man can win. Physical love means reaction, being panic in essence, and Maurice saw now how natural it was that their primitive abandonment at Penge should have led to peril. They knew too little about each other—and too much. Hence fear. Hence cruelty" (196). At this point they "give over talking" and, in clasping hands, they come together as comrades. This is an example of the imperative "Only connect...," the epigraph from *Howards End* (1910). Nor is this manner of men coming together a one-off in Forster's oeuvre: for instance, in *A Passage to India* (1924) there is Dr. Aziz and Cyril Fielding's friendship that transgresses strict racial boundaries in colonial India. In *Maurice*, the the titular character gives up his family, career, and social position, and Alec turns his back on opportunities for a better life in Argentina. Class is a limit whose transgression is a source of pleasure and possibility. Inspired by Carpenter and Merrill—and in contrast to Oswald and Imre—Maurice and Alec "must live outside class, without relations or money" (207); they live outside the social order as outlaws of the greenwood.

It is worth pointing out that the novel swaps one form of philosophy to order and justify the male-male relationship for another. Relations without a set of structuring ideals are also portrayed in a negative light. There are three instances of this in *Maurice*. The first of these is Maurice's attraction to Dickie Barry. Maurice peers into the young man's bedroom as he "lay unashamed, embraced and penetrated by the sun" (124). The use of the word "penetrated" here is suggestive as Maurice's gaze penetrates into the guest room of his mother's house where Dickie sleeps. The young man's "lips were parted, the down on the upper was touched with gold, the hair broken into countless glories, the body was a delicate amber" (124). Again, the parted lips and bare chest are blatantly sexual. Maurice is nearly predatory in his pursuit of Dickie. "This episode nearly burst Maurice's life to pieces": "His feeling for Dickie required a very primitive name. He would have sentimentalised once and called it adoration, but the habit of honesty had grown strong. What a stoat he had been! Poor little Dickie! He saw the boy leaping from his embrace, to smash through the window and break his limbs, or yelling like a maniac until help came. He saw the police—" (127). He realises that no high-minded idealism or talk of Platonic love could disguise that the primitive urge termed "lust" was what he had felt for the young man. He looks at himself in the mirror and notes the incongruity between his respectable middle-class appearance and his inner life: "Was it conceivable that on Sunday last he had nearly assaulted a boy?" (130). Lytton Strachey, who read the novel in 1915, quite rightly criticized the portrayal in this scene, finding nothing unusual in the protagonist's desire for the boy and certainly not warranting such a harsh portrayal (Furbank 2: 15). The second instance is Maurice's attraction to the young working-class men who attend his boxing lessons. After Dickie, he vows "to keep away from boys and young men" (127) and comes to recognize his actual motivations underlying his volunteer work in the East End. "The feeling that can impel a gentleman towards a person of lower class," he reasons, "stands self-condemned" (128). Hence the text seems to repudiate sexual exploitation of the lower classes and the hypocrisy which supports a system of prostitution sanctified by intellectualism or pedagogy, à la Oscar Wilde, or even Symonds. Although he finds happiness with a member of the working class, the two men have declassed themselves and come together as comrades. With the young men of his boxing class, Maurice would have stood above as a patron; with Alec, he stands alongside as an equal. But this was not always the case. The third instance of the negative portrayal of male-male relations without philosophy is Maurice and Alec's "primitive abandonment" at Penge.

Therefore the novel demonstrates its reliance upon some form of philosophy. When Hellenism fails, Maurice is left to grope about until he can fashion for himself a model for conducting relations with another man. Maurice leaves behind the crippling aspects of Clive's Hellenism, and he and Alec are free to express the physical dimension of their love. And yet history is not rejected. It still represents a source of strength for the present and future. By appropriating Greek love and employing it in new ways, Carpenter offered a powerfully affirmative homosexual identity and model for relations which reverberate in Forster's text. The physical expression of love was a source of angst for many of the inheritors of Greek love, and thus is a concern in all four literary texts considered here. In the relationship Maurice forms with Alec, physical desire is no longer repressed, sublimated, or disavowed. However, sex and sexual desire outside of a philosophical framework is threatening in *Maurice*.

Conclusion

Forster's *Maurice* and Prime-Stevenson's *Imre* are indebted to Greek love and share a great deal in common in regards to the Whitmanian visions of same-sex identity and relations they portray and advocate. In contrast to the German works of fiction that I discussed above, which portray intergenerational love of men for teenage boys, the English examples depict intragenerational love, in other words, love between adult males. This physical attraction is, or may be, in the German texts one-sided. This is certainly the case in *Der Puppenjunge*, where the young man is only interested in the monetary exchange, but it is less clear in *Der Tod in Venedig*, in which mute Tadzio's feelings about Aschenbach's adoration are intimated at points in the narrative, but are never voiced. On the other hand, in the English novels, desire is mutual, although still based on a form of sexual difference, and is organized in lifelong partnerships, rather than transient mentorships. Thus, the English novels do not depict Greek pederasty, instead, the mode of desire which has become the prevailing norm in gay subcultures and in gay literature. This chapter demonstrates that the texts position themselves in relation to Greek love in ways that initiate an expansion of this discourse. The result is a broader space in which to discuss and depict love and desire between males.

Part 3

Science and Sex

Chapter 4

The Highest Being Drawn Down into Decadence

The German poet Stefan George lamented the fact that in *Der Tod in Venedig* "the highest is drawn down into the realm of decadence" (Mann, *Letters* 96) ("sei das Höchste in die Sphäre des Verfalls hinabgezogen"; Mann, *Briefe* 179). Of course, the problem that George actually had with the novella was that it did nothing to bring "the highest"—George believed the love between an older and younger man to be the highest form of love—out of the realm of decadence, to which many commentators had already consigned it for some time. Mann's seemed yet another voice that either entirely or partially considered same-sex sexuality to be indicative of degeneration.

Although *Der Tod in Venedig* was written after Freud's *Drei Abhandlungen zur Sexualtheorie* (*Three Essays on the Theory of Sexuality*, 1905) began to effect a shift in thinking about same-sex sexuality, how influential Freud's writings on homosexuality were on the novella is a matter of debate (see Schmidt, "Childhood, Pedagogy, and Psychoanalysis" 301–02, note 8; see also Wysling, "Thomas Manns Rezeption der Psychoanalyse" 201–22; Symington, "The Eruption of the Other" 127–41; Widmaier-Haag, *Es war das Lächeln des Narziss*; Dierks, "Thomas Mann und die Tiefenpsychologie" 284–300). Mann, who knew Freud personally, admitted his debt to the psychoanalyst in an interview in 1925 with the Italian newspaper *La Stampa*, stating that *Der Tod in Venedig* "originated under the immediate influence of Freud. Without Freud, I would never have thought of treating this erotic motif, or would have certainly formed it differently" ("unter dem unmittelbaren Einfluss von Freud entstanden [ist]. Ich hätte ohne Freud niemals daran gedacht, dieses erotische Motiv zu behandeln, oder hätte es gewiß anders gestaltet"; qtd. in Dierks 284; Widmaier-Haag 156). Nevertheless, Hans Wysling suggests that this may have been a retrospective assessment on the author's part. "Regarding the treatment of the homoerotic motif, *Death in Venice* can have as much to do with Krafft-Ebing as with the *Three Essays*." ("*Der Tod in Venedig* kann, was das homoerotische Motiv angeht, ebensowohl mit Krafft-Ebing wie mit den *Drei Abhandlungen* zu tun haben"; Wysling 203). Freud, it is worth pointing out, writes against regarding homosexuality as the product of hereditary degeneration: "it may well be asked whether an attribution of 'degeneracy' is of any value or adds anything to our knowledge" (Freud, *On Sexuality* 49) ("man [darf] fragen, welchen Nutzen und welchen neuen Inhalt das Urteil "Degeneration" überhaupt noch besitzt"; Freud, *Drei Abhandlungen* 17). In the *Drei Abhandlungen*, he points out several facts which to him indicate that homosexual men and women cannot be regarded as degenerate: the fact that homosexuality is found in people who in no other respects deviate from the "normal"; that it is found "in people whose efficiency is unimpaired, and who are indeed distinguished by specially high intellectual development and ethical culture" ("bei Personen, deren Leistungsfähigkeit nicht gestört ist, ja, die sich durch besonders hohe intellektuelle Entwicklung und ethische Kultur auszeichnen"); and that homosexuality is found "among the peoples of antiquity at the height of their civilization" (50) ("bei den alten Völkern auf der Höhe ihrer Kultur"; 18) as well as "among many savage and primitive races" (50) ("bei vielen wilden und primitiven Völkern"; 18). However, degeneration is an essential concept to the portrayal of same-sex desire in the novella. Hence it is evident that the text is still influenced by and comments upon degenerationist theories.

Of the two schools of sexological thought that influence the novella, the more evident is the degenerative theory which the Austrian psychiatrist Richard von Krafft-Ebing developed in the earlier editions of *Psychopathia Sexualis* (first edition, 1886). Aschenbach's passion for another male consumes him in a way parallel to the cholera epidemic which spreads through the canals of Venice. Moreover, Aschenbach is not the only "degenerate" homosexual in the novella. The old dandy on the ship to Venice is clearly a homosexual character, as is indicated by various markers such as dress, physical attributes, effeminacy, and the suggestive sign he gives Aschenbach as he disembarks from the ship. This character also displays physical signs of degeneration, namely, his bad teeth, weak voice, and pale skin. Tadzio too shows some of the physical characteristics associated with degeneration. Robert Tobin observes this link in his essay, "Queering Thomas Mann's *Der Tod in Venedig*": "They have yellowish, perhaps slightly sickly, skin, linking them to medical discourses of the time. Some of them are effeminate, going so far as to wear make-up, suggesting gender inversion. They seem to signal their membership in this group with a number of fashion markers—rakishly tilted and colorfully beribboned straw hats, red ties and sailor's outfits, for instance" (72). Mann does not, however, entirely denigrate same-sex sexuality by associating it with disease, argues Anna Katharina Schaffner, who charts the thematic influence of Krafft-Ebing's work in Mann's first novel *Buddenbrooks: Verfall einer Familie* (*Buddenbrooks: Decline of a Family*, 1901). She writes that in Mann's fictional framework, "sexual deviance and the signifiers of physical and psychological disintegration are associated with metaphysical, intellectual, and artistic progress; in fact they are the prerequisites for the advent of the artist" (*Modernism and Perversion* 175). Certainly this holds true for *Der Tod in Venedig*.

Psycho-degeneration was not the only school of sexological thought current at the time. Magnus Hirschfeld proposed from around the turn of the twentieth century onwards the third- or intermediate-sex theory, which viewed homosexual men and women as belonging to a sex between the male and female sexes. Hirschfeld's theory may have worked some degree of influence on Mann's portrayal of Aschenbach. In the 2002 essay "Making Way for the Third Sex," Tobin discusses the influence of sexological theories of homosexuality, particularly Hirschfeld's third-sex theory, on Mann's early writings. Tobin asserts that the turn from the "liberal" medical understanding of same-sex desire that is manifest in the early short fiction to "antiliberal" historicizations of love between males as Greek love is nowhere "more apparent that in *Der Tod in Venedig*" (331). Although Aschenbach strives to clothe his desire for another male in the garb of classicism, argues Tobin, these efforts are "undercut by the novella" (331) and, "in the end, the late nineteenth-century view of homosexuality based on gender inversion . . . outlasts the anti-liberal" (333). Therefore, Tobin suggests that medical theories are still a powerful force in the novella. He develops his thesis further in the 2012 essay "Queering Thomas Mann's *Tod in Venedig*" where he argues that "the novella presents in Gustav von Aschenbach a powerful proponent of a Hellenizing, masculinist, anti-liberal and anti-medical understanding of sexuality" (79) which is in contrast to the voice of the "authorial narrator" whom Tobin identifies as a "liberal emancipationist" (72). "The narrator's narrative seems to undercut [Aschenbach's] approach with liberal presumptions of homosexual identity as a characteristic of a fixed, biological, pathological, and gender-inverted minority" (79). It is "the queer ironic structure of the novella," concludes Tobin that allows the novella to confront "the conflict between these two approaches dialectically" (79). Tobin presents two late nineteenth- and early twentieth-century cultural forces in conflict: sexology versus antisexology. What I wish to stress here is that "liberal sexology" was by no means a unified voice as Tobin would have it in his essays. It is understandable, though, that the strands of sexological thought represented by Krafft-Ebing and Hirschfeld are conflated since it seems that this is also the case in the novella. In the following, I tease out the differences and the ways they affect the portrayal of the characters. Aschenbach is an intermediary figure in terms of his gender and sexuality, but this intermediacy seems also to be in close alliance with decadence and degeneration, indeed perhaps is the root of this disintegration (or rather vice versa). Mackay, on the other hand, in his fiction recognized the distinct character of the two schools of sexological thought, but he condemned both, the one as physicians taking up the reins of societal power from priests and judges and the other as a misguided effort at liberating same-sex love by brokering a deal with the physicians.

John Henry Mackay's rejection of sexological models is well traversed terrain in the secondary literature on *Die Bücher der namenlosen Liebe* (see Fähnders, "Anarchism and Homosexuality in Wilhelmine Germany" 138–46; Kennedy, *Anarchist of Love*; Ivory, "The Urning and His Own" 334, 338, 345; J. Bauer, "On the Nameless Love and Infinite Sexualities" 1–26). James Jones writes that, in spite of the author's fervent opposition to sexological inquiry, the novella, *Fenny Skaller: Ein Leben der namenlosen Liebe*, unconsciously internalizes the thought structures of this field of knowledge. "While [Mackay's] stance against the 'Third Sex' theory would seem to allow him to create a literary discourse ranging beyond the medical model, the very opposite proves to be the case. His works portray the homosexual character almost exclusively within a conception of him as Other and he is defined according to his love for other males" (*We of the Third Sex* 263). I concur with Jones's observation of the minoritizing understanding in *Fenny Skaller* and Mackay's other writings, but I disagree with the interpretation he draws from it. He argues that a conception of sexuality defining the individual is the influence of the medical model. Jones's conclusion might rest on an interpretation of the first volume of Michel Foucault's *The History of Sexuality* (1976), one that views sexual subjectivity as the product of medical discourse. But, as David Halperin writes, such an interpretation—one that argues "that before the modern era sexual deviance could be predicated only of acts, not of persons or identities"—is as "inattentive to Foucault's text as it is heedless of European history" ("Forgetting Foucault" 97). Foucault, Halperin writes, is writing about legal/medical discourses, not about personal or private feelings. I suggest that the novella *Fenny Skaller* and the novel *Der Puppenjunge*, as well as other nameless love writings, prove that an essentialist, minoritizing view of same-sex sexuality need not be part and parcel of sexology. A significant debt to sexual science exists in *Fenny Skaller*, but it is in terms of reaction, not the unconscious adoption of the modes of thought of this system of knowledge. On the other hand, neither does Mackay fully embrace the vision touted by the *Gemeinschaft der Eigenen*. Members of the GdE imagined same-sex desire in universal terms, as a potential for all men, and conceived sexual desire as possessing fluidity. Mackay's nameless love is both minoritizing and essentialist, providing an alternative discourse to understanding and expressing same-sex love that neither surrenders itself to the hands of the scientists, nor indulges in an anachronistic Hellenic fantasy.

This chapter explores the influence of and reactions to sexology in the two German works of fiction. It first considers the development of two distinct schools of thought in German inquiry into same-sex sexuality, then examines Mann's incorporation of elements of degenerationist and third-sex conceptions, and finally Mackay's rejection of sexological thought, which is a central theme of the novella *Fenny Skaller* and is more subtly woven into the narrative of *Der Puppenjunge*.

The Inception of a Scientific Discipline

During the first decade of the twentieth century, the term "Sexualwissenschaft" ("sexual science" or "sexology") was coined to denote this diverse and rapidly expanding field of scientific inquiry which was most actively undertaken in Germany and Austria (see Hekma, "A Female Soul in a Male Body" 233, 544, note 37). The aim of this system of knowledge was to study the sexual life of the individual within a scientific context, and the forms which received, especially in the formative years of the discipline, the greatest attention were those that deviated from societal norms, such as same-sex sexuality (Irvine, *Disorders of Desire* 5; Roberts, "Medicine and the Making of a Sexual Body" 83; Bristow, *Sexuality* 13). The origins of medical interest in same-sex sexuality can be traced to the mid-nineteenth century when some forensic physicians in France and Germany began to take note of cases of sodomy passing through the courts (Hekma 214–18). One of these physicians was Johann Ludwig Casper (1796–1864), who, in his essay titled "Über Nothzucht und Päderastie und deren Ermittlung seitens des Gerichtsarztes" (On Rape and Pederasty and Their Investigation on the Part of the Forensic Physician, 1852), was the first medical figure to consider the possibility that same-sex sexuality was an inborn phenomenon rather than an acquired vice (Beachy, "The German Invention of Homosexuality" 811). Other psychiatrists, including Wilhelm Griesinger (1817–1868) and Carl Westphal (1833–1890), made significant interventions in this area. The medical practitioner who would have the greatest influence in directing this school of thought, who would develop the idea of homosexuality as a marker of hereditary degeneration, was Richard von Krafft-Ebing (1840–1902). "In 1877," writes Chiara Beccalossi, "Richard von Krafft-Ebing published an important article in the *Archiv für Psychiatrie und Nervenkrankheiten* in which he explained *conträre Sexualempfindung* as a 'functional sign of degeneration.' This would go on to become the dominant psychiatric view of sexual inversion until the 1890s, paving the way for further sexological studies on various sexual deviations" (*Female Sexual Inversion* 6). His magnum opus was *Psychopathia Sexualis*, which ran through twelve editions in his lifetime. So pervasive was his influence that his was not merely a key voice in the medical discourse on sexual perversion, but also in the broader cultural discourse of decadence of the European fin de siècle.

Psychopathia Sexualis set the standard for all following studies of sexuality to imitate or react against. It is a compendious study, treating more than just homosexuality—although this is the nonnormative mode of sexuality which, particularly in later editions, received the most attention—but also sadism, masochism, fetishism, bestiality, necrophilia, and others. For Krafft-Ebing, aberrations come in two forms: they are either a form of "perversion" ("Perversion") or of "perversity" ("Perversität"); the former is a congenital form of sexual pathology, whereas the latter is a form of acquired vice (*Psychopathia Sexualis: A Medico-Legal Study* 53; *Psychopathia Sexualis: Eine medicinisch-gerichtliche Studie* 65). As Beccalossi describes, Krafft-Ebing regarded homosexuality as "a functional sign of degeneration" (223) ("ein funktionelles Degenerationszeichen"; 242) which is closely associated with other forms of degenerative mental conditions. "As a rule," writes Krafft-Ebing, these perversions are "constitutional, having its root in congenital conditions" (223) ("Diese ist in der Regel eine constitutionelle, in angeborenen Bedingungen wurzelnde"; 242). He argues that "In almost all cases where an examination of the physical and mental peculiarities of the ancestors and blood-relations has been possible, neuroses, psychoses, degenerative signs, etc., have been found in the families" (223–34) ("Fast in allen Fällen, die einer Erhebung der körperlich geistigen Zustände der Ascendenz und Blutsverwandtschaft zugänglich waren, fanden sich Neurosen, Psychosen, Degenerationszeichen u.s.w. in den betreffenden Familien vor"; 243). Homosexuality, however, was not considered a hereditary condition, but the underlying degeneration was, and it was likely to be compounded in succeeding generations. Yet there was a silver lining to these dark clouds of degeneration. Unlike his contemporary Max Nordau (1849–1923), in his work *Entartung* (*Degeneration*, 1892), Krafft-Ebing associates degeneration with artistic creativity. As Schaffner explains, homosexuality was in his view "cast as both socially destructive and culturally redemptive" (*Modernism and Perversion* 48). "Insanity of a degenerative character" (223) ("Irrsein mit dem Charakter des degenerativen"; 243) is to be found side by side with "brilliant endowment in art, especially music, poetry, etc." (223) ("glänzende Begabung für schöne Künste, besonders Musik, Dichtkunst, u.s.w."; 243). Out of the sphere of decadence, disease, and disintegration springs art and beauty.

This psycho-degenerative theory may have been the dominant school of thought in fin-de-siècle sexology, but it was not uncontested. In the 1860s, Karl Heinrich Ulrichs (1825–1895) developed in his writings, *Forschungen über das Räthsel der mannmännlichen Liebe* (*Research into the Riddle of Man-Manly Love*), which were published between 1864 and 1880, the theory of the third sex, arguing that homosexual men and women were not mentally ill, but belonged to a third sex between the male and female sexes. This concept formed the foundation of Magnus Hirschfeld's theory of sexuality. Hirschfeld (1868–1935) referred to the third sex as naturally occurring sexual intermediaries ("sexuelle Zwischenstufen"). In contrast to Krafft-Ebing's more clinically neutral approach to the study of sexual variance, which sought to systematize and classify diverse forms of nonnormative sexual behavior, the writings of Ulrichs and the studies of Hirschfeld are driven by their efforts at penal reform. There was, however, much interaction between these two schools of thought on homosexuality. Ulrichs consulted Krafft-Ebing in 1869, and Krafft-Ebing admitted his debt to Ulrichs in a letter he wrote him in 1879 (Oosterhuis, *Stepchildren of Nature* 139), which Ulrichs published in his final treatise "Critische Pheile: Denkschrift über die Bestrafung der Urningsliebe" ("Critical Arrows: Memoir of the Punishment of Uranian Love," 1880). "From the day when you sent me your writings—I believe it was in 1866—I have turned my full attention to this phenomenon . . . ; and it was only the knowledge of your books which motivated me to study this highly important area" (*The Riddle of "Man-Manly" Love* 2: 685) ("Von dem Tage an, wo Sie mir—ich glaube, es war 1866—Ihre Schriften zusandten, habe ich meine volle Aufmerksamkeit der Erscheinung zugewendet . . . ; und die Kenntniß Ihrer Schriften allein war es, was mich veranlaßte zum Studium in diesem hochwichtigen Gebiet"; *Forschungen* 4: 92). Krafft-Ebing eventually came to support the cause of homosexual liberation by signing Hirschfeld's petition for the amendment of Paragraph 175 (Oosterhuis, *Stepchildren of Nature* 172–73). Thus, these two schools of thought, the two medical conceptions of homosexuality were not always and in every respect in conflict. In Krafft-Ebing's last piece of writing on homosexuality, which was published in the third edition of Hirschfeld's *Jahrbuch für sexuelle Zwischenstufen* in 1901, he spoke against his earlier degenerative hypothesis, arguing that same-sex desire was not only a fixed orientation, but should be viewed neither as vice nor even as sickness (Beachy, "The German Invention of Homosexuality" 819).

In the late nineteenth century, at a time when most viewed same-sex acts as sins or crimes, leaders in the medical community, such as Westphal and Krafft-Ebing, as well as Albert Moll (1862–1939) and Iwan Bloch (1872–1922), saw this behavior as a matter for special medical and psychological attention. For many of these researchers, homosexuality was an indicator of underlying moral, mental, and physical degeneration. The taint of depravity associated with sexual relations between men remained, only from then on it suggested a diseased body and mind rather than a corrupt soul. "Though the terminology and scientific scaffolding were new," writes David Greenberg, "the fundamental opposition between normal sex and abnormal paresthesias was largely based on traditional oppositions. Sex was perverse if reproduction was not its goal" (*The Construction of Homosexuality* 414). For the literary texts of the following decades, these medical conceptions remained central, with all four works responding to this epistemological rebranding. In *Puppenjunge*, as well as *Imre* and *Maurice*, this influence is in terms of clear reaction: consequently these texts assert the health, vitality, and manliness of their protagonists in order to negate degeneration. *Der Tod in Venedig*, in contrast, is informed to a significant extent by degenerationist theories, but not these theories alone. Both of the degenerationist and third-sex conceptualizations of homosexuality are influential in the shaping of Mann's treatment of Aschenbach's desire.

Homosexual Love in the Time of Cholera

An oft-cited letter to Carl Maria von Weber written in 1920 assists in locating the views that directed Mann's portrayal of homosexual desire in *Der Tod in Venedig*. In the letter, the author explains that the depiction of Aschenbach's passion for Tadzio was determined in large part by "the naturalistic bent of my generation . . . which compelled me to see the 'case' *also* in a pathological light" (*Letters* 94) ("die *naturalistische* . . . Einstellung meiner Generation, die mich zwang, den 'Fall' *auch* pathologisch zu sehen"; *Briefe* 177). Mann argues to Weber, a young poet, that pathology, degeneration, effeminacy, and gender intermediacy are not necessarily bound together with same-sex passions—for instance, he references Michelangelo, Frederick the Great, Winckelmann, Platen, and Stefan George as exemplars of those who are by no means "unmanly or feminine men" ("unmännliche oder weibische Männer"). Yet degeneracy is a factor, argues Mann, which experience teaches often is the root of same-sex sexuality. "Experience refutes the idea that an attraction to the same sex is necessarily allied to 'effeminacy.' Experience also teaches, to be sure, that degeneracy, hermaphroditism, intermediate creatures, in short, repulsively pathological elements may be and frequently are involved" (95) ("Die Erfahrung widerlegt die Behauptung, daß 'Effemination' dazu gehöre, damit es sich vom gleichen Geschlecht angezogen fühle. Sie lehrt freilich auch, daß Entartung, Zwittertum, Zwischenstufenwesen, kurz, abstoßend Pathologisches der Grund sein kann und häufig der Grund ist"; 178). The letter provides documentary evidence which serves to highlight the influence of medical, specifically degenerationist, theories of homosexuality on the novella. In order to understand the novella's portrayal of homosexuality as pathology, it is essential to note that in the letter Mann views two distinct branches of sexological thought as one. On the one hand is the belief that homosexuality is resultant from degeneration and pathology, which was disseminated in the writings of a group of psychiatrists which includes Krafft-Ebing; and on the other hand is Hirschfeld's intermediate-sex theory. Homosexual men and women, argued Hirschfeld, formed a third or intermediate sex between the male and female sexes. Such intermediaries were not the product of physical and mental degeneration, but rather were naturally occurring anomalies. But this seems not to be the case for Aschenbach. He is a crossing of the bourgeois and the bohemian, of male and female; his intermediacy seems to underlie the degeneration which manifests itself in the form of homosexuality.

The letter to Weber also serves to show that Mann was uneasy allying homosexuality with degeneration and medicine. "Stefan George has said that in *Death in Venice* the highest is drawn down into the realm of decadence—and he is right; I did not pass unscathed through the naturalistic school. But disavowal, denunciation? No" (96) ("[Stefan] George hat zwar gesagt, im 'T. i. V.' sei das Höchste in die Sphäre des Verfalls hinabgezogen,—und er hat recht; nicht ungestraft bin ich durch die naturalistische Schule gegangen. Aber Verleugnung, Verunglimpfung? Nein"; 179). He insists it was not his intent to condemn, disavow, or vilify the all-consuming passion of a middle-aged man for a fourteen-year-old boy. After all, same-sex desire is the force that Mann recognized, writes Hans Vaget, as "the most vital source of his creativity" ("Confession and Camouflage" 585). Yet, on the other hand, neither does the novella present an unequivocal defense of this passion. There are three ways in which sexological concepts influence the text. The first is in the metaphor which likens homosexuality to disease, in the overt parallel trajectories of the cholera epidemic which overtakes Venice and Aschenbach's homosexuality and overruns his reserve and consumes him. Second are the physical markers displayed by Tadzio that suggest that he, like the character Hanno Buddenbrook from Mann's debut novel, is the scion of a degenerate line. And the third, the least explicit, is the text's casting of the protagonist as a sexual intermediary.

In the first chapter, Aschenbach's encounter with the nemesis figure invokes in him distant visions of the jungles of the Ganges Delta: "a tropical swampland under a cloud-swollen sky, moist and lush and monstrous, a kind of primeval wilderness of islands, morasses and muddy alluvial channels" (199) ("ein tropisches Sumpfgebiet unter dickdunstigem Himmel, feucht, üppig und ungeheuer, eine Art Urweltwildnis aus Inseln, Morästen und Schlamm führenden Wasserarmen"; 64). Later in the narrative, the English travel clerk describes a similar scene: "that wilderness of rank useless luxuriance, that primitive island jungle shunned by man, where tigers crouch in the bamboo thickets" (256) ("jener üppig-untauglichen, von Menschen gemiedenen Urwelt- und Inselwildnis, in deren Bambusdickichten der Tiger kauert"; 142). Aschenbach sees the breeding ground of the cholera epidemic to which Venice eventually succumbs (Reed, "Notes" 159). Also in the vision, there is lying in wait in this ancient tropical wilderness a "crouching tiger" ("kauernde[r] Tiger"), ready to spring from its hiding place in a bamboo thicket. This tiger is not only a metaphor for the disease, but also for Aschenbach's latent sexuality, the confrontation with which makes "his heart throb with terror and mysterious longing" (200) ("sein Herz pochen vor Entsetzen und rätselhaftem Verlangen"; 65). He desires this confrontation, for it to be revealed to him, and yet he fears the consequences. After Aschenbach admits to himself his love for Tadzio at the climax of the fourth chapter (244; 126), at the beginning of the fifth the cholera outbreak becomes apparent to him and other hotel guests despite the Italian authorities' best efforts to cover the epidemic up. Does this visibility also extend to the protagonist's desire? The disease invokes in Aschenbach an irresistible urge to remain in Venice, similar to the mysterious longing that brought him to the city in the first place. "Thus Aschenbach felt an obscure sense of satisfaction at what was going on in the dirty alleyways of Venice, cloaked in official secrecy—this guilty secret of the city, which merged with his own innermost secret and which it was also so much in his own interests to protect" (246) ("So empfand Aschenbach eine dunkle Zufriedenheit über die obrigkeitlich bemäntelten Vorgänge in den schmutzigen Gäßchen Venedigs,—dieses schlimme Geheimnis der Stadt, das mit seinem eigensten Geheimnis verschmolz, und an dessen Bewahrung auch ihm so sehr gelegen war"; 128). As the city is increasingly consumed by plague, Aschenbach's desublimating homosexuality ever more rapidly consumes him; he takes pleasure in both. He frantically pursues Tadzio on his forays through the filthy narrow alleyways and infested canals of Venice, surrendering himself to the mania of his passion, to which he symbolically succumbs by eating soft overripe strawberries, an act which also infects him with the disease (see Kitcher, 125–91 for an alternate interpretation).

The allusion, the affinity between homosexuality and cholera, was not lost on the novella's early critics. As cited above, the poet Stefan George lamented that in the work "das Höchste" (George believed that pederastic Eros structured upon ancient Greek models was the "highest" form of love) was drawn down into "the realm of decadence" (*Letters* 96) ("die Sphäre des Verfalls"; *Briefe* 179). And Kurt Hiller, writing in an essay published in Hirschfeld's *Jahrbuch für sexuelle Zwischenstufen* in 1914, describes the novella's portrayal of homosexual desire, in which "it is diagnosed as a symptom of decline and described almost like cholera" ("[es] wird da als Verfallssymptom diagnostiziert und wird geschildert fast wie die Cholera"), as "an example of moral narrowness" ("ein Beispiel moralischer Enge") (qtd. in Shookman, *A Novella and Its Critics* 24–25). And this aspect of the novel has been discussed by contemporary Mann scholars. T. J. Reed notes the complicity between Aschenbach and the city of Venice: to the protagonist, the "cholera seems not a threat but a confirmation, an accomplice even, of his passion; the city has its own dark secret, and one kind of disorder winks at another" (*Making and Unmaking a Master* 61; see also Binion, *Sounding the Classics* 37–38). This "naturalistic bent" serves a necessary practical function. The ambivalent treatment, which considers the pathological side of the protagonist's case (thus reflecting the direction in which Krafft-Ebing and Moll had taken the fin-de-siècle study of sexual perversions) ensured against scandal. Reed writes that "there was no expression of moral outrage from the guardians of public decency; there were repudiations of homosexuality, but no suggestion that Mann had been defending it. It was clearly assumed that a specialist in decadence had treated another aspect of it" ("Homosexuality and Taboo and *Der Tod in Venedig*" 130–31).

Second, the influence of degeneration theory shows up in the object of desire. Tadzio himself is "real" but also not entirely of this world. For Aschenbach, he is Hermes Psychagogos, who summons Aschenbach's soul to the eternal; his beauty is ethereal and is not associated with health and vitality (as in the case of the other objects of desire from the texts under discussion in this study) but is associated with illness and death. Aschenbach first notices this motif in connection with the youth's skin. "Was he in poor health? For his complexion was white as ivory against the dark gold of the surrounding curls" (220) ("War er leidend? Denn die Haut seines Gesichtes stach weiß wie Elfenbein gegen das goldige Dunkel der umrahmenden Locken ab"; 92). This contrast is at once aestheticized: his skin is like ivory against golden locks. This simile further objectifies the boy; he is an object of art, a living statue. Although this simile describes his poor health, it further reinforces his beauty. It serves to suggest the linkages between beauty and disease as well as love and death. Other factors indicate Tadzio's weakness and poor health; they occur twice in the narrative as Aschenbach notes Tadzio's teeth. "He had noticed that Tadzio's teeth were not as attractive as they might have been: rather jagged and pale, lacking the lustre of health and having that peculiar brittle transparency which is sometimes found in cases of anaemia. 'He's very delicate, he's sickly,' thought Aschenbach, 'he'll probably not live to grow old.' And he made no attempt to explain to himself a certain feeling of satisfaction or relief that accompanied this thought" (228) ("Er hatte jedoch bemerkt, daß Tadzios Zähne nicht recht erfreulich waren: etwas zackig und blaß, ohne den Schmelz der Gesundheit und von eigentümlich spröder Durchsichtigkeit, wie zuweilen bei Bleichsüchtigen. Er ist sehr zart, er ist kränklich, dachte Aschenbach. Er wird wahrscheinlich nicht alt werden. Und er verzichtete darauf, sich Rechenschaft von einem Gefühl der Genugtuung oder Beruhigung zu geben, das diesen Gedanken begleitete"; 103). And, towards the novella's climax, Aschenbach notes it again. "'He's sickly, he'll probably not live long,' he thought again, with that sober objectivity into which the drunken ecstasy of desire sometimes strangely escapes; and his heart was filled at one and the same time with pure concern on the boy's behalf and with a certain wild satisfaction" (255) ("'Er ist kränklich, er wird wahrscheinlich nicht alt werden,' dachte er wiederum mit jener Sachlichkeit, zu welcher Rausch und Sehnsucht bisweilen sich sonderbar emanzipieren; und reine Fürsorge zugleich mit einer ausschweifenden Genugtuung erfüllte sein Herz"; 140). Critics have attempted to elucidate the "Genugtuung" Aschenbach receives from the indicators of Tadzio's mortality. Esther Leser for instance explains that "The motif of physical weakness is closely related to the theme of decadence, and Beauty is not related to life, but to Death; for the Greeks, it never referred to fruitfulness and fertility. Tadzio's fragility suited Aschenbach's mental concept of Beauty because he related the boy's beauty to the unearthly and the eternal" (*Thomas Mann's Short*

Fiction 171). Additionally, Tadzio's pale skin and bad teeth are signifiers of degeneration. These motifs are neither singular in Mann's oeuvre nor in the novella. Hanno from *Buddenbrooks* is the homosexual final issue of the degenerate eponymous family of the novel and is marked, among other attributes, by his fragility, pale skin, bad teeth, and musical genius (Schaffner, *Modernism and Perversion* 175). And in the novella they appear in the form of Tadzio's antithesis—in the sense that the one figure inspires love and desire in the protagonist whereas the other inspires loathing and disgust—the aged dandy whom Aschenbach encounters on the ship to Venice. His physical condition too is neither robust nor healthy: his voice is shrill, he cannot hold his alcohol, his teeth are poor, and the reader can assume that beneath the rouge is pale skin (211; 79–80). These "characteristics are part of a package," writes Robert Tobin, "that identified the queer men in *Der Tod in Venedig*"; not just the aging dandy, but the "sickliness of Tadzio reflects the general pathologization of same-sex desire by the sexologists" ("Queering" 74). The protagonist is not the only character whose homosexuality has a degenerative etiology. Beauty and pathology are also linked in the object of desire.

And finally, sexology influences the literary text through the third- or intermediate-sex theory. Mann signed Hirschfeld's petition for the abolition of Paragraph 175 (Tamagne, *A History of Homosexuality in Europe* 83; Sigusch, *Auf der Suche nach der sexuellen Freiheit* 69), but in the letter to Weber he writes negatively of Hirschfeld's efforts at achieving homosexual liberation through scientific research, calling his *Wissenschaftlich-humanitäres Komitee* "ghastly" (*Letters* 96) ("gräßlich"; *Briefe* 180). However, Tobin suggests in his essays that the third-sex theory influences the novella ("Third Sex" 330–33; "Queering" 67–79). Robert Martin too writes that, in *Der Tod in Venedig*, Karl Heinrich Ulrichs's and Hirschfeld's "biologistic formula has evolved . . . into a subtle analysis of divided identity" ("Gender, Sexuality, and Identity in Mann's Short Fiction" 58). In the novella as well as in many of Mann's other works, queer characters are outsiders, "foreign" in some way; and, with regard to homosexual artists, this foreignness is internalized as the mixed-race motif. Therefore, race is a central concern of *Der Tod in Venedig*. So far in this study, I have not much discussed this issue. In *Imre*, "race" or nationality—not age, gender, or social class—is the desirable difference in the relationship between Oswald and Imre (see chapter 1). It is not surprising that race should come up when considering homosexuality, as it was during this era that both discourses emerged, not parallel to one another, as Siobhan Somerville shows, but through one another: "the simultaneous efforts to shore up and bifurcate categories of race and sexuality in the late nineteenth and early twentieth centuries were deeply intertwined" (*Queering the Color Line* 3). Carpenter and Prime-Stevenson both, in their respective writings, make analogies between race and sexuality. "Between [the] whitest of men and the blackest of negro stretches out a vast line of intermediary races as to their colours: brown, olive, red tawny, yellow" (*The Intersexes* 14). This metaphor indicates that, for Prime-Stevenson, neither race nor sex were matters of discrete binary pairs, but rather subtle variations from one pole to the other. Hirschfeld, ironically, argues against categories of race, regarding them basically as social constructions, specifically the distinction between Jew and Aryan, while at the same time upholding categories of sex (see H. Bauer "'Race,' Normativity and the History of Sexuality"). Reflecting the attitudes of society at large, in *Der Tod in Venedig*, the crossing of sexes and genders is articulated in and is analogous to the crossing of races. The novella suggests that the homosexual artist inhabits a liminal space between sexes, races, and nationalities: a location which grants him, and others like him, special insight and self-awareness which is the wellspring of their artistic genius.

This contrasts markedly with the treatment of degeneration in *Buddenbrooks* in the character of Hanno. Although he is a crossing of the staid German Buddenbrooks and the more artistic Dutch Arnoldsens, Hanno is less an intermediary and more the final issue of two degenerate families (Schaffner, "Richard von Krafft-Ebing's *Psychopathia sexualis* and Thomas Mann's *Buddenbrooks*" 490–91). He is characterized by his poor health, homosexuality, and outstanding musical talent. Aschenbach shares more in common with the eponymous protagonist of the short story "Tonio Kröger" (1903). In their cases, emphasis is upon the volatile mixing of the bourgeois and the bohemian and of the North and the South. Literarily inclined, Tonio belongs neither to his father's hanseatic mercantile world nor that of his musical, exotic mother. "My father . . . was of a northern temperament: contemplative, thorough, puritanically correct, and inclined to melancholy. My mother was of a vaguely exotic extraction, beautiful, sensuous, naïve, both reckless and passionate, and given to impulsive, rather disreputable behaviour. There is no doubt that this mixed heredity contained extraordinary possibilities—and extraordinary dangers" ("Tonio Kröger" 193–94). ("Mein Vater . . . war ein nordisches Temperament: betrachtsam, gründlich, korrekt aus Puritanismus und zur Wehmut geneigt; meine Mutter von unbestimmt exotischem Blut, schön, sinnlich, naiv, zugleich fahrlässig und leidenschaftlich und von einer impulsiven Liederlichkeit. Ganz ohne Zweifel war dies eine Mischung, die außerordentliche Möglichkeiten—und außerordentliche Gefahren in sich schloß"; *Gesammelte Werke* 8: 337). Tonio does not belong entirely to either world, nor does he fit into either sex. His first love is his foil, Hans Hansen, who embodies all that is manly, bourgeois, and German. "But my deepest and most secret love belongs to the fair-haired and the blue-eyed, the bright children of life, the happy, the charming and the ordinary" (194) ("Aber meine tiefste und verstohlenste Liebe gehört den Blonden und Blauäugigen, den hellen Lebendigen, den Glücklichen, Liebenswürdigen und Gewöhnlichen"; 338). Tonio's artistic temperament is born of his intermediacy in terms of race and sexuality. This theorization plays a central role in *Der Tod in Venedig*, for Aschenbach too is a product of racial mixing. "A strain of livelier, more sensuous blood had entered the family in the previous generation with the writer's mother, the daughter of a director of music from Bohemia. Certain exotic racial characteristics in his external appearance had come to him from her. It was from this marriage between hard-working, sober conscientiousness and darker, more fiery impulses that an artist, and indeed this particular kind of artist, had come into being" (202–03) ("Rascheres, sinnlicheres Blut war der Familie in der vorigen Generation durch die Mutter des Dichters, Tochter eines böhmischen Kapellmeisters, zugekommen. Von ihr stammten die Merkmale fremder Rasse in seinem Äußern. Die Vermählung dienstlich nüchterner Gewissenhaftigkeit mit dunkleren, feurigeren Impulsen ließ einen Künstler und diesen besonderen Künstler erstehen"; 68–69). This mixing of "blood" produces a great artist. Clayton Koelb points out that if his readership had not recognized the pattern from Mann's previous works, they would have from Goethe's autobiography *Aus meinem Leben: Dichtung und Wahrheit* (*Truth and Poetry: From my Own Life*, 1811–1833), in which the poet recounts his parentage in similar terms. "It would seem reasonable and fitting to Mann's audience that a great artist would be born of such a mixture of the homely and exotic, the staid and the impetuous, the bourgeois and the bohemian" (Koelb, "Death in Venice" 98–99). The novella incorporates a racialized discourse of "blood" through the motif of the divided, mixed-blood identity, but this mixture, if not tainted, is at least a volatile combination. Gerhard Härle writes that with the topos of blood mixing, which is a thematic set piece in Mann's work, in the case of Aschenbach there is a trade-off. This crossing of races grants him recourse to the exotic, allows him to transgress boundaries, and is full of potential, but at the price of heightened aesthesia and morbidity (Härle, *Männerweiblichkeit* 147, 348, note 13). Tonio admits to his confidante Lisaweta Iwanowna that in this crossing of boundaries lie "extraordinary possibilities—and extraordinary dangers" (194) ("außerordentliche Möglichkeiten—und außerordentliche Gefahren"; 337).

There are key differences between these two protagonists however. "Unlike Tonio," Martin argues "who as a young man is immersed in the maternal world of feeling, Aschenbach has constructed his life out of resistance to this darker self" ("Gender, Sexuality, and Identity in Mann's Short Fiction" 63). He must overcome his own physical limitations in order to do so. His physical fragility is a recurrent topic. At the outset of the narrative, the pressures of the author's duties have overstimulated him (197; 61). In the second chapter, the narrator explains "that Aschenbach's native constitution was by no means robust, that the constant harnessing of his energies was something to which he had been called, but not really born" (203) ("daß [Aschenbachs] Natur von nichts weniger als robuster Verfassung und zur ständigen Anspannung nur berufen, nicht eigentlich geboren war"; 69). His health is too poor to allow him to attend school as a boy, and at age thirty-five he falls ill because he has lived his life like a clenched fist. "They were not broad, the shoulders on which he thus carried the tasks laid upon him by his talent; and since his aims were high, he stood in great need of discipline" (204) ("Da er also die Aufgaben, mit denen sein Talent ihn belud, auf zarten Schultern tragen und weit gehen wollte, so bedurfte er höchlich der Zucht"; 70). His motto—"durchhalten!"—epitomizes the "discipline" ("Zucht") and "composure" ("Haltung") that enables his art: the figures of Frederick the Great and Saint Sebastian embody to Aschenbach his struggle. Without this moderating force, his talent would threaten to burn too fiercely for his frail body to contain. "Aschenbach had nevertheless had to recognize in good time that he belonged to a breed not seldom talented, yet seldom endowed with the physical basis which talent needs if it is to fulfill itself—a breed that usually gives of its best in youth, and in which the creative gift rarely survives into mature years" (203) "[Aschenbach] hatte doch zeitig erkennen müssen, daß er einem Geschlecht angehörte, in dem nicht das Talent, wohl aber die physische Basis eine Seltenheit war, deren das Talent zu seiner Erfüllung bedarf,—einem Geschlechte, das früh sein Bestes zu geben pflegt und in dem das Können es selten zu Jahren bringt"; 70). The term "Geschlecht" here is suggestive. The term has a broader meaning in German than merely biological sex or gender. David Luke, for instance, translates this passage as Aschenbach belonging to a "breed" of artist. Nevertheless it reinforces the idea that Aschenbach, like Tonio Kröger, belongs to a separate (perhaps a third) sex. The protagonist seems to recognize this in his final monologue: "yes, though we may be heroes in our fashion and disciplined warriors, yet we are like women, for it is passion that exalts us, and the longing of our soul must remain the longing of a lover—that is our joy and our shame" (265) ("ja mögen wir auch Helden auf unsere Art und züchtige Kriegsleute sein, so sind wir wie Weiber, denn Leidenschaft ist unsere Erhebung, und unsere Sehnsucht muß Liebe bleiben,—das ist unsere Lust und unsere Schande"; 153). He says that "we are *like* women" ("so sind wir *wie* Weiber"; emphasis added) thereby suggesting gender inversion, the intermediate role of the homosexual in general and the homosexual artist in particular (see Tobin, "Queering" 76). *Der Tod in Venedig* continues Mann's exploration of the relationship between racial, gender, and sexual intermediaries, variations of which would recur in later works. In addition, it reinforces the ties between homosexuality and the artistic temperament, which by this time were well established not only in medical literature. This employment of the motif of the crossing of genders and sexes is allied with the metaphor which links cholera and homosexuality. The novella's interpretation of intermediary sexuality is not the same as the developmental concepts advocated in the research of Ulrichs and Hirschfeld, which conceived *sexuelle Zwischenstufen* as a form of naturally occurring, not necessarily pathological, sexual variation. Instead the text situates it as the root of decline and degeneration, a volatile mixing of North and South, artistic and mundane, of man and woman, and of masculine and feminine: but a mixing from which vitality and creativity can also spring.

The psychopathological view of homosexuality has a great degree of impact upon the text, by the author's own admission. Mann writes in his letter to Weber that not unpunished did he pass through the naturalistic school, but he claims that his intent was not to condemn or disavow (*Letters* 96; *Briefe* 179). Pairing love and beauty with death is by no means a condemnation or disavowal of this love. As August von Platen writes in "Tristan," from his *Sonette aus Venedig* (*Venetian Sonnets*, 1824): "Whoever has gazed at beauty eye to eye / Is given over, signed and sealed, to death" ("Wer die Schönheit angeschaut mit Augen / Ist dem Tode schon anheimgegeben"; Platen 172–73). Mann's essay on Platen (as in chapter 2) can help illuminate the themes of the novella. The two figures, the poet and the fictional author, are meant to belong to the same "Geschlecht" of artist. Mann writes of Platen in a way that indicates that he was a model for the fictional character: "At thirty he was already showing serious organic symptoms of tension and exhaustion. After a further nine years' stress of emotions and their suppression, he died at Syracuse of a vague typhus attack which was nothing but a pretext for the death to which obviously he was devoted from the first" (*Essays of Three Decades* 269) ("Mit dreißig schon treten schwere organische Anzeichen der Überreizung und Erschöpfung zutage. Nach neun Jahren weiterer Gefühlsüberlastung und -abschnürung stirbt er zu Syrakus an einer undeutlich typhösen Krankheit, die nichts war als der Vorwand des Todes, dem er von Anbeginn wissentlich anheimgegeben war"; *Gesammelte Werke* 9: 280–81). Both writers possess talent of too great an intensity for their bodies to contain. Aschenbach ought not to have made it to age fifty. The *Zucht* that rules his life can be credited with this feat; it has harnessed and tamed his creative genius and extended his life, but may have done so at the cost of reaching his full artistic potential. The repression of his maternal legacy has earned him acclaim, respectability, and a title of nobility, yet, as Caroline Picart argues, "the tyranny of the Apollonian in him leaves him decadent and effete rather than healthy and vital" (*Thomas Mann and Friedrich Nietzsche* 20). The artist cannot worship at the altar of Apollo alone, neither can he forsake the former god and turn all his attention to Dionysus. In Mann's world, the artist was an intermediary figure, a bridge between intellect and sexuality, between the masculine and the feminine, Harry Oosterhuis explains ("The Dubious Magic of Male Beauty" 185). Schaffner writes that "in Mann's representations of the homosexual artist, the highest and the lowest coexist, the degenerate is also the sublime," through which he invests "the pathological with metaphorical significance" (*Modernism and Perversion* 181). In *Der Tod in Venedig* death and disease are linked to artistic genius, as well as "beauty, love, [and] eternity" (*Essays of Three Decades* 261) ("Schönheit, Liebe, [und] Ewigkeit"; *Gesammelte Werke* 9: 271).

"False and dangerous" Theories

Hirschfeld's theory of the third sex and sexual intermediaries was not without vocal critics. One of the quarters from which this opposition was voiced was the segment of the German "homosexual" community that promoted the masculine model of same-sex relations. In Adolf Brand's journal *Der Eigene*, in Elisar von Kupffer's literary anthology, *Lieblingminne und Freundesliebe in der Weltliteratur*, and in Benedict Friedländer's studies, the third-sex and masculine models were viewed as largely mutually exclusive. The program proposed by the *Gemeinschaft der Eigenen* and the nameless love fictionalized by Mackay resist medical typology and nomenclature essentially on the same grounds. First, they argue that love and desire between men is not pathological, not a manifestation of inherited degeneration. Second, they insist that this love is a thoroughly manly impulse. They object to the reification of gender, basic to the third-sex theory, whereby love for a man is characterized as a fundamentally female drive. Thus they reject the cross-sex or cross-gender hypothesis. For them, the man-loving man is just that: a man who loves other men.

The leaders of the GdE rejected and opposed various aspects of modern life, perhaps none more so than sexology and its minoritizing concept of same-sex desire. Kupffer, in his essay "Die Ethisch-politische Bedeutung der Lieblingminne" (1899), and Friedländer, in *Renaissance des Eros Uranios*, both cite and dismiss Ulrichs's theory of the third sex. Kupffer writes: "It has now become the fashion in humane-scientific and, on the other hand, closely concerned circles to speak of a 'third' sex, whose spirit and body are said not to agree with one another" ("The Ethical-Political Significance of *Lieblingminne*" 36) ("Es ist nun mal in human-wissenschaftlichen und anderseits in nahbeteiligten Kreisen Mode geworden, von einem 'dritten' Geschlecht zu reden, dessen Seele und Leib nicht zusammenstimmen sollen"; *Lieblingminne und Freundesliebe in der Weltliteratur* 3). He insists that it has become "a moral duty" (36) ("eine moralische Pflicht"; 3) to contradict such a "mire of lies and filthiness" (36) ("Sumpf von Lügen und Unflätigkeiten"; 3), which, of course, is the aim of his writings. Friedländer, approaching the subject from a scientific rather than a cultural-historical point of view, argues that "the main error of Hirschfeld's intermediate-sex theory" ("der Hauptirrthum der [Hirschfelds] Zwischenstufentheorie") is that it considers "same-sex love as exclusively the affair of a small, almost always unmarried minority" ("die gleichgeschlechtliche Liebe ausschliesslich [als] die Angelegenheit einer kleinen, fast immer unverheiratheten Minderzahl"; *Renaissance des Eros Uranios* 264). His study details a biological, physiological, and historical basis for universal bisexuality. Love and desire for a man is not an essentially feminine drive, rather, man possesses "the capability to love in both directions" ("[die] Fähigkeit zu beiden Richtungen des Liebestriebes"; 263), but Judeo-Christian asceticism forces most men to repress their homoerotic and homosocial desires. The central issue to which the German masculinist movement objected was sexology's casting of same-sex desire as a trait found in a segment of humanity, regardless of whether the scientists believed that this segment suffered from hereditary mental illness (Krafft-Ebing) or that their sexuality was a harmless natural anomaly resultant from cross-gendering (Ulrichs, Hirschfeld). They sought to counter these conceptions in their writings.

Mackay's fiction, which would otherwise share this opposition to medico-scientific conceptions of homosexuality, differs in one essential way. Despite its protestations against the sexologists' placing of individuals into pigeon-hole intermediary levels, it depicts love between males in minoritizing terms. Although the mode of relations portrayed is intergenerational, like *Lieblingminne*, Mackay's protagonists do not love in both directions; instead their sexualities are fixed and directed only toward teenage boys. A particular passage from the first book "Die Namenlose Liebe: Ein Bekenntniss" seems to suggest the universality of same-sex attraction: "a Greek inheritance ineradicably lives on in the breast of each man, each youth" (*Books* 56) ("ein hellenisches Erbteil in der Brust jedes Mannes, jedes Jünglings unausrottbar weiterlebt"; *Bücher* 78). Not each man who loves men, but this inheritance lives on in the hearts of *all* men. This is not, however, the conception of same-sex desire portrayed in Mackay's fiction. Skaller in the novella and Graff in the novel are "those who from youth on felt themselves draw to their own sex, who as boys and adolescents, and as adults, always loved only their own sex" (*Books* 125) ("einmal Die, die sich von Jugend an überhaupt nur zu ihrem eigenem Geschlecht hingezogen fühlten, die als Knaben und Jünglinge, wie als Erwachsene immer nur ihr eigenes Geschlecht lieben"; *Bücher* 223). Thus, unlike the vision championed by the GdE, Mackay's characters are a minority marked by their same-sex desire, whose orientation is fixed. Moreover, sexological studies play a key role in Fenny Skaller's development, allowing him to forge an identity resistant to theories of psychopathology and sexual intermediacy. It can be inferred from the novel *Der Puppenjunge* that Herman Graff undergoes a comparable confrontation with sexological writings on same-sex desire. As a consequence, Graff can conceive of his love as natural, self-evident, and thus in no need of medico-scientific explanation.

Mackay's resistance and opposition to sexological inquiry translates into his fiction as an effort to portray same-sex subjectivity and same-sex love beyond the medical model, an aim which, in terms of his nameless love writings, is most successfully realized in the novel *Der Puppenjunge*. In large measure, the novel's lack of interest in sexology owes something to the writer's earlier working-through of his anxiety about being classed with the mentally ill and third-sex psychic hermaphrodites in the autobiographical novella *Fenny Skaller: Ein Leben der namenlosen Liebe*. The novella vehemently reacts against sexological thought, especially the third-sex theory, because this conception's emphasis on gender inversion seems to represent to the protagonist a direct threat to his masculinity and identity as a manly lad-lover. Despite this rejection of both major schools of sexual science, the text does not adopt the universalizing and retrogressive cultural-historical stance common to the writings of other contributors to Brand's literary journal. In the novel, which was published thirteen years after *Fenny Skaller*, the masculine, lad-lover identity with its essentialist and minoritizing understanding of sexuality appears again, while the unconcealed vitriol directed at the perceived imperialistic expansion of sexual science into the realm of love between men takes on a subordinate role in the narrative. The following charts the overt reaction to sexological thought in the earlier work of fiction and then considers how the positioning of the Sagitta texts in relation to this discourse is articulated more subtly in *Puppenjunge*.

In Prime-Stevenson's *Imre*, the man of science assumes the role of champion, but in Mackay's writings the physicians and sexologists are conquerors. The author positively rejects the scientific study of sexuality, terming it a misguided intellectual effort that seeks artificial unity of sexual diversity, forcing love into categories devised from observations made by doctors on patients in asylums. In the polemic introduction to *Die Bücher der namenlosen Liebe*, he spells out his repudiation. "This love, persecuted by judges and cursed by priests, has fled to the medical doctors as if it were a sickness that could be cured by them. But it is no sickness. Doctors have as little to look for and examine here as judges, and those who have accepted it as a sickness taken them on as if they are not ill are mistaken if they believe they can free themselves from the clutches of power by making a pact with this power" (45) ("Diese Liebe, verfolgt von den Richtern und verflucht von den Priestern hat sich zu den Ärzten geflüchtet, als sei sie eine Krankheit, die von ihnen geheilt werden könne. Aber sie ist keine Krankheit. Ärzte haben hier so wenig zu suchen und zu untersuchen, wie Richter, und die sich ihrer angenommen haben wie keiner Kranken, irren sich, wenn sie glauben, sie könnten sie aus den Fängen der Gewalt befreien, indem sie mit dieser Gewalt paktieren"; 62–63). They are a newly emergent power, fulfilling a role once held by the priest and judge. J. Edgar Bauer writes that "The 'physicians' Mackay depicts support a long-standing cultural pattern of using social pressure to deny natural differences in sexual constitution and thus distort the true nature of the 'nameless love'" ("On the Nameless Love and Infinite Sexualities" 9). And those who think they can broker a deal with this social force—here Mackay indicates Hirschfeld and the WhK—are deluding themselves. On the whole, this summarizes how *Fenny Skaller* treats the scientific study of same-sex sexuality. This is not to say that sexology in this novella is cast solely in an antagonistic role. For instance, the protagonist's reading of sexological studies plays a central function in the formation of his own sexual identity.

Krafft-Ebing's *Psychopathia Sexualis* appears in the novella as "a large, yellow book" which has "a curious Latin title, a title in two words" (*Books* 119) ("einen seltsamen lateinischen Titel, einen Titel in zwei Worten"; *Bücher* 211). Mackay's biographers point to the scene as a dramatization of the author's own reckoning with his sexual desire. Walter Fähnders and K. H. Z. Solneman write that Mackay became aware of his homosexuality at around the age of twenty-two, certainly by 1886, when he read Krafft-Ebing's study, whose first edition appeared that year (Fähnders, "Anarchism and Homosexuality in Wilhelmine Germany" 141; Solneman, *Der Bahnbrecher John Henry Mackay* 210). Thomas Riley writes that the novella seems "to describe the whole sexual development of Mackay himself, a case history turned into a novel by a master poet" (*Germany's Poet-Anarchist* 108). In the novella, the sexological study and the others which Skaller would eventually seek out fulfill a complementary, twofold role in the narrative: first, through the study he learns that he is not alone and second, sexological methodology and pronouncements set the protagonist against this field of knowledge. Through sexology he begins to learn about his desire and eventually fashions his identity in opposition to it.

The case histories that Skaller reads shock and excite him in equal measure. "But he reads and reads. About things he has never heard of, and which he nevertheless knows; which he had never held to be possible, and which he nevertheless understands; which he had never imagined, and yet recognizes; he reads of things monstrous" (*Books* 119–20) ("Er aber liest und liest . . . Von Dingen, von denen er nie gehört, und die er doch weiß; die er nie für möglich gehalten und die er doch versteht; die er nie geahnt und doch gekannt, von Dingen liest er, ungeheuerlichen"; *Bücher* 213). Skaller discovers himself in the scientific study, but his initial response is one of mixed emotions. He knows not whether his excitement is jubilation or outrage. "*There are others like him!* He is no longer alone among people, no longer alone on this earth! Now it is to be his too, this earth. . . . He no longer had a horror of himself. Quite secretly, inwardly, there arose a shy hope: that he, too, would one day be fortunate in this love" (120) ("Es giebt Andere gleich ihm! Er ist nicht mehr allein unter den Menschen, nicht mehr allein auf dieser Erde! Nun soll sie auch die seine werden, diese Erde, und er will auf ihr leben! . . . Ihm graute nicht mehr vor sich selbst. Ganz heimlich, in seinem Innern, erhob sich eine schüchterne Hoffnung: daß auch er einmal glücklich sein würde in dieser Liebe"; 213–14). This text is a conduit to a wider community where same-sex desire, sexual identities, and emotions associated with it and its repression are shared experiences. Skaller is still isolated and cannot speak about his love, "But he kept silent no longer within himself, and from then on no longer silent about his love" (120) ("Aber zu sich selbst schwieg er fortan nicht mehr von seiner Liebe"; 214), he no longer must carry the burden and guilt of his isolation. Once he begins to grasp the import of his newly acquired knowledge, Skaller questions whether it truly describes his love and whether it opens the door to a community with which he wants to associate. "He understood only so much: they had locked up his love in science's wax-figure cabinet of monsters, of deformities and monstrosities of all kinds—there they had also classified him: among people with whom he had nothing in common, and could and would have nothing in common. But the love *existed*. It was there, and among those pages, filled with the confessions of the desperate, who did not understand themselves and who hoped for salvation from the doctor" (120–21) ("Nur so Viel begriff er: in ein Wachsfigurenkabinett der Wissenschaft von Scheusäligkeiten, von Mißgeburten und Monstrositäten aller Art hatte man auch seine Liebe gesperrt—dorthin hatte man auch ihn klassificiert: unter Menschen, mit denen er Nichts gemein hatte und Nichts gemein haben konnte und wollte. Aber die Liebe gab es. Sie war da . . . zwischen diesen Blättern, gefüllt mit den Bekenntnissen Verzweifelter, die sich selbst nicht kannten und Rettung von dem Arzte erhofften"; 214–15). As described above, *Psychopathia Sexualis* is a compendious study which treats a broad range of sexual behaviors that deviate from societal norms, and an early edition, from which the protagonist is likely to be reading, would contain shorter, more factual accounts collected from hospitalized patients. Skaller feels himself a cut above the subjects of the study. His love is not an illness; it does not belong among what he views as the confessions of desperate individuals whom the medical community brands mentally ill degenerates. He rejects the idea of seeking absolution from physicians, which is a position that is one of the benchmarks of the author's liberationist campaign for the nameless love. Nonetheless, the text is useful to Skaller in proving that he is not alone. Further reading of sexology conducted years later provides the protagonist with what he considers a more complete perspective of the field of scientific inquiry into same-sex desire.

From his critical reading, Skaller observes that two schools of sexology exist: on the one hand is the segment of the medical community who, viewing same-sex desire as mental illness, attempt to cure this condition, whereas on the other is a camp who, recognizing that same-sex desire is not illness and cannot be cured, attempt to liberate this love as the third sex. "Cursed by parsons of all religions and all sects as an unmentionable sin; prosecuted by judges . . . , it had now luckily fallen into the hands of the doctors, some of whom still sought to cure it as a sickness, but the others, who knew that it could not be a sickness, sought to rescue it by placing it between the sexes" (148–49) ("Von Pfaffen aller Religonen und aller Art als unnennbare Sünde verflucht; von den Richtern . . . als Verbrechen verfolgt, war sie nun glücklich in die Hände von Aerzten gefallen, von denen die einen sie immer noch als eine Krankheit heilen, die anderen aber, die wußten, daß sie keine Krankheit sein konnte, sie zu retten versuchten, indem sie sie zwischen die Geschlechter stellten"; 264). But this emancipationist platform only perpetrates, for Skaller, an error as egregious as casting this love in the role of sin, crime, or disease. In defiance of the newly constructed third sex and the artificially unified categories that he considers these physicians employ to systematize human emotion into "intermediates" ("Übergänge"), Skaller argues for infinite sexualities, "the tremendous variety of love" (125) ('[die] ungeheur[e] Verschiedenheit der Liebe"; 223) (see J. Bauer, "On the Nameless Love and Infinite Sexualities" 11). In support of his vision, he points to the diversity of homosexual experience. "Within the circle of this love for the same sex there was a huge, unbridgeable contrast . . . : that between the masculine man, whose masculine inclination was for masculine youth—the ancient love of the Greeks—and that of the man with a feminine disposition, or perhaps better said, of the outwardly masculine female who is inclined to men" (148) ("Es [gab] innerhalb des Kreises dieser Liebe zu dem eigenen Geschlecht einen ungeheuren, durch Nichts zu überbrückenden Gegensatz . . . den zwischen dem männlichen Manne, dessen männliche Neigung der männlichen Jugend galt—die alte Liebe der Hellenen; und dem des weiblich gearteten Mannes, oder, wohl besser gesagt, des äußerlich männlich gearteten Weibchens, das sich dem Manne gab"; 263). Skaller identifies two extremes in the spectrum of men who are drawn to their own sex, and owing to this irreconcilable diversity he considers the third-sex category a fiction constructed by physicians. This is by no means an unreasonable argument. He resists being typologized by sexology; but he does not evade typology. He defines himself in the narrative by way of his desire for young men. He argues for the specificity of his own form of same-sex sexuality. However, his protestations against sexological imperialism are undercut by the frankly denigratory language he employs in regard to effeminate homosexual males in this passage and at other points in the narrative. Skaller inverts the language of the third sex and thereby constructs a foil against which to justify his mode of desire via its masculinity. "He, Skaller, was a man and he felt himself entirely as such. Noting in his being, his manner, his inclination was feminine. So much so, that everything called feminine repelled him, above all in love" (148) ("Er, Skaller, war ein Mann, und er fühlte sich ganz als ein solcher. Nichts in seinem Wesen, seiner Art, seiner Neigung war weiblich. So sehr, daß Alles, was weiblich hieß, ihn abstieß, vor Allem in der Liebe"; 264). It is clear that he finds the basis of the third-sex theory insulting, the idea that love for a man is essentially a feminine attribute, and thus a man who loves men must have a female/feminized soul. Again, this is not an unreasonable objection owing to the fact that this reification of gender is the greatest weakness of the third-sex concept. But what is unreasonable is that when the protagonist presents his own classifications of male sexuality, which comprise four orientations, his plan is far more restrictive than that which is on offer from Hirschfeld and other third-sex advocates. According to Skaller, men can be divided into four groups: (1) heterosexual men; (2) those like him who "from the very beginning on were drawn *only* to the younger one of their own sex, always so strongly only to the younger that for them the love for an older one was completely impossible" (126) ("die es ebenso von allem Anfang an nur zu dem Jüngeren ihres Geschlechts hinzog, so stark immer nur zu dem Jüngeren, daß ihnen die Liebe zu einem Aelteren gänzlich unmöglich war"; 224); (3) effeminate men who always love adult or older men; and (4) the elusive group within which Skaller can find mutual attraction and love: "those who in their youth were able to return the love of an older one of their sex just as well as later that of a woman, whose feelings in their youth did not yet go in a definite direction" (125–26) ("Die, welche in ihrer Jugend die Liebe eines Aelteren ihres Geschlechts ebensogut erwidern konnten, wie später die einer Frau; die, deren Empfinden in ihrer Jugend noch in keiner bestimmten Richtung ging"; 224). He admits that "these were theories which life would never exactly fit" (126) ("dies waren Theorien, in die das Leben sich nie so fügen würde"; 224), but it is from this perspective, utilizing this biased view of male sexuality, that homosexual subcultures are presented in the novella (150–51; 267–68) and through this that the author's own exclusively intergenerational mode of desire is championed. This is not the idea of infinite sexualities, the diversity of love, which the text advocates only shortly before in the narrative. The greatest failing point of the novella, in terms of didactic intent, is this inconsistency.

Der Puppenjunge engages with sexology less directly than *Fenny Skaller*. Medical science is personified by only one figure in the novel. This physician is an agent of the state, employed by the prison to conduct an examination of Graff after having been incarcerated for violating Paragraph 175. Graff finds the specialist's insistence that he is ill preposterous. "Sick? No, he was not sick. Nothing was the matter with him. What indeed was supposed to be the matter with him?" (280) ("Krank? . . . Nein, er war nicht krank.—Ihm fehlte Nichts. Was sollte ihm wohl fehlen?"; 323). Like the judges and the jailers who place him in prison, this character is merely the functionary of the repressive regime. Furthermore, whereas Skaller's emotional reckoning with his desire is graphically depicted as he peruses the case histories of *Psychopathia Sexualis*, Graff has progressed past this point in his personal trajectory. "He knew his sexual disposition. He knew how it stood for him. He still read a great deal, but did not trouble himself for an explanation where there was nothing to explain. What was self-evident, natural, and not in the least sick did not require an excuse through an explanation. Many of the theories now posed he held to be false and dangerous. It was a love just like any other" (158) ("Er kannte seine Veranlagung. Er wußte, wie es um ihn stand. Er las noch immer Viel, bemühte sich aber nicht um Erklärungen, wo es Nichts zu erklären gab.—Was selbstverständlich, natürlich und nicht im Geringsten krankhaft war bedurfte nicht der Entschuldigung durch eine Erklärung. Viele der jetzt aufgestellten Theorien hielt er für falsch und gefährlich. Es war eine Liebe wie jede andere Liebe auch"; 184). Graff understands his "disposition," but the narrator withholds how the protagonist gains this knowledge. This is partially answered, though, when the narrator acknowledges that Graff still reads much but is not concerned with "an explanation where there was nothing to explain." What and why he reads is still withheld. In light of the scene from the 1913 novella explored above, it is reasonable to assume that Graff is reading medical, scientific, and possibly cultural-historical treatments of homosexuality. And since he does not seek an explanation, or at least is not seeking one any longer, Graff must read for the same reason that Skaller furtively immersed himself in Krafft-Ebing's sex study. These unnamed texts serve as his only conduit to a wider community of man-loving men; they are a means to enter the experiences of other persons, to discover that one is not alone and that, despite the taboo, same-sex desire is a shared experience. Thus, Graff accepts and understands his sexual desires, not in spite of sexological studies, but rather because of these works. His reading of these case histories allows him to shape his understanding of his desire for other men in terms of its self-evidence and naturalness: a love like any other. In this way, as Oosterhuis's study shows, the character Hermann Graff has this in common with many late nineteenth-century homosexual readers of *Psychopathia Sexualis*. The sexological texts initiate awareness and allow Graff to progress beyond a reliance on these frameworks of knowledge.

Sexology, in the books of the nameless love, is presented as a force, like religious and legal structures, that perpetuates myths, errors, and misconceptions about same-sex love. In *Puppenjunge*, the theories are declared "false and dangerous." And yet, in the same way that sexological writings on homosexuality empower Fenny Skaller to forge an identity in opposition to sexological pronouncements, for Herman Graff they are a point of reference against which he can build an identity as a healthy, manly lad-lover. The nameless love, in spite of its contradictions and denigration of effeminate models, is nevertheless a powerful image and conceptualization of male-male love. For the numerous men who struggled against medical concepts and felt more constrained than liberated by the third-sex identities, *Die Bücher der namenlosen Liebe* and *Der Puppenjunge* offer other alternatives. Mackay's writings are a means of building an affirmative concept of oneself as a lover of other males. And, for the modern reader, the novel's disruption of discourse means that the narrative is not dated in the same way as in Edward Prime-Stevenson's *Imre: A Memorandum*. *Der Puppenjunge* has the advantage of its accessibility. It refuses to name this desire with contemporary terms (most of which are now antiquated) while depicting the protagonist's love for a young man within recognizable literary conventions. Mackay's novel is more accessible despite the fact that the love relationship between Oswald and Imre is one that we today recognize, egalitarian and between two adults, in contrast to Mackay's ephebophilia which seems a throwback to earlier Victorian writings.

Conclusion

The scientific study of sexuality, particularly same-sex sexuality, was a pervasive cultural force from the late nineteenth century into the early twentieth, especially in Germany and Austria, where the inquiry was most active. *Der Tod in Venedig* demonstrates influence from degenerationist and third-sex theories, as well as from Freud. The intermediate-sex individuals in Mann's fiction are gifted with special insight, which is the source of their artistic powers, but are at the same time cursed with "sympathy with the abyss" (207) ("Sympathie mit dem Abgrund"; 74). In *Der Tod in Venedig*, as well as others of Mann's works of fiction, from degeneration springs artistic genius, beauty, and passion. On the other hand, *Der Puppenjunge* strives to treat love between members of the same sex outside of sexological discourse, but, like the author's earlier, autobiographical novella, *Fenny Skaller*, it betrays some influence from sexology, in particular in the form of opposition. Mann's novella is the odd one out in that it is the only work of fiction under discussion not to take an unambiguous stance against psychopathological models of homosexuality. Perhaps writing for a broader audience meant making concessions to these scientific and cultural discourses. But Mann's novella also subverts these discourses by privileging Krafft-Ebing over Nordau, by allying regeneration through the production of art with degeneration. Hence Mann comments on this school of sexological thought more subtly than, but nonetheless as effectively as, the other works of fiction.

Chapter 5

Health, Masculinity, and the Third Sex

Both Edward Prime-Stevenson's *Imre: A Memorandum* and E. M. Forster's *Maurice* are fiercely resistant to medical theories which identify same-sex sexuality as a marker of degeneration and mental illness; both emphasize the health and vitality of their central characters; and both are influenced by third-sex theories, which is explicit in *Imre* and implicit in *Maurice*. The greatest difference here is not in substance, but in stylistic concerns; whereas the treatment of these themes in *Imre* can often feel heavy handed, Forster executes his with more subtlety and lightness of touch. But behind the humor with which Forster depicts motifs representing aspects of medical discourse (i.e., the embodiments of "Science" in Dr. Barry and the hypnotist Lasker Jones) lies a seriousness which is parallel to the direct didacticism of *Imre*.

Havelock Ellis writes of *Imre* in the third edition of *Sexual Inversion* that "it embodies a notable narrative of homosexual development which is probably more or less real" (*Studies in the Psychology of Sex* 340). It would thus seem that Ellis did not primarily regard the novel as an imaginative work of fiction, but as "more or less" autobiographical. The text itself would lead a reader to believe this. *Imre* is influenced by the concepts, nomenclatures, and most importantly the sexological mode of narration, the medical case history. Harry Oosterhuis argues that the self-narration undertaken in the autobiographies which private patients penned for psychiatric studies are the forerunner of the "coming-out" narrative, the gay variation of the bildungsroman genre (Oosterhuis, "Richard von Krafft-Ebing's 'Step-Children of Nature'" 81). *Maurice* is without a doubt an artistically accomplished rendering of this genre, which would become the cornerstone of gay and lesbian literature, whereas Prime-Stevenson's novel is in form and content conceived as a literary sexological case history and, owing to the middle ground it inhabits, is like a "missing link" between the autobiographical medical case history and the fully formed "coming-out" novel. It includes most of the components that define the actual case histories, such as those which homosexual men and women contributed to researchers including Richard von Krafft-Ebing, the memoir Claude Hartland published "for the consideration of the medical fraternity" (Hartland, *The Story of A Life*), and those John

Addington Symonds and Edward Carpenter penned for *Sexual Inversion* (1897). In the novel, the affinity to the case history format is reinforced by its prefatory letter, in which Oswald addresses Xavier Mayne, offering this "episode" to him (32–33). This is a literary device that simulates the case history, as if this "autobiography" could be inserted into Mayne's study, *The Intersexes: A History of Similisexualism as a Problem in Social Life*. Although it was not an actual case history itself, *Imre* was inspired by one, found in Otto de Joux's *Die Enterbten des Liebesglücks; oder, das dritte Geschlecht: Ein Beitrag zur Seelenkunde* (The Disinherited of Love's Happiness; or, The Third Sex: A Contribution to the Study of the Mind, first edition 1893, expanded edition 1897). Prime-Stevenson selectively translates and reproduces this autobiography in *The Intersexes* (109–11) which is by "a young scion of a novel family of the Continent" narrating his love for a "German or Austrian army-officer" named Rudolph (110). "I have absolutely nothing feminine in me as to my looks; my bearing indeed is noted for its genuine masculinity. But, for all that, I have a soul like a woman's. I am a man; but I love another man, burningly, passionately, to death itself. I know too it is a mad hopeless struggle that I have kept up against my all too-tender nature, since my boyhood's years. So I have given up struggling against my fate" (*Intersexes* 110). The subject of this case history prefigures both Oswald and Imre. Prime-Stevenson's rendering of de Joux's case history is a text distinct from the original, adapting it, as Matthew Livesey demonstrates, to meet the liberationist needs of *The Intersexes* (see Livesey, "The Homosexual Origins of the Gay Novel" 103–18). This text, then, engenders another, the novel. This work of fiction, in turn, could lead readers back to the original sexological works. For Prime-Stevenson, writes Margaret Breen, "literature functioned as a mediating force, one that linked a general public with the world of scientific research" ("Homosexual Identity, Translation, and Prime-Stevenson's *Imre* and *The Intersexes*" 5). The novel could, writes Christopher Looby, "serve as a guide, for less well-educated readers, toward the burgeoning archive of sexually progressive literature" ("The Gay Novel in the United States" 422). The narrative conventions of sexology, the liberationist case history, direct the narrative, and, additionally, the theory of the female soul in the male body shapes the ways in which the characters arrive at an understanding of their sexual subjectivities. I argue elsewhere, though, against reading *Imre* as merely a literary mouthpiece for sexology, suggesting that while sexology is powerful in the novel, it is not the only or perhaps even the chief influence upon the text (see Wilper, "Sexology, Homosexual History, and Walt Whitman" 52–68). Nevertheless, sexology plays a crucial role in shaping the narrative structure, the identities of the protagonists, and their relations.

Similarly, Forster's *Maurice* advances the idea of homosexuality as an immutable biological component to the central characters' sexual constitutions. "It's not the least good—I've changed," declares Clive, to which Maurice responds: "Can the leopard change his spots?" (107). Prime-Stevenson employs the same metaphor for sexual identity in *The Intersexes*. When addressing whether homosexuality can be cured, Prime-Stevenson rhetorically asks: "Can we 'cure' Nature? Can we make the leopard change his spots?" (120). But Clive does fight his body to "change his spots," consequently crippling it in the process. In the writings of Symonds and Carpenter, sexual fulfillment is associated with health. Ellis narrates in his case history of Symonds, "Case XVIII," in the first edition of *Sexual Inversion* that "[Symonds] feels absolutely certain that in early life his health was ruined, and his moral repose destroyed, owing to the perpetual conflict with his own inborn nature, and that relief and strength came with indulgence. . . . He is convinced that his sexual dealings with men have been thoroughly wholesome to himself, largely increasing his physical, moral, and intellectual energy, and not injurious to others" (Ellis and Symonds 147). And Carpenter, in "Case VI," writes that, before finding sexual satisfaction "by embraces and emissions" with "special friends," "I was once or twice on the brink of despair and madness with repressed passion and torment" (132). While Carpenter's theories of comrade love are recognized as underlying the relationship between Maurice and Alec, most scholars agree that his sexological theories of the "homogenic love" of intermediate sexes are absent from the text. In his writings, Carpenter presents a romanticized and idealized conceptualization of Uranian men, believing that these individuals represent a vanguard of human sexual evolution. John Fletcher writes, "Carpenter wishes to see the 'healthy' Uranian male supplementing his masculine constitution with certain 'feminine virtues'—tenderness, sensuality, intuition, emotionality, altruism, and self-sacrifice" ("Forster's Self-Erasure" 73). It is in many of these same terms that Carpenter describes himself in the case study he provided for *Sexual Inversion* (Ellis and Symonds 132–33). Fletcher argues, though, that the intersex model is problematic in Carpenter's writings. The third-sex theory and Whitmanian comrade love are mutually exclusive, Fletcher suggests, thus a "contradiction between Ulrichs and Whitman marks the writings of both Symonds and Carpenter" (73). "The ideological danger in any crossing of genders is that the feminine will supplant or improperly dominate the masculine in the mixed type, that instead of an extension of the masculine beyond its traditional sphere a subversion of masculinity may result" (Fletcher 74). Fletcher concludes that "the absence of a theory of inversion, of intermediacy of cross-gendering" in *Maurice*, sets the novel apart from Carpenter's writings as well as from the writings of many of Forster's homosexual contemporaries (90). Howard Booth agrees that the sexological theories are excluded from *Maurice*, but he questions the assumptions that Fletcher and others reach about the motives underlying this absence. "There are surely dangers though to suggesting that the exclusion of inversion theory from the novel is simply the result of an accommodation on Forster's part between models of inversion and societal pressure to be manly" ("Maurice" 183). Booth suggests that Forster creates a novel which avoids sexological models, unlike Radclyffe Hall's *The Well of Loneliness*, which draws overtly on Krafft-Ebing and inversion theory. Instead, Booth argues that "*Maurice* often 'inverts' what the reader expects to find," and thus "The novel's lack of interest in the inversion of the sexes is perhaps itself another of these inversions" (183). Yet I question in what follows whether the third-sex concept is truly absent from *Maurice*.

This chapter explores the influence of third- or intermediate-sex sexology in Prime-Stevenson's *Imre* and Forster's *Maurice*. It first considers the development of the third sex theory by Karl Heinrich Ulrichs and Magnus Hirschfeld in the struggle for homosexual liberation, which directly influenced Prime-Stevenson's writings. Then the chapter considers the work of Symonds, Ellis, and Carpenter in bringing German third-sex sexology to Britain. Next, the two literary analyses follow: first an examination of the way in which *Imre* argues against the psycho-degenerative hypothesis, incorporates the third-sex theory, and simultaneously undermines the authority of scientific discourse, and second an exploration of *Maurice* and its responses to embodiments of scientific discourse and the novel's subtle incorporation of Symonds's, Ellis's, and Carpenter's intermediate- or third-sex ideas.

Science and Homosexual Liberation: Theorizing the Third Sex

Homosexual individuals, as Harry Oosterhuis claims, were not merely the "passive victims of a medical juggernaut, with no other choice than to conform to medical stereotypes" (*Stepchildren of Nature* 11). Indeed, some of these individuals employed science in the aims of homosexual liberation. Not merely employing a "reverse discourse," as Michel Foucault argues (*The History of Sexuality* 101), with the third-sex theory, the homosexual individual, in the role of sexual theorist, would wield a great deal of influence upon sexological discourse. Preeminent among these figures in Germany are Karl Heinrich Ulrichs and Magnus Hirschfeld, who, in their politically motivated essays, treatises, and sexological studies, spoke on behalf of homosexual men and women and demanded an end to persecution, seeking above all the abolition or reform of laws criminalizing sex acts between men.

Writing under the pseudonym Numa Numantius in 1864–65, the Hanoverian civil servant Ulrichs published the first five essays of a twelve essay project collectively titled *Forschungen über das Räthsel der mannmännlichen Liebe* (*Research into the Riddle of Man-Manly Love*, published between 1864 and 1880). The texts of the *Forschungen* series are bold legal polemics that deploy the authoritative language of science, drawing on recent research into embryology, to challenge moralistic and penal persecution of a sex of humans he terms *Urnings* or Uranians. "It is a fact that there are individuals among us whose body is built like a male, and, at the same time, whose sexual drive is directed toward men," Ulrichs begins his first essay, "Vindex: Social-juristiche Studien über mannmännliche Geschlechtsliebe" ("Vindex: Social and Legal Studies on Man-Manly Love," 1864), "I have termed these individuals Urnings" (*The Riddle of "Man-Manly" Love* 1: 34) ("Thatsache ist es, daß es unter den Menschen Individuen gibt, deren Körper männlich gebaut ist, welche gleichwohl aber geschlechtliche Liebe zu Männern [empfinden.] . . . Diese Individuen nenne ich nachstehend 'Urninge'"; *Forschungen* 1: 1). In Ulrichs's view, the "true" man, a *Dioning* or Dionian, possessed a man's body and a man's psyche, while the *Urning* possessed the body of a true man and the psyche or psychical elements of a true woman. He drew on the language of Hellenism to formulate his terms for sexual orientations. The terms "Uranian" and "Dionian" derive from the speech of Pausanias in Plato's *Symposium* where he discusses two types of love: the Heavenly variety exclusively between men from Aphrodite Urania, and the Common type from Aphrodite Dione (Plato, *Symposium* 13–14). It is clear that Ulrichs took some interpretational liberties with his source, as those led by so-called "Common" love "are attracted to women as much as boys, and to bodies rather than minds" (Plato, *Symposium* 13). Uranians belong to a "third sex" ("ein[em] dritte[n] Geschlecht"), similar to but independent from the male and female sexes, "we are independent of the male or female sex, fully separate from both" (*The Riddle of "Man-Manly" Love* 1: 36) ("Selbstständig stehen wir da, neben Männern und neben Weibern, völlig abgesondert von beiden"; *Forschungen* 1: 5).

In his seventh text of the series, which was published (like all others after the sixth essay) under his own name, "Memnon: Die Geschlechtsnatur des mannliebenden Urnings" ("The Sexual Nature of the Man-Loving Uranian," 1868), Ulrichs elaborates upon his developmental hypothesis of homosexuality. Uranism is a form of "physio-psychic hermaphroditism" ("körperlich-seelische[m] Hermaphroditismus"), which Ulrichs expressed in the Latin phrase "anima muliebris virili corpora inclusa" (a female psyche confined in a male body). He stresses that in the case of Uranians this hermaphroditism was manifest only in terms of sexual attraction and gender—inversion was limited to the soul, not the body—and takes care to disassociate the third sex from any possible suggestion that it is a mistake or accident of nature. "In vain will you search for something pathological or deformed either emotionally or physically in male as well as female Urnings. Both are the fruit of a completely wholesome course of development of nature, even if it is an irregular one" (*The Riddle of "Man-Manly" Love* 1: 303) ("Etwas Krankhaftes oder Verkrüppeltes, geistig oder körperlich, wird man beim männlichen, wie beim weiblichen Urning vergeblich suchen. Beide sind die Frucht des wenn schon unregelmäßigen, so doch durchaus gesunden Entwicklungsganges der Natur"; *Forschungen* 2: 7). The text seems to anticipate the turn that the study of same-sex desire would take the following year starting with Westphal's "Conträre Sexualempfindung," that of viewing this mode of attraction as indicative of mental illness caused by hereditary degeneration.

Toward the end of the nineteenth century in Germany, Ulrichs's studies were rediscovered and reprinted and incorporated into the expanding body of scientific texts published with the intent of bringing about legal and social change (Steakley, *The Homosexual Emancipation Movement in Germany* 23–24). In 1896, the physician and sexologist Magnus Hirschfeld published a pamphlet titled *Sappho und Sokrates; oder, Wie erklärt sich die Liebe der Männer und der Frauen zu Personen des eigenen Geschlechts?* (Sappho and Socrates; or, How Does One Explain the Love of Men and Women to Persons of Their Own Sex?, 1896), in which he draws on historical and scientific sources to argue the case for homosexual rights. The following year he led the founding of the *Wissenschaftlich-humanitäre Komitee*, an organization whose main objectives were securing the abolition of Paragraph 175 of the German Criminal Code, educating the public, and involving homosexuals in defending their own rights (see Steakley, *The Homosexual Emancipation Movement in Germany* 30; Stümke 34–35; Steakley, "Per Scientiam ad Justitiam" 139). One of the organs for achieving the committee's aims was the journal *Jahrbuch für sexuelle Zwischenstufen* (Annual for Sexual Intermediaries), whose first issue appeared in 1899. Hirschfeld's activities were not limited to the German-speaking countries; he also founded the World League for Sexual Reform, which held congresses in Berlin in 1921, Copenhagen in 1928, and London in 1929 (Dose, "The World League for Sexual Reform" 242–43). The *Institut für Sexualwissenschaft* (Institute for Sexual Research), which he founded in 1919 and later ran as director under the aegis of the German state, was world renowned (Wolff, *Magnus Hirschfeld* 174–75). The English-American novelist Christopher Isherwood, who lived at the institute in the early 1930s, describes it in his autobiography, *Christopher and His Kind* (1976). "It was a place of education for the public, its lawmakers, and its police. Hirschfeld could invite them to the sex museum and guide them through a succession of reactions—from incredulous disgust to understanding of the need for penal reform" (*Christopher and His Kind* 18–19). Isherwood recalls his first reaction to the ethnographic collections: "Christopher giggled because he was embarrassed. He was embarrassed because, at last, he was being brought face to face with his tribe. . . . He was forced to admit kinship with these freakish fellow tribesmen and their distasteful customs. And he didn't like it. His first reaction was to blame the Institute. He said to himself: How can they take this stuff so *seriously?*" (16–17).

The efforts of the WhK and other organizations with which Hirschfeld was involved were organized around his third- or intermediate-sex research. Hirschfeld's oeuvre is vast, comprising more than 2,000 works (Mancini, *Magnus Hirschfeld* ix). One of his principle studies is *Die Homosexualität des Mannes und des Weibes* (*Homosexuality of Men and Women*, 1914) which is a multifaceted exploration of homosexuality in men and women, equally for the first time, as both a biological and a sociological phenomenon (see H. Bauer, *English Literary Sexology* 44). He theorizes that the third sex comprised "sexual intermediaries or sexual transitions" ("sexuell[e] Zwischenstufen oder Geschlechtsübergänge") existing between constructed polar opposites: the "absolute sex type" ("absolut[e] Geschlechtstypus") (*Homosexuality* 61; *Homosexualität* 30). Diagnosing "true" homosexuality, Hirschfeld writes, "is in no way easy in every case" (76) ("ist keinesweges in allen Fällen eine leichte [Aufgabe]"; 40); key to this, apart from the observable physical characteristics, is recognizing the homosexual "psyche." "Decisive for the diagnosis is proof of a homosexual psyche, of a homosexual drive that is distinguished from the emotional complex defined as love, which attracts men to women and women to men, in that they turn to persons who belong to their own sex" (76) ("Maßgebend für die Diagnose ist der Nachweis einer homosexuellen Psyche, einer seelischen Triebrichtung, die sich von dem als Liebe bezeichneten Gefühlskomplex, der den Mann zum Weibe und das Weib zum Manne zieht, nur dadurch unterscheidet, daß sie sich Personen zuwendet, die dem gleichen Geschlecht angehören"; 40). Elena Mancini explains that because Hirschfeld believed that "sexual differences were expressed in the variation of four different categories: the sex organs, other physical characteristics, the sexual drive, and psychological characteristics," homosexuality could not be traced to one factor, instead it "was the product of a composite of factors that could not be isolated" (*Magnus Hirschfeld* 63), and thus could not singled out and "cured." Both Ulrichs and Hirschfeld believed in the liberating potential of science. For them, science proved that there was no fault to be assigned to the homosexual man or woman for his or her desires, and thus they did not deserve to be persecuted for them. Enlightened discourse and public education could bring about legal and social reform. In England, this belief also had followers.

The Third Sex in England

Ulrichs's third-sex theory reached English readers through John Addington Symonds. Two months after meeting Ulrichs in Italy in 1891, he privately published the essay "A Problem in Modern Ethics," which, in dealing with homosexuality and its role in society, references Ulrichs and his *Forschungen* as well as critically assesses contemporary research being undertaken on the Continent in the field of sexual science. Symonds challenged degenerationist sexology through historical and cultural discourses, namely through Greek love. "The truth is that ancient Greece offers insuperable difficulties to theorists who treat sexual inversion exclusively from the points of view of neuropathy, tainted heredity, and masturbation" (*Symonds and Homosexuality* 147). He argues that "An Englishman or a Frenchman who loves the male sex must be diagnosed as tainted with disease; while Sophocles, Pindar, Pheidias, Epaminondas, Plato, are credited with yielding to an instinct which was healthy in their times because society accepted it. . . . The bare fact that ancient Greece tolerated, and that modern Europe refuses to tolerate sexual inversion, can have nothing to do with the etiology, the pathology, the psychological definition of the phenomenon in its essence" (146). Symonds felt that if he were to correct these "errors," he would "need somebody of medical importance to collaborate with" (*Letters* 3: 797). So he began work on a psychological study of "sexual inversion" with a young and then unknown physician named Henry Havelock Ellis (1859–1939). Sean Brady posits, however, that although Ellis was the medical authority on the project, "*Sexual Inversion* was Symonds' brainchild" (*Masculinity and Male Homosexuality in Britain* 191). Joseph Bristow notes that "Given Symonds's extensive reservations about sexology" the collaboration with the young scientist was perhaps atypical for the poet and scholar ("Symonds's History, Ellis's Heredity: Sexual Inversion" 91). Although Symonds did not completely reject physiology playing a role, the "task of *A Problem in Modern Ethics* was to contest practically every major sexologist and scientific theorist who engaged with the vexed topic of homosexuality" (87). Heike Bauer explains that Symonds found sexology lacking because science did not historicize same-sex desire "in relation to its high status within Greek culture, and hence fails to see the social value of the phenomenon" (*English Literary Sexology* 61). Symonds did not live to witness the realization of this work which produced *Sexual*

Inversion (first published in Germany in 1896 and in England the following year), the first English medical textbook of homosexuality.

In *Sexual Inversion*, Ellis posits that "true homosexuality"—as opposed to situational perversion which might occur in prison or other places where usual sexual outlets were unavailable—was simply a harmless sexual abnormality resultant from a congenital predisposition toward inversion. Symonds compared homosexuality to color-blindness, whereas Ellis preferred an analogy to color-hearing "in which there is not so much defect, as an abnormality of nervous tracks producing new and involuntary combinations. Just as the colour-hearer instinctively associates colours with sounds, . . . so the invert has his sexual sensations brought into relationship with objects that are normally without sexual appeal" (Ellis and Symonds 204). For Ellis, inverted sexual instinct is a manifestation of abnormality, meaning deviation from norms of a given social situation; he distinguishes between abnormality and disease and adopts the term "anomaly" in order to better emphasize that "the study of the abnormal is perfectly distinct from the study of the morbid" (205). Both "A Problem in Modern Ethics" and *Sexual Inversion*, writes Ivan Crozier, were written with the intent to advance legal views of same-sex relations ("The Medical Construction of Homosexuality" 79). The latter study concludes with a solid appeal for legal reform in which Ellis argues that laws forbidding sex acts between males do nothing to curb these practices, but instead persecute individuals whose sexual nature is no fault of their own. "I am of the opinion that neither 'sodomy' . . . nor 'gross indecency' ought to be penal offences, except under certain special circumstances. . . . It should be the function of the law in this matter to prevent violence, to protect the young, and to preserve public order and decency" (Ellis and Symonds 220). This appeal itself may seem to the modern reader tentative, but to assume this position two years after the Wilde trials was certainly daring, hence incurring the wrath of Scotland Yard, and even more so considering that not even this modest aim would be achieved for another seventy years. Banned in Britain upon its publication, the second edition was released through an American publishing house in 1901, becoming the second volume of Ellis's long-term project *Studies in the Psychology of Sex*. From this edition onwards, *Sexual Inversion* did not carry Symonds's name at his family's request (Crozier, "Introduction" 65–67).

Edward Carpenter's vision of the Uranian love of comrades (discussed in chapter 3) is a key aspect of a wider platform of "sexual Utopianism" and social reform. He clearly saw himself as carrying on Symonds's work, posits Brady. Carpenter takes steps to combine the cultural-historical approach of Symonds with the biomedical framework of Ellis. But he does so in a way which allowed him to develop "his ideas on the subject in a direction that was a distinct departure from either Ellis' or Symonds'" (Brady, *Masculinity and Male Homosexuality in Britain* 204). What resulted was an ennoblement of the third sex by means of invocations of Greek love, Hellenic ideals, and an interpretation of the homoerotic aesthetic of Whitman's verse, through which Carpenter fashions a powerfully affirmative homosexual identity. In one of his most circulated texts, *The Intermediate Sex*, he expounds a theory of homosexuality—in which he refers to Ulrichs's scientific underpinnings and employs the German theorist's terms—that insists upon the health and normality of Uranians. Although extreme cases of inversion do occur, he writes, these are rare; sexual intermediates are mostly "quite normal and unsensational" physically (*The Intermediate Sex* 31). "In fact, while these extreme cases are of the greatest value from a scientific point of view as marking tendencies and limits of development in certain directions, it would be a serious mistake to look upon them as representative cases of the whole phases of human evolution concerned" (32). Carpenter does not only assert the health, sanity, and vitality of Uranians against prevailing discourses of pathology or vice and sexual license; he also insists upon the superiority of intersexed individuals, arguing that intersexuality is a sign of evolutionary progress. In the future, they will be instrumental in bridging rifts between the sexes and between the classes. "It is probable that the superior Urnings will become, in affairs of the heart, to a large extent the teachers of future society." Their intermediary qualities, the blending of male and female characteristics, place them in a unique position: "it is not difficult to see that these people have a special work to do as reconcilers and interpreters of the two sexes to each other" (*The Intermediate Sex* 14). Furthermore, the intermediate sex holds the key to lasting social reform as "Eros is a great leveller. Perhaps true Democracy rests, more firmly than anywhere else, on a sentiment which easily passes the bounds of class and caste, and unites in closest affection the most estranged ranks of society" (114–15). The relationship between Carpenter, an upper-middle class social-sexual activist, and Merrill, a working class man, attempts to enact this belief. With his novel, *Maurice*, Forster fictionalizes this relationship as well as the intermediate or third-sex theories that accompany it.

"Those cold psychic-sexual terms"

Prime-Stevenson had read Symonds and Ellis's *Sexual Inversion*, but it appears as if he was not terribly impressed with it. "There is nothing of the sort in English," he writes of his own study, *The Intersexes*, "in spite of numerous contributions toward this or that aspect, by English-writing psychiaters of more of less weight. For, such larger things as those by Havelock Ellis and John Addington Symonds . . . are far from adequate; dealing with pathologic conditions, with only limited 'typic' aspects, and are too much from and for exclusively a professional-psychiatric standpoint" ("Letter to Paul Elmer More" 135). The liberationist intent of *Sexual Inversion* was overlooked by one the very individuals it hoped to assist. It was the German sexologists, the works of both Ulrichs and Hirschfeld, as well as that of Krafft-Ebing, which enabled Prime-Stevenson to formulate his own vision of a "Uranian" identity. The debt he owes to German sexology is evident in his defense of homosexuality *The Intersexes*, which was published two years after the novel, but, as the author explains in the study's preface, was prepared around 1900 (x). Prime-Stevenson explains that the primary intent of his study was to summarize current research and trends in the science of sexuality in order to make them accessible to an English-speaking readership. He describes *The Intersexes* as offering the reader, particularly "the individual layman, intelligently inclined to social sciences," a condensed survey of the field of sexological inquiry into homosexuality as these studies "are not primarily in English." He writes that his study is not intended for "active professional psychiatrists, of any nationality," but he notes also that as "British and American physicians are not well-informed on such lines," they too "may find the present survey of service" (x). The main way he achieves his aim with this study is through translation. In addition to printing original case histories of homosexual individuals, *The Intersexes* translates cases and extracts from Ulrichs, Hirschfeld, Krafft-Ebing, and others. His presentation of a third-sex conception, with homosexual men (Uranians) and women (Uraniads) forming "intersexes" between the male and the female (16), indicates his primary theoretical debt to the writings of Ulrichs and the studies of Hirschfeld. The aim of his study is first to offer homosexual men and women positive images of themselves and their "race" and a self-concept liberated from societal opprobrium through the means of science, and second to educate the heterosexual reader in order to earn tolerance, understanding, and respect from the majority for this minority. In the same vein as his contemporaries in Britain, Symonds, Carpenter, and Ellis, Prime-Stevenson employs sexology in his writings as a tool in the effort toward homosexual liberation. *Imre: A Memorandum* is the other essential component in Prime-Stevenson's writing campaign. The novel and the study work in different, but nevertheless complementary, ways toward achieving his goal.

In *Imre*, the pathological hypothesis, whose "narrow psychologic conventions" (32) characterize same-sex desire as a "diseased, leprous, [and] gangrened" hereditary taint (89), forms a chief moralistic censure of same-sex sexuality from which the characters struggle to liberate themselves. When Oswald is confronted directly by a character personifying conventional morality, this attack is loaded not in terms of the Sin of Sodom—as it is when Maurice confesses he is an "unspeakable of the Oscar Wilde sort"—but rather is phrased in terms of disease and crime. "Society needs more policemen than it has," declares a character to whom Oswald makes a confession of his sexuality, "to protect itself from such lepers as you!" (99). Before Oswald can free himself of this opprobrium and arrive at an understanding of his Uranian sexual and gender identity as the "supreme phase" of masculinity, he first conceptualizes his desire in terms of pathology. Degenerationist sexological thought is channeled most insidiously through the American physician whose pronouncements initially seem to offer hope to the protagonist. Oswald recounts to Imre that he read "a serious work, on abnormalisms in mankind; a book partly psychologic, partly medico-psychiatric" (90–91) by "a specialistic physician in nervous diseases [and] abnormal conditions of the mind" (91). Akin to Fenny Skaller's reading of Krafft-Ebing's *Psychopathia Sexualis*, Oswald discovers himself in the study. "It described myself, my secret, unrestful self, with an unsparing exactness" (91). He learns "that responsible physicians, great psychologists . . . knew of men like myself and took them as serious problems for study" (91). At this point in his personal trajectory toward self-awareness, he is desperate for answers; the fact that the text speaks of homosexual desire as pathological and "Curable, absolutely 'curable'" (91) does not cause him alarm. When the author of this treatise visits London, Oswald arranges a consultation, but the diagnosis he receives only serves to complicate his quest for self-knowledge. "Your case, my dear sir, is the easier [to cure]," the physician informs him, "because you suffer in a sentimental and sexual way from what we call the obsession of a set, distinct Type, you see; instead of a general—h'm, how shall I style it—morbidity of your inclinations. It is largely mere imagination! You say you have never really 'realized' this haunting masculine Type which has given you such trouble? My dear sir, don't think any more about such nonsense! You never will 'realize' it in any way. . . . Too much *thought* of it all, my dear friend! Too much introspection, idealism, sedentary life, dear sir! Yes, yes, you must *marry*" (91–92). Thus, unlike most of this specialist's patients who suffer from a "morbid state of certain sexual-sensory nerve-centers," Oswald is not diseased at all; rather his homosexual desire is "nonsense," "mere imagination," a fixation which has been exacerbated by an intellectual, leisure-class life. Initially, this figure seems to represent advanced and enlightened views, but he merely regurgitates old prejudices disguised as cutting-edge diagnoses and treatments. This issue was obviously a pressing one for Prime-Stevenson, who devotes a chapter to marriage as a false "cure" for homosexuality in *The Intersexes* (530–54). Despite the seeming setback for Oswald, this episode is of importance as it helps Oswald realize that, contradictory to the physician's pronouncement, his passion is neither a mental "abnormalism" nor a product of his imagination. This medical diagnosis empowers him to formulate a very different self-diagnosis.

    The theme of the Uranian as the extreme on the spectrum of manhood is recurrent in *Imre*. This is a key defense against not merely cultural discourses that associated same-sex desire with effeminacy and decadence (see chapter 6), but also related medical theories that placed same-sex desire in the realm of pathology and nervous disorder. Oswald discourses to Imre that Uranians are men who "have not in body, in mind, nor in all the sum of our virility, in all the detail of our outward selves, any womanish trait! Not one! It is only the ignoramus and the vulgar who nowadays think or talk of the homosexual as if he were a—hermaphrodite. In every feature and line and sinew and muscle, in every movement and accent and capability, we walk the world's ways as men" (85). It is not surprising, given the prevailing attitudes of the era, that Oswald conflates biological sex with gender, the latter of which has come to be recognized as more largely a matter of culture than the former. On the one hand, Oswald asserts that physically the Uranian is indistinguishable from a Dionian, a "normal" man. On the other hand, he speaks of the homosexual as manly in terms of "accent and capability," in "traits," and "outward selves." Thus, in other words, the homosexual fulfills the masculine gender role as well as (if not better than) any heterosexual man. In the author's study *The Intersexes*, Prime-Stevenson stresses that in most cases the Uranian or Uraniad (homosexual man and woman, respectively) are not physically distinguishable from ordinary men and women. "Nothing in the Uranistic physique necessarily differs in the least from the normal man. What is more, a magnificently masculine physique often conceals the sex—the intersex from observation" (78). Differing to Hirschfeld, who sought indications of intermediate sexuality in the "homosexual psyche" as well as in physical attributes, the crossing of genders and sexes in the novel is limited to the soul, and does not extend to the body (see also Fone, *Homophobia* 361). Masculinity, manliness, and health are tightly bound together in this literary text. It is intimated that femininity or "womanishness" in the male is indicative of degeneration. The crossing of sexes/genders is radically restricted, manifest exclusively in terms of sexual attraction.

This theme is communicated not only in Oswald's confession to Imre, but also by his characterization of the beloved, which fills much of "Masks," part one of the novel (35–69). It is an exposition which is overtly geared to support his claims about the Uranian. Imre is described as follows: "Of middle height, he possessed a slender figure, faultless in proportions, lightness, and elegance. His athletic powers were renowned in his regiment. He was among the crack gymnasts, vaulters, and swimmers . . . . Yet all this force, this muscular address, was concealed by the symmetry of his graceful, elastic frame. Not till he was nude, and one could trace the ripple of muscle and sinew under the fine hairless skin, did one realize the machinery of such strength" (51–52). This rendering of the character's athleticism and physique no doubt serves an aesthetic function in the narrative: it is homoerotic titillation. Gifford writes that Imre is a "masturbatory figure, a hyper-masculine ideal" epitomizing "the apotheosis of a gay man's desire" (Introduction 20). But its central purpose is to support the didactic and reform aims of the novel. Imre symbolizes the "high-grade Uranian" as the physical apex of manhood. Prime-Stevenson draws on Greek sculptural imagery (as Aschenbach does with Tadzio): Imre possesses a "Hellenic exterior," his body is hairless (unlike Maurice's), a trait which reinforces the affinity to Hellenic representations of ideal male beauty. These images of manly vitality and male beauty, writes George Mosse, derived from classical sources which, in addition to being essential reference points for the depiction of homoeroticism and male-male desire, were central to society's construction of masculine gender discourses. In the eighteenth century, "As the male body assumed ever-more importance as symbolic of true masculinity, greater attention had to be paid to its development, as well as to setting a specific standard of masculine beauty" which "took its inspiration from Greece" (Mosse, *The Image of Man* 28). The homosexual or sodomite, writes Mosse, was thought to represent a "countertype" to normative masculinity, threatening to the masculine role in his ability to cross gender barriers (66–67). Furthermore, the wide ranging economic, social, and cultural changes of the second half of the nineteenth century contributed to anxiety about "degeneration" reaching fever pitch, fuelled by writings such as Max Nordau's *Entartung* (English translation published in 1895). Manliness and physical fitness were regarded as the means to avoid national crises (see Greenslade, "Fitness and the Fin de Siècle" 45–49). Prime-Stevenson subverts these discourses in order to prove that an assumed "countertype" of masculinity in actuality embodies these ideals better than most "normal" men. Imre's physical prowess asserts the health and virility of the homosexual man, refuting conceptualizations that presuppose same-sex desire as a "diseased, leprous, gangrened" sexual impulse (89).

Oswald recounts to Imre that after his consultation with the American specialist he intends to follow his recommendation and marry (93). These plans, though, are derailed when Oswald meets a man who "quickened within me the same unspeakable sense of a mysterious bond of soul and of body—the Man-Type which owned me and ever must own me, soul and body together" (93–94). Oswald discovers that the intensity of such emotion could not be written off as "mere imagination." He confesses himself and his love to this man; however, this disclosure reaps scorn rather than understanding (99). His life is shattered, and he becomes estranged from his previous existence. Painful though the experience is, it allows Oswald to begin to gain more understanding of himself and his sexual subjectivity. He describes to Imre that he realizes that "I had no disease. I was simply what I was born!—a complete human being, of firm, perfect physical and mental health; outwardly in full key with all the man's world: but in spite of that, a being who from birth was of a vague, special sex; a member of a sex *within* the most obvious sexes; or apart from them. I was created as a man perfectly male, save in one thing which keeps such a 'man' back from [the] possibility of ever becoming integrally male—this terrible, instinctive demand for a psychic and physical union with a man—not with a woman" (95–96). After he arrives at this plainly third-sex understanding of himself and his love for other men, Oswald accidentally encounters "a mass of serious studies, German, Italian, French, English, from the chief European specialists and theorists on the similisexual topic" (96), through which he learns of "the theories and facts of homosexualism, of the Uranian Love, of the Uranian Race," and that "secondary sexes" exist between the male and female sexes (96). This is an overt incorporation into the text of this liberationist school of sexological thought. In this way it is as if the novel were an essay in the form of a work of fiction. The author writes of it in *The Intersexes* as being penned "with more serious purpose than entertainment" (369). That Oswald deduces the existence of an intermediate, third sex before encountering sexological treatises, which deal with same-sex sexuality in these terms, indicates the understanding that the author seeks to put forward, that this conception reflects the actuality of homosexual experience and thus the truth of the homosexual disposition, rather than him being merely influenced by these works.

The reader might expect Oswald's confession to impart knowledge or even awakening to Imre, but this is not the case as the latter is also well acquainted with the psychiatric study of homosexuality. He has consulted a "great Viennese psychiater" who diagnoses his "inborn homosexualism" (118). This is Prime-Stevenson's tribute to Krafft-Ebing, whom he describes as the inspiration behind his study, *The Intersexes*, and to whom he dedicated that work. Prime-Stevenson writes in a letter to Paul Elmer More that Krafft-Ebing "himself urged me to write this book: went (years ago) over every detail of its plan with me, chapter by chapter; and gave what he saw of it before his sudden death in Vienna, his fullest approval" ("Letter to Paul Elmer More" 136). It seems a contradiction that the psychiatrist most responsible for the conception of same-sex desire as a morbid phenomenon, a sign of hereditary degeneration, should receive a positive mention in this novel which actively resists this manner of characterization of homosexuality. Krafft-Ebing's work, despite assigning pathology to homosexual desire, was an important resource for homosexual men and women. Oosterhuis and Heike Bauer describe how increased contact with homosexuals caused Krafft-Ebing to readdress his theories (Oosterhuis, *Stepchildren of Nature* 211–71; H. Bauer, *English Literary Sexology* 32–33). Oosterhuis characterizes the contact as a dialogue between physician and patient in which the latter "began to influence the production of medical knowledge." He posits that the "case histories and autobiographical accounts of Krafft-Ebing's patients demonstrate that perverts did not always passively accept external conditions of action; they rather responded to social constraints in different ways, reflected upon them, and reconstituted them in the light of their particular circumstances" (12). These homosexual readers were able to cause the psychiatrist to change his attitude toward their sexuality. Heinrich Ammerer explains: "Krafft-Ebing's relationship with homosexuality transformed between his first treatise in 1877 and his death. From an interested, but clinically neutral, observer, he became an advocate for homosexuals who campaigned with a great deal of empathy for their exemption from punishment" ("Krafft-Ebings Verhältnis zur Homosexualität wandelte sich zwischen seiner ersten Abhandlung 1877 und seinem Tod. Aus einem interessierten, aber nüchternen Beobachter wurde ein Fürsprecher der Homosexuellen, der sich mit großer Empathie für deren Straffreiheit einsetzte"; *Am Anfang war die Perversion* 283). Oosterhuis argues that the case histories of a study like Krafft-Ebing's offered homosexuals a resource for forging identities and created a space for self-expression (229–30). This must have been how the author of *Imre* viewed it. The Viennese specialist whom Imre consults stands in contrast to the "well-meaning but far too conclusive Yankee doctor" (96): the former offers consolation, advising Imre not to marry (118). "The Austrian doctor had not a little comforted and strengthened Imre morally; warning him away from despising himself: from thinking himself alone, and a sexual pariah; from over-morbid sufferings" (118).

The taxonomy, thought structures, not to mention methods of liberationist sexology (i.e., the use of the case history with its emphasis placed upon confession) leave an indelible imprint upon the text; but this novel is more than just a fictionalization of a medical case history. There are two elements which enact a criticism of the field of sexological inquiry. First, the text indicates that its coalescence with this discourse is not entirely harmonious: the recurrent motif of the "mystery of love" provides a certain degree of resistance to the methods of sexual science. At one point in the narrative, Imre rails against the assumptions and methods of sexology: "thou [Oswald] art made in thy nature as God makes mankind, as each and all. . . . We are what we are! This terrible life of ours . . . this existence that men insist on believing is almost all to be understood nowadays—probed through and through—decided! . . . but that ever was and will be just *mystery*" (104; emphasis added). Oswald too doubts that the riddles of the human heart can be dissected and systematized by medicine. Even as he assigns, or at least attempts to assign, sexological labels to his friend. "Uranian? Similisexual? Homosexual? Dionian? Profound and often all too oppressive, even terrible, can be the significance of those cold psychic-sexual terms to the man who—'*knows*'! *To the man who 'knows'!* Even more terrible to those who understand them not" (64). The "mystery of love" motif recurs in the text, allowing it to access literary discourses beyond the rational and empirical, thus representing a source of resistance to the novel's immersion in sexological thought.

Second, shortcomings in the third-sex theory platform become evident when contrasting Imre's sense of his sexual identity with that of Oswald. As noted above, both characters have had access to progressive sexology. Imre's consultation with the "great Viennese psychiater" brings him little consolation; from this humane platform he merely gains some respite from societal contempt and learns to accept "himself as an excusable bit of creation" (120). Science and sympathy prove simply not to be enough. Imre twice contemplates suicide, sensing "how widely despised, mocked, and loathed is the Uranian Race" and "how sordid and debasing are the average associations of the homosexual kind" (120). He does not view his intermediacy in terms of gender and sexuality as an advantage, primarily because he has not had access to the cultural and historical discourses which empower Oswald to speak of Uranism in terms of vitality, creativity, and superiority. Imre lacks the discourses of Greek love that form the core of Oswald's identity.

Third-sex sexology impacts the text greatly. It provides a framework for conceptualizing love and desire between men, a nomenclature for naming this sexuality and the men who experience it, and it shapes the narrative form, but sexology is not the sole discourse to direct the text. Cultural-historical models and romantic literary topoi are key determining elements of this "autobiography," this "mysterious and profoundly personal incident" from Oswald's and Imre's lives (32).

"'Rubbish, rubbish!' was his natural reply"

In *Maurice*, medical discourse does not encroach on the narrative until after the protagonist has passed from under the sway of Clive's Hellenism. For Maurice, his same-sex desire becomes an affliction after an encounter in a commuter train compartment with a "stout and greasy-faced" elderly man, who propositions him with "a lascivious sign." This incident is a warning for Maurice because he "saw in this disgusting and dishonourable old age his own" (131). He attempts to avoid this fate by turning to the medical community for help. Maurice "loathed the idea of a doctor," but he invites the idea of punishment for his sexual desire and "he assumed a doctor would punish him": "He could undergo any course of treatment on the chance of being cured, and even if he wasn't he would be occupied and have fewer minutes for brooding" over how "he had failed to kill [his] lust singlehanded" (131). His consultations with two doctors demonstrate a generational gap in the medical community concerning sex psychology and how to classify homosexuality. First, Maurice casually asks a younger doctor, Jowitt, about "unspeakables of the Oscar Wilde sort." Dr. Jowitt associates homosexuality with psychological illness, but claims no knowledge of the field, "that's asylum work, thank God" (131). Although disappointed by the doctor's disavowal, Maurice adopts medical nomenclature. He considers consulting a "specialist, but did not know whether there were any for his *disease*" (132; emphasis added). Later, he admits to "trustworthy" Dr. Barry that he belongs to this unspeakable sort. However, the older and more conservative Dr. Barry views sex psychology as "suspect" because of the recentness of the studies and the fact that they are published in German (136)—presumably either Barry cannot read German or the fact that they are published in German necessarily entails suspicion, or both.

Both doctors in *Maurice* demonstrate what Brady describes as a "deliberate 'unknowning'" of homosexuality (*Masculinity and Male Homosexuality in Britain* 212), and in particular they highlight resistance among British medical professionals of the late nineteenth and early twentieth centuries "to regard homosexuality as a subject fit for scientific enquiry" (10). Thus, for Barry, Maurice's condition is neither a medical nor a psychological issue: it is an "evil hallucination," a "temptation from the devil" (134). Dr. Barry "held that only the most depraved could glance at Sodom, and so, when a man of good antecedents and physique confessed the tendency, 'Rubbish, rubbish!' was his natural reply" (136). However, a contradiction exists in Dr. Barry's opinion. First, same-sex desire is a "temptation from the devil" that conceivably anyone, even Maurice or he himself, could fall under. Second, the sodomite is a type of person, "the most depraved," someone from poor antecedents and of weak physical condition who has a "tendency" toward this behavior. Although he rejects homosexuality as a medical condition, he echoes the views held by the psycho-degenerative theorists. Maurice cannot be "an unspeakable of the Oscar Wilde sort" (134), so Dr. Barry reasons, his health, heredity, and sanity contradict the possibility. Maurice begs Dr. Barry for help, "What is it? Am I diseased? If I am, I want to be cured" (134), but he gains nothing from his encounter with medical science "except the belief that doctors are fools" (138). This is a difficult lesson for Maurice, but a valuable one nonetheless. As with Oswald, Maurice learns that his desire is neither a form of mental illness, nor "imagination," nor an "evil hallucination." Both characters' encounters with the medical profession enable them to be critical of the purported authority of so-called science.

Maurice's attempt to seek a cure for his sexuality does not stop here though. Risley offers him the name of a hypnotist, to whom Maurice turns in the hope of re-orientating his sexual desire. Nevertheless, he mistrusts this "science"; he feels that he "was putting himself into the hands of a quack" and associates "hypnotism with séances and blackmail" (155). Maurice's opinion changes somewhat when he meets Jones who is "what an advanced scientific man ought to be," namely, he is "sallow and expressionless" and offers Maurice a "bloodless hand" (155). The session is marked by detachment. "It was as if they met to discuss a third party." Jones "neither praised nor blamed nor pitied" (155). During the first session, though, "Maurice yearned for sympathy" (156); however, later he readjusts his expectations and, in the second session, delights in the scientific dispassionateness. "What a comfort the man was! Science is better than sympathy, if only it is science" (183). Maurice still questions whether hypnotism really is science, and thus his skepticism never completely leaves him. From the case history Maurice provides, Jones diagnoses "congenital homosexuality." Maurice asks, "Congenital how much? Well, can anything be done?" (158). This is the first time this term is used in the narrative. Jones provides the label, "homosexual," an interpellation which Maurice never uses to identify himself. Jones then employs hypnosis to test how deeply the "tendency" is rooted (156). This is no doubt an intentional mixing of terminology. That Maurice's homosexuality is "congenital," or inborn, but the hypnotist tests how deeply it is rooted, highlights the flaws in this "science." The novel is primarily taking aim at the belief that sexual orientation can or ought to be cured. The portrayal in *Maurice* is an amalgamation of elements of sex psychology, popular pseudoscience, and psychoanalysis (then in its infancy in Britain), which are mixed in order to highlight the absurdity, not to mention the error, of attempting to realign natural sexual constitutions to conform to arbitrary cultural norms. Jones seems to run a good business treating deviant desire; he admits to Maurice upfront that three fourths of his patients approach him for this treatment—while only fifty per cent of these are successfully re-orientated toward women. What happens to this other half? For Maurice, who is counted among the unsuccessful cases, exile is proffered as the only option: "I'm afraid I can only advise you to live in some country that has adopted the Code Napoleon" (183). A key difference to the earlier encounters with embodiments of medical science is that neither hypnosis nor the sessions with Jones are rejected outright by the novel. They do have their use as a plot device: initiating Maurice's estrangement from his position in society, triggering the dream that brings Alec to his room (165–66), and allowing Maurice to form his own vision of love between men. The second session with Jones opens Maurice to the possibility of reaching his own conclusions. Maurice acquires the knowledge he needs to build a sexual identity apart from Clive's romanticized Hellenism and Dr. Barry's demonized "evil hallucination." "It comes to this then: there always have been people like me and always will be, and generally they have been persecuted." But they need not necessarily be. "Men of my sort could take to the greenwood" (183). Hypnosis and the sessions with Jones are no "cure" for homosexuality; they are however a plot device that catalyzes important events. Hypnosis and the field of knowledge Jones represents are foreign, cold, and impersonal, but allow Maurice to conceptualize an "English" greenwood relationship with Alec.

The novel portrays Maurice as a "healthy normal Englishman" (58). The pairing of health and manliness in a homosexual character is Forster's greatest challenge to many of the prevailing medical discourses; but unlike *Imre*, *Maurice* does not overplay these attributes of the central character. The way in which the author accomplishes this is by fashioning "a character who was completely unlike myself or what I supposed myself to be," as he writes in the novel's terminal note. Maurice is "handsome, healthy, bodily attractive, mentally torpid, not a bad business man and rather a snob" (216). Above all he appears to be a "normal" Englishman, read "heterosexual." For instance, Clive's impression of Maurice is that "Hall was a man who only liked women—one could tell that at a glance"

(57). Forster realizes that an effete or artistic homosexual would not challenge prevailing stereotypes in the way he intended with this text. His character must be radically different. For defying psychopathological discourses, the constellation of the attributes "handsome, healthy, [and] bodily attractive" is key. As a boy, Maurice is no bookish weakling; instead "He was a plump, pretty lad, not in any way remarkable" (2). Upon reaching manhood he is a perfect specimen of health and virility. Looking in the mirror, Maurice "thought, 'A mercy I'm fit.' He saw a well-trained serviceable body and a face that contradicted it no longer. Virility had harmonized them and shaded either with dark hair" (95). And in the epilogue to the novel, which the author cut from the final version, Maurice's health reaches its climax. "Beneath the exterior a new man throbbed—tougher, more centralized, in as good form as ever, but formed in a fresh mould, where muscles and sunburn proceed from an inward health" (222). Like Imre, Maurice is not only a desiring subject, but also an object of desire. These two characters contrast with the evocations of male beauty in the two German texts that rhapsodize adolescent, ephebic beauty which is associated with immaturity or often with feminine ideals. Whereas Aschenbach compares Tadzio to "Boy with Thorn," Imre is an Adonis or Antinous; *Maurice*, though, breaks away from this recourse to the Greeks. That his face and body are "shaded" with dark hair and his skin is "sunburned" emphasize that Maurice is a living specimen, in contrast to the sculptural imagery applied to the other objects of desire. This juxtaposition is made explicit when Maurice and Alec are in the British Museum. Maurice's "colour stood out against the heroes," they are "perfect but bloodless" (194). Maurice's beauty is not idealized; the character is constructed in terms of his typicality, Englishness, Imperial prowess: he is a pillar of British society. "What a solid young citizen he looked—quiet, honourable, prosperous without vulgarity. On such does England rely" (130). This is where the attributes "mentally torpid, not a bad business man and rather a snob" come into play. Maurice is not an exceptional figure, but an ordinary one. And herein is invested *Maurice*'s subversiveness. In the way that Imre embodies a transnational discourse of masculinity based upon Greco-Roman ideals which were circulated, according to Mosse's research, throughout Western Europe since the eighteenth century (Mosse, *The Image of Man* 17–39), Maurice epitomizes a nineteenth- and early twentieth-century image of English Imperial masculinity, whereby the novel asserts the normality, health, and above all the Englishness of this homosexual figure.

The third-sex theory, I argue, is a powerful force behind the narrative action of *Maurice*. While Hirschfeld charted feminization of the body of the homosexual male in his research into sexual intermediaries, for Ulrichs, Carpenter, and Prime-Stevenson, physique was not an indicator of sex: the third-sex body was a "true" man's body. Ulrichs writes, in "Memnon," only the soul, not the body, belongs to the other sex. "The actual physical build of an Urning, when naked, never shows any femininity" (*The Riddle of "Man-Manly" Love* 1: 305, note 88) ("Der eigentliche bloße Körperbau eines Urnings, Construction und Form, zeigt wohl nie etwas weibliches"; *Forschungen* 2: 9, note 6). Carpenter reiterates this belief in *The Intermediate Sex*: "in bodily structure there is, as a rule, nothing to distinguish the subjects of our discussion from ordinary men and women" (27). For Symonds and Carpenter, the feminine soul does not manifest itself overtly in the subject, who is able to pass in every respect as "normal" in society, except through his sexual preference. Indeed, as in the way that Forster portrays Maurice, many Uranians are the epitome of physical masculinity: "many are fine, healthy specimens of their sex, muscular and well-developed in body . . . with nothing abnormal or morbid of any kind observable in their physical structure or constitution" (*The Intermediate Sex* 23). Thus the contradiction between the work of Ulrichs and Whitman that allegedly marks the work of Symonds and Carpenter is perhaps overestimated in Fletcher's essay. In the Uranian, writes Carpenter, "we find a man who, while possessing thoroughly masculine powers of mind and body, combines with them the tenderer and more emotional soul-nature of the woman" (32). Forster's novel hints at this "soul-nature" through the protagonist's inner sensitivity. "A slow nature such as Maurice's appears insensitive, for it needs time even to feel. . . . Once gripped, it feels acutely, and its sensations in love are particularly profound. Given time, it can know and impart ecstasy; given time, it can sink to the heart of Hell" (45). Although Maurice conforms outwardly to ideals of masculinity at school, such notions run counter to his temperament. "He did not enjoy being cruel and rude. It was against his nature. But it was necessary at school, or he might have gone under" (19). Living up to what society expects of the young man is a struggle. He passes as "normal," but not without a degree of anguish. The capacity for self-sacrifice is in the novel the most prominent indicator of the "gentle, emotional disposition" of the Uranian (*The Intermediate Sex* 27). It takes the form of the willingness to sacrifice for one's "friend." Maurice dreams of this friend as a boy: "He could die for such a friend, he would allow such a friend to die for him; they would make any sacrifice for each other, and count the world nothing, neither death nor distance nor crossness could part them" (12). In Alec he discovers this "friend," and they willingly relinquish society to take to the greenwood as outlaws.

The third-sex theory is not overt in *Maurice*, and sexological language does not play a key narrative function as it does in *Imre*. Physicians are not the champions of enlightenment that they are in Prime-Stevenson's text, and Maurice and Alec do not employ the taxonomical structures of sexology to understand and discuss their sexual drives toward other men as Oswald and Imre do. Nonetheless, the intermediate sex interpretation of homosexual desire is present in the text. Maurice and Alec illustrate the type of homosexual man described by Symonds and Carpenter. From the beginning, critics have recognized the underlying debt Forster owed to Carpenter in his portrayal of comrade love. One of the earliest of these readers was Lytton Strachey, who criticized the love relationship as "shades of Edward Carpenter" (*Maurice* 219). However, supporting this comrade love are Carpenter's interpretations of scientific theories of the intermediate sex.

Conclusion

Although the four literary texts that are analyzed here and in previous chapter assume different and divergent approaches to fictionalizing contemporary sexological thought, all four are united in that they bring sexology further into the literary sphere. The third-sex theories of Ulrichs and Hirschfeld were an indispensible point of reference for Prime-Stevenson both in his own engagement with sexology, *The Intersexes*, and in his novel. The third sex reached Forster by way of Symonds's and Carpenter's efforts at sexual reform. *Imre* and *Maurice* novelize the third sex, the former overtly and the latter subtly, while at the same time emphasizing the health of the homosexual man which empowered them to reject medical and cultural discourses which characterize him as degenerate and mentally ill. Both texts, in their own distinct way, draw upon and concomitantly reach beyond sexological conceptions and the limits of sexological typification, thereby opening up the discourse for further-reaching depictions and discussions of same-sex desire.

Part 4

Wild about Oscar Wilde?

Chapter 6

A Tough Act to Follow: Homosexuality in Fiction after Oscar Wilde

Nineteenth-century Britain witnessed many public scandals involving "attempted sodomy" or, as it became known after 1885, "gross indecency." The Oscar Wilde trials were preceded by the Boulton and Park case (1871) and the Cleveland Street Scandal (1889). Furthermore, Charles Upchurch finds that sensationalist newspaper reporting of same-sex scandals occurred throughout the century. He argues that between the 1820s and 1870s newspapers ran "hundreds of articles pertaining to sex between men" attesting to the fact that this phenomenon was a regular topic of public discourse (*Before Wilde* 2). Wilde's scandal was unique, because it resulted in what Alan Sinfield describes as a crystallization of the homosexual image in the public figure of Wilde (*The Wilde Century* 125). Out of the hazy nexus of concepts, argues Sinfield, emerged a brilliantly clear image as well as a signifier for "unspeakable" acts and identities.

In February 1895 Wilde received an illegibly scrawled note on a calling card from the Marquis of Queensberry, father of his lover Lord Alfred Douglas, which either accused him of being a "posing Somdomite" or a "ponce and Somdomite" (Ellmann, *Oscar Wilde* 411–12). Wilde sued for libel, which was unsuccessful owing to the fact that opposing council was able to provide sufficient evidence attesting to the fact that he had indeed engaged in sex acts with twelve men, ten of whom were named (Ellmann 417). This led to Wilde's arrest and two subsequent trials for gross indecency. The first of these trials opened on 26 April 1895, with the jury unable to reach a verdict, and by 25 May 1895 the next trial ended with a conviction (Ellmann 434–49). The high profiles of the personages involved made for a particularly appealing scandal for the reading public. "With Wilde and the Marquis of Queensberry vying for top billing among a remarkable cast of characters (including several legal luminaries and a potential parade of young working-class men), and with much of the dialogue provided by one of the West End's most popular playwrights himself," writes Ed Cohen, "the drama promised to be highly entertaining" (*Talk on the Wilde Side* 132). Despite the interest, Cohen points out that for the most part the public, who greedily consumed the reporting, were left to read between the lines to infer what crime had actually been committed. Newspapers were compelled to broach same-sex acts delicately. "Indeed, the criminal activities themselves were never directly named in any newspaper account of the case but instead were designated by a virtually interchangeable series of euphemisms . . . that directly conveyed nothing substantive about the practices in question except perhaps that they were nonnormative" (Cohen 184). The iconography of the scandal, the cartoons, drawings, and illustrations produced to accompany the courtroom accounts, are as important in communicating Wilde's crime as the thinly veiled language used to intimate "the Love that dare not speak its name." They would also exert "widespread influence on how the public came to perceive him," writes Joseph Bristow, leaving "a lasting impression on how his name has been preserved in cultural memory" (*Wilde Writings* 9–10). In these cartoons, Wilde becomes more "arrogant, bloated, and voluptuous than he ever was" in reality (Bristow 10). During the trials, the newspaper reports and cartoons made the aesthete as grotesque as possible, attributing to him the physical marks of racial degeneration popularized in Max Nordau's widely discussed *Entartung*, which had been recently translated and made available in the months before the trials (Bristow, "Homosexual Writing on Trial" 28; Bristow, "Picturing His Exact Decadence" 23; see also Nordau, *Degeneration* 317–22).

Despite the ambiguity that the veil of propriety cast over the issue at hand, the intense public discourse spawned by the three trials and ensuing media circus proved to make the name of the love that no one dared speak speakable. Sinfield argues in *The Wilde Century* that the trials brought together tenuously related cultural phenomena under Wilde's public persona. He writes that an important impact on the public imagination resulted, "produc[ing] a major shift in perceptions of the scope of same-sex passion" (3) and the solidification of a queer image as "the entire, vaguely disconcerting nexus of effeminacy, leisure, idleness, immorality, luxury, insouciance, decadence and aestheticism, which Wilde was perceived, variously, as instantiating, was transformed into a brilliantly precise image. The parts were there already, and were being combined, diversely, by various people. But, at this point, a distinctive possibility cohered, far more clearly, and for far more people, than hitherto" (118). Before this "queer moment," the tastes Wilde had cultivated and the traits he had incorporated into his public personality were associated mainly with the aristocracy and were thus a protest against bourgeois conventions. During the trials the queer image emerged when the aristocratic effeminate role, which Eve Sedgwick writes "has existed since at least the seventeenth century" (*Between Men* 93), merged with the homosexual in the figure of Wilde. "Oscar Wilde" became for decades afterward the only signifier available to many to name same-sex acts and "afforded a simple stereotype as a peg for behaviour and feelings that were otherwise incoherent and/or unspeakable" (Sinfield 125). Eventually, writes Sinfield, representations of the leisure-class, Wildean homosexual "consolidated the queer image, to the point where, unless there were really explicit signs, queers were generally assumed to be leisure-class. And conversely, leisure-class men might fall under suspicion, regardless of their actual preferences" (137). For many early homosexual activists and writers, primarily in the English-speaking context, "Oscar Wilde" would be an image to negate.

This chapter investigates two of the English-language literary responses to Wilde's scandal, Edward Prime-Stevenson's *Imre* and E. M. Forster's *Maurice*, by exploring the ways in which the novels foreground masculine homosexuality over the effeminate Wildean stereotype. The former novel, along with the author's *The Intersexes*, is forthright in its rejection of the Wildean stereotype and attempts to wrestle interest in literature and the fine arts away from effeminacy. Although, in Forster's novel, Maurice identifies himself as "an unspeakable of the Oscar Wilde sort" (134), this vision of homosexuality never provides him with a means for understanding, expressing, and living his sexual desire. Lesley Hall explains that Maurice "did not mean he was witty, politically radical, intellectually subversive, or a dandified aesthete: he meant he desired other men" (*Sex, Gender, and Social Change in Britain* 54). "Oscar Wilde" names homosexuality twice—both instances trigger instantaneous recognition of the signified "unspeakable" practices (131, 134). This is a lasting effect of the Wilde trials: "Oscar Wilde," writes Sinfield, became for decades after the trials "the one form in which speech might occur" (*The Wilde Century* 125). Regarding *Maurice*, he writes that "It was hard to be queer without a model" and thus "Maurice first recognizes homosexuality in Risley" (140), who was based on the writer Lytton Strachey (1880–1932), who had adopted the Wildean model for himself (141). However, Sinfield posits, "The novel is designed to show that Maurice doesn't have to be like Oscar Wilde" (140). "The Wildean stereotype is still powerful in the novel, though by negation. Maurice and Alec make off to the woods, whereas Forster himself stayed in Cambridge, with the knowing dons and adventurous, leisure-class students. Forster thereby excludes from his happy ending not only himself but also men like Strachey—the most prominent and progressive homosexuals of the time; so determined is he to pursue the repudiation of effeminacy" (142). I disagree with Sinfield in that I see the role of the Wildean image extending beyond mere negation or repudiation, something which is especially clear when *Maurice* is contrasted to *Imre* as well as Mackay's books of the nameless love. Risley is crucial to Maurice's education and serves a key function in the plot's progression. Claude Summers posits that one of "the most significant literary influences on Forster's novel is the work of Victorian England's most famous homosexual outlaw, Oscar Wilde," whose *De Profundis* in particular "informs Maurice at every turn" (*E. M. Forster* 148; *Gay Fictions* 22, 85). Risley is a "child of light," a figure that Wilde describes in *De Profundis*: "His chief war was against the Philistines. That is the war every child of light has to wage. Philistinism was the note of the age and community in which [Jesus] lived. In their heavy inaccessibility to ideas, their dull respectability, their tedious orthodoxy, their worship of vulgar success, their entire preoccupation with the gross materialistic side of life, and their ridiculous estimate of themselves and their importance, the Jews of Jerusalem in Christ's day were the exact counterpart of the British Philistine of our own" (*Collected Works* 2: 182). Summers argues that "Maurice himself will after assume the same struggle" (*E. M. Forster* 152; *Gay Fictions* 88). If Risley is the "child of light," a burden which Maurice and Alec in the end assume, he and the Wildean model of homosexuality cannot be relegated to merely a negative image against which the novel defines its protagonists. There are three points in the novel when Risley stretches Maurice "a helping hand" (23). Before the literary analyses, though, three of the components that form the core of the nexus that is Wilde's public persona and, after the trials, homosexual image are discussed: effeminacy, dandyism, and aestheticism. Although *Imre* rejects all that Wilde had come to represent in the popular imagination, *Maurice* is more subtle in its depiction of the interaction between the more masculine and more effeminate models of homosexuality. Aspects of Wilde's legacy would be carried on, in a manner of sorts, in Forster's eponymous hero.

Aestheticism as Rebellion

In England in the final decades of the nineteenth century, a model of homosexuality took shape and gained attention concomitantly with the masculine and democratically egalitarian vision advocated in the writings of John Addington Symonds and Edward Carpenter (see chapter 3). Although Greek love and Walt Whitman were also key discourses which shaped and influenced this other homosexual model (see M. Robertson, *Worshipping Walt* 139–97), instead of back-to-nature manliness and socialist Utopianism being its defining characteristics, this alternative model is distinguished by effeminacy, dandyism, aestheticism, and was embodied in Oscar Wilde. This section considers these aspects of Wilde's public persona which, through their association with him, became so tightly bound up in the effeminate homosexual role.

From the time Wilde left Oxford in 1879, he marketed himself as a "liminal figure" in London society, writes Cohen (*Talk on the Wilde Side* 135). He became the embodiment of the Aesthetic Movement and the consummate "dandy-aesthete." Martin Green points out that although the dandy and the aesthete are distinct figures in many respects, the example of Wilde shows that they "are very closely related, and frequently the same person is both. Very often the two phases are alternative ways of embodying the same idea, the same temperamental drive" (*Children of the Sun* 32–33). Thus Green proposes the term "dandy-aesthete" to designate these "twin aspects of one identity" (33). Aestheticism is a movement which resists attempts to define it. Jonathan Freedman writes that there is no "single, unitary definition of a diverse, fractious, and ultimately disjunctive group of writers, artists, and critics" (*Professions of Taste* 4). The one unifying trait of British aestheticism, Freedman writes, "is the desire to embrace contradictions, indeed the desire to seek them out the better to play with the possibilities they afford" (6). Dennis Denisoff, who identifies the heyday of the Aesthetic Movement between 1880 to 1895, argues that "the term 'aestheticism' came to be associated with a multiplicity of high-art and popular constructs and products including literary and visual works, artistic styles, household decor, personae, and philosophical views" (*Aestheticism and Sexual Parody* 6). Max Beerbohm (1872–1956) in the essay "1880" (1895) retrospectively described that year as a time when

> Fired by [Wilde's] fervid words, men and women hurled their mahogany into the streets and ransacked the curio-shops for the furniture of Annish days. Dados arose upon every wall, sunflowers and the feathers of peacocks curved in every corner, tea grew quite cold while the guests were praising the Willow Pattern of its cup. A few fashionable women even dressed themselves in sinuous draperies and unheard-of greens. Into whatsoever ballroom you went, you would surely find, among the women in tiaras and the fops and the distinguished foreigners, half a score of comely ragamuffins in velveteen, murmuring sonnets, posturing, waving their hands (loc. 342).

These dandy-aesthetes, whom Beerbohm describes as "comely ragamuffins in velveteen," were "interested in fashioning themselves as art," writes Denisoff, they belonged to "an elite class that possessed refined tastes and values—a class in many ways beyond the dictates of everyday society." Such exclusiveness, suggests Denisoff, was "a factor in determining whether people with unconventional sexual desires were likely to turn to those interests when formulating their identities" (7).

One of the key figures in the Aesthetic Movement and one of the most important influences on Wilde was the Oxford don Walter Pater (1839–1894), whose *The Renaissance: Studies in Art and Poetry* (1873) Wilde had read during his first term at Oxford and would later call "that book which has had such a strange influence over my life" (*Collected Works* 2: 168; see Raby, *Oscar Wilde* 16; Wright, *Oscar's Books* 102–03). Pater insists that, to become truly conscious of the Greek spirit of beauty, one should live life as a series of intense moments. "To burn always with this hard, gemlike flame, to maintain this ecstasy, is success in life" (*The Renaissance* 152). The highest wisdom comes not from the intellectual or analytical faculties, but from the senses and immediate experience. "Of such wisdom, the poetic passion, the desire of beauty, the love of art for its own sake, has most. For art comes to you proposing frankly to give nothing but the highest quality of your moments as they pass, and simply for these moments' sake" (Pater 153). The imperative here is to live one's life as a work of art: to cultivate rare and exotic tastes and interests, to deck oneself in and furnish one's abode with only the most exquisite, to draw on philosophies of Individualism that set one above the common man. "I put all my genius into my life," Wilde claimed to André Gide, "I put only my talent into my works" (qtd. in Raby 7).

Joseph Bristow writes that Wilde was celebrated for "his unmanly mode of self representation," his silks and velvets, and not "only did his unorthodox dress sense catch the public's attention, his powers of conversation usually managed to make their mark" ("A Complex and Multiform Creature" 201). This effeminate dandy-aesthete image that he fostered did not at this point indicate same-sex sexuality, but enabled him to critique and to challenge ideals of middle-class masculinity. During the nineteenth century, the middle-class man began in earnest to distinguish himself from the aristocrat. The characteristics which he stressed in order to accomplish this were above all his work ethic and moral seriousness (see Tosh, "The Old Adam and the New Man" 72–77). Aestheticism, for many children of the middle class, including Wilde, was a "strategic response," writes Freedman, which enabled them to "claim authority for themselves in that world" that was heretofore reserved for the aristocracy (*Professions of Taste* 48). The Regency dandy, who had "cultivated refinement to con the upper classes into accepting him" (Bronski, *Culture Clash* 57), offered a useful precedent. Stephen Calloway writes that the Regency dandies had made an art of their lives, and for their inheritors, the dandy-aesthetes of the fin de siècle, this was an aim to be emulated ("Wilde and the Dandyism of the Senses" 36). Wilde sought entry into the reserves of the upper classes; in particular he sought recourse to the freedoms ceded to aristocratic masculinity. And upset the social certainties he certainly did. "In contrast to the 'manly' middle-class male," writes Cohen, "Wilde would come to represent—through his writing and his trials—the 'unmanly' social climber" ("Writing Gone Wilde" 803).

This dandy-aestheticism merged with a theory of personality and Individualism in opposition to the mandates of British middle-class manliness. Josephine Guy explains that Wilde engaged with Individualism (uppercase "I"), a political platform which emerged in Britain in the 1880s and faded from view after 1910, rather than individualism (lowercase "i"), "the methodological atomism that underlay much nineteenth-century social thought, and that was often interpreted as a justification for egoism" ("A (Con) Textual History" 69–70). Wildean Individualism is communicated across his oeuvre, but is articulated straightforwardly in the essay "The Soul of Man under Socialism" (1891) where Wilde establishes a case for socialism based upon the opportunities this economic system could afford for unhampered personal development. Wilde writes that instead of the masculine imperatives to produce and to accumulate inherent in the capitalist system, in a socialist society man's individuality will grow organically, "flower-like, or as a tree grows" (*Collected Works* 4: 239). It is a paradoxically individualistic socialism, distinct from the no-less-Utopian socialism which Carpenter envisioned. Guy writes that the essay's "attempt to reconcile such diametrically opposed doctrines as Socialism and Individualism" features the wit and iconoclasm for which Wilde's writings have become famous ("A (Con) Textual History" 67). Under Wilde's Socialism the individual will be able to realize himself or herself perfectly. "'Know thyself' was written over the portal of the antique world. Over the portal of the new world, 'Be thyself' shall be written" (240). Being oneself would involve overturning normative gender mandates. Robert Smythe Hichens (1864–1950) captures (or rather parodies) "the higher philosophy," Wilde's subversion of middle-class masculinity, in *The Green Carnation* (1894): "The philosophy to be afraid of nothing, to dare to live as one wishes to live, not as the middle classes wish one to live; to have the courage of one's desires, instead of only the cowardice of other people's" (109). To achieve this new world which Wilde envisions, dandy-aestheticism becomes a form of disobedience to gender roles and the economic system which underpin them, and it is through such disobedience that they can be overturned. "Disobedience, in the eyes of anyone who has read history, is man's original virtue. It is through disobedience that progress has been made, through disobedience and through rebellion" (235). The obstacle to Wilde's new world is Philistinism. "He is the Philistine," explains Wilde in *De Profundis*, "who upholds and aids the heavy, cumbrous, blind mechanical forces of Society, and who does not recognise the dynamic force when he meets it either in a man or a movement" (*Collected Works* 2: 188). Wilde's was "a life that had been a complete protest against [Philistinism], and from some points of view a complete annihilation of it" (*Collected Works* 2: 129). Wilde's effeminate self-styling, his dandy-aesthete persona, his philosophy of Individualism undermined Victorian morality and masculine gender codes which he equates with Philistinism and selfishness. "Selfishness is not living as one wishes to live, it is asking others to live as one wishes to live. And unselfishness is letting other people's lives alone, not interfering with them. Selfishness always aims at creating around it an absolute uniformity of type. Unselfishness recognizes infinite variety of type as a delightful thing, accepts it, acquiesces in it, enjoys it" (*Collected Works* 4: 263–64). During and after his trials for acts of gross indecency, the cultural phenomena Wilde cultivated in his public persona would come to be regarded as part and parcel of homosexuality.

In the Aftermath of Wilde

The Wilde trials brought male homosexuality into public discourse and contributed to the formation of a homosexual stereotype. Another effect was, writes Havelock Ellis in later editions of *Sexual Inversion*, that it "contributed to give definiteness and self-consciousness to the manifestations of homosexuality" and as a consequence "aroused inverts to take up a definite attitude" (*Studies in the Psychology of Sex* 352). And yet, for many contemporary homosexual activists in Britain and elsewhere, disassociating themselves and their desire from this Wildean homosexual role became one of the most pressing issues. Many of the post-Wilde writings by homosexual authors react against the effeminate model. Prominent among these are Marc-André Raffalovich's (1864–1934) "L'Affaire Oscar Wilde" (1895) and Carpenter's writings, such as his literary anthology *Ioläus: An Anthology of Friendship* and his sexological treatise *The Intermediate Sex*. This group also includes Prime-Stevenson with his novel *Imre: A Memorandum* and his study *The Intersexes: A History of Similisexualism as a Problem in Social Life*.

As the earliest of the four literary texts discussed in this study, *Imre* was written and published very much in the wake of the Wilde scandal, which accounts for the text's response to the effeminate role as the least nuanced of the four works of fiction. In comparison to the other works under discussion, Prime-Stevenson's text is the most straightforward in its rejection of the effeminacy model of same-sex subjectivity. The novel never mentions Wilde by name, but it leaves no doubt that the effeminate figures against which the protagonists build their identities represent Wilde and the stereotype of homosexuality his trials allowed the Victorian popular press to manufacture. Effeminacy in the novel is associated with and condemned in terms of psychopathology, dissolution, and immorality. This response to Wilde is communicated even more openly in *The Intersexes*, where Wilde is cited by name and the Wildean model of homosexuality is confronted head on. The following first considers the overt rejection of Wilde in Prime-Stevenson's study and then explores how this stance is thematized in the novel, including an effort to wrestle interest in the arts away from the effeminacy model and situate them within the sphere that belongs to the masculine Uranian.

In addition to its medical justification and defense of manly Uranian same-sex desire, *The Intersexes* is an impassioned cultural-historical celebration of homosexuality, an exercise in establishing a queer cultural unity, which includes a sweeping exploration of same-sex love in world literature. This part of the study does not spare glowing praise for Walt Whitman and his verse, but this is not the case when it comes to Wilde. The study rejects Wilde's fiction and criticism and opposes the stereotype Wilde came to represent and the role he played for contemporary homosexual subcultures. This fervent rejection of Wilde demonstrates on the one hand just how crucial the Wildean counter-discourse had become for many within homosexual subcultures in the first decade after his death. "An exaggerated personal cult for Wilde," writes Prime-Stevenson, "and a corresponding exaggerated estimate of his intellectualism have become noticeable in circles of English homosexuals" (362–63). The author tries to downplay Wilde, but for a modern reader of the text, he inadvertently makes evident the profundity of Wilde's impact. The text reacts to the canonization of Oscar Wilde as a homosexual martyr figure, suggesting that Prime-Stevenson believed that this is not the type of figurehead homosexual men and women needed to assist in their struggle for liberation. *The Intersexes* attempts to discredit Wilde on two points: in terms of his standing as an artist and as a homosexual.

Chapter 9 of *The Intersexes* attempts to construct a homosexual literary legacy to which there are but few contributions by English-language writers (255–408). Prime-Stevenson writes that "The Anglo-Saxon uranian presents himself to us less frequently as a man of letters than does his Continental colleague. He dares not. Social ostracism and criminal prosecutions can easily follow" (347) which was the fate "of the gifted Irish novelist, essayist, and dramatist, Oscar Wilde" whose "literary tragedy [is] remembered by many contemporaries with grief" (362). Wilde's *The Picture of Dorian Gray*, which Prime-Stevenson describes as "a novel of vague homosexual suggestiveness" (362), is one of the few contributions to this legacy. What appears at first to be a sympathetic treatment of Wilde and his writings and an acknowledgement of their place in the Uranian literary canon quickly turns into derision of Wilde's art and its underlying aesthetic theories. "The brilliancy of Wilde, at its brightest, did not reach the level of genius. His originality of thought, and even of expression in his writings, his suggestiveness as an aesthetic theorist, his epigrammatic independence in conversation and print, all are highly discutable traits" (363). In other words, Prime-Stevenson intimates that Wilde was a literary and aesthetic charlatan. He was not as brilliant as his posthumous reputation makes him out to be, and his originality as a writer and critic are doubtful. *The Intersexes* is not the first place this view was expressed by a contemporary homosexual man. Raffalovich, in "L'Affaire Oscar Wilde," which was first published in 1895 and the following year incorporated into his sexological study *Uranisme et Unisexualité: Étude sur différentes manifestations de l'instinct sexuel* (Uranism and Unisexuality: Study of Different Manifestations of Sexual Instinct, 1896) (Roden, "Marc-Andre Raffalovich" 131), writes of *The Picture of Dorian Gray* that it is "an unoriginal novel (Oscar Wilde has never been original)" which "is artificial, superficial, and effeminate. Unisexuality reigns there, but without vigor: in a half-light of affectation and fear." He goes on to condemn Wilde: "Oscar Wilde, having neither common sense nor talent, can only treat sexual inversion or perversion feebly, deceitfully, languishingly" (qtd. in Roden, "Marc-Andre Raffalovich" 133). These diatribes against Wilde and his novel are undoubtedly to a large extent sour grapes by two writers whose fiction is, it could be argued, mediocre; but they are also important as two voices who resisted the Wildean stereotype in their own writings in an effort to challenge popular (mis)-conceptions and offer homosexual men a broader range of images of themselves.

Prime-Stevenson does not stop with Wilde's fiction though; he also casts aspersions at Wilde's homosexuality, which he calls "eccentric intimacies with young men of far inferior station" and "notoriously venal pederasty" (362). "Wilde's type of uranianism was in no sense classic. It was far below the level of idealism which his intellectuality would lead one to expect. His sexual instincts were concentrated on vulgar boy-prostitutes of the town" (363). This charge is leveled against Wilde by Raffalovich too. "It is clear," Raffalovich writes, "that Wilde never understood the obligations imposed by a love based on Plato, Shakespeare, Michelangelo" (qtd. in Roden 134). Despite what Wilde claimed in his speech in defense of "the Love that dare not speak its name," his chosen form of same-sex relations was far from Socratic and thus was not the ideal it posed as. Furthermore, Prime-Stevenson charges that Wilde died "reformed." "His receiving the halo of a 'martyr' to homsexualism is also the less well-bestowed, since he repudiated in his last writings though perhaps with his constitutional insincerity the morality of the homosexual instinct, and so died 'repentant.' That Wilde was a victim of British social intolerance and hypocrisy, and of the need of new and intelligent English legislation as to similisexual instincts is perfectly true: but Wilde himself was not a little a shrewd and superficial *poseur*, to the very last" (363). It can be assumed that by Wilde's "last writings" Prime-Stevenson means primarily *De Profundis* in its 1905 edition, which was, as Michael Doylen points out, regarded by many contemporary readers as "evidence of Wilde's genuine contrition for his past transgressions" ("Oscar Wilde's *De Profundis*" 547). But Prime-Stevenson also suggests that Wilde may not have been sincere in this repudiation, an opinion which, according to Doylen, *De Profundis* also engendered in its early readers. They saw it as "yet another pose struck by the incorrigible aesthete" (547). What is undeniable from this section of *The Intersexes* is that Prime-Stevenson treats Wilde only in a bid to write him out of the homosexual literary and (sub)cultural legacy. This stance toward Wilde is less directly evident in the novel and is mainly manifest in its repudiation of homosexual effeminacy and its valorization of homosexual manliness. In striving to proffer images of homosexual masculinity, the novel seeks to counteract those in wide circulation after the trials—an aim perhaps too ambitious for a small book published privately by an out-of-the-way book press. Nevertheless, the novel challenges the discursive links between effeminacy and homosexuality, primarily through the trope of the Uranian comrades-in-arms, while at the same time it reestablishes the link between art and homosexuality. Appreciation for the arts plays a key role in the Uranian relationship portrayed in the novel, and images of homosexual artists, musicians, and thinkers are a crucial element of the means through which the protagonists build their identities and oppose the opprobrium attached to their desire by the forces of normativity. After the unequivocal link between aesthetic appreciation and the effeminate homosexual role emerged from the trials, the novel fights this association, striving to recoup aestheticism for the manly Uranian.

Whereas the other three literary texts feature characters that demonstrably identify with the effeminacy model—the two dandy characters in *Der Tod in Venedig*, various minor characters in *Puppenjunge*, and Risley in *Maurice*—in *Imre* evocations of the Wildean homosexual are few. These images are not absent from the text, though, instead they haunt the periphery—they materialize behind every use of the adjective "womanish." Despite the text's side-lining of effeminate homosexual figures in favor of images of masculinity, a glimpse of the Wildean homosexual does cohere briefly. As Oswald confesses his secret to Imre, he describes the models through and against which he formed his sexual subjectivity. He recalls positive images that inspired him such as "Socrates and Plato," "Alexander, Julius Caesar, Augustus, and Hadrian," and "Platen, Grillparzer, Hölderlin, Byron, [and] Whitman" (87). But the "Race-Homosexual" also includes "countless ignoble, trivial, loathsome, feeble-souled and feeble-bodied creatures" (86). "Those, those, terrified me, Imre! To think of them shamed me; those types of man-loving-men who, by thousands, live incapable of any noble ideals or lives. Ah, those patently depraved, noxious, flaccid, gross, womanish beings! perverted and imperfect in moral nature and in even their bodily tissues!" (86). As examples of this class of homosexual, he lists the third-century Roman Emperor Heliogabalus, also known as Elagabalus, (ca. 203–22 CE), the French nobleman and general Gilles Baron de Rais (1404–1440), Henri III of France (1551–1589), and the Marquis de Sade (1740–1814). These historical figures do not directly allude to Wilde, but merely suggest effeminacy, excess, or debauchery. Oswald then turns his rant onto more contemporary figures. "The effeminate artists, the sugary and fibreless musicians! The Lady Nancyish, rich young men of higher or lower society twaddling aesthetic sophistries; stinking of perfume like cocottes! The second-rate poets and the neurasthenic, *précieux* poetasters who rhyme forth their forged literary passports out of their mere human decadence; out of their marrowless shams of all that is a man's fancy, a man's heart, a man's love life!" (87). These are the very "rubbish of humanity" (86), discourses Oswald. He employs language which may indicate a pathological or hereditary etiology, not of the homosexuality of these types, but of their effeminacy. They are "perverted and imperfect" in "their bodily tissues." Within this class, there are "effeminate artists" who "twaddl[e] aesthetic sophistries" as well as "second-rate poets and neurasthenic, *précieux* poetasters," or second-rate poets, whose muse is "mere human decadence." Byrne Fone writes that Oswald's catalogue of homosexual effeminacy "is staggering and it includes every homophobic cliché." The character is a voice in a campaign to argue that while the effeminate and therefore visible garner the public's attention, most homosexual men do not stand out and are outwardly "normal." "Protesting too much, perhaps, Oswald insists that weakness, effeminacy, and ineffectuality are found in only a small segment of the homosexual population" (*Homophobia* 358). This rant leaves little doubt that Oswald condemns a type of effeminate artist which Wilde came to represent (see also Gifford, *Dayneford's Library* 113). The entire essay (84–89) demonstrates that there is a positive and negative strand to the homosexual historical and literary legacy which the novel and *The Intersexes* forges. Both strands can be traced from the ancient world to the fin de siècle. The positive strand culminates in Whitman, whereas the negative one culminates in Wilde. There is a Whitman/Wilde dialectic that shapes the novel and its depiction of homosexual identities. The novel recalls not Wilde in any specific sense (as is the case in *The Intersexes*) but those images which the popular press constructed. The source of Oswald's anger is the stereotype in circulation, coined to make Wilde seem depraved and degenerate, but Oswald does not direct this rage at the perpetrators of this image, he blames the effeminate homosexuals themselves, attacking their aesthetic philosophies and the quality of their poetry.

The novel employs a strategy of depicting homosexuality which seems to throw the "bad," effeminate homosexuals (the Wilde type) under the proverbial bus in order that the "good," "normal" homosexuals (the Whitman type) can be accepted by the mainstream. Thus the text (over)stresses the masculinity of the Uranian, the man "who is too much man": "So super-male, so utterly unreceptive of what is not manly, so aloof from any feminine essences, that we cannot tolerate woman at all as a sexual factor! Are we not the extreme of the male?" (86). Uranians ought not to be condemned, but respected because they are even manlier than heterosexual men. Offered to the reader in support of Oswald's claim is the portrayal of the eponymous character who is an amalgam of manly virtues. Although he is a perfect specimen of manly beauty, he is not at all vain. "United with all this capital of a man's physical attractiveness was Imre's extraordinary modesty. He never seemed to think of his appearance for so much as two minutes together. He never glanced into a mirror when he happened to pass near that piece of furniture" (52–53). Neither is he dandyish. "He never posed; never fussed as to his toilet, nor worried concerning the ultrafitting of his clothes, nor studied with anxiety details of his person. . . . He detested all jewelry in the way of masculine adornments, and wore none: and his civilian clothing was of the plainest" (53). He is a lieutenant in the army, possessing renowned martial and athletic prowess (51–52), which is a fact that is key to the text, as the homosexual soldier is a central trope in *Imre*, whose importance is explained in *The Intersexes*. "It would seem that, being himself so robustly male, there is no place in a soldier's heart, or sexual impulse, for anything not vehemently manly. Here advances the theory of the Uranian as a super-virile, not sub-virile, sex" (*The Intersexes* 187).

Rather than reject the social value placed upon attitudes, ideas, emotions, and behaviors labeled in contemporary society as "manly," the novel appropriates this discursive formation for its own use, arguing that the homosexual man, although he might possess a feminine soul, can be, and in the case of the two characters portrayed in the novel is, super-manly. Femininity is in *Imre* radically restricted to sexual desire. The Uranian comrades-in-arms topos supports this claim.

Breaking the association between effeminacy and art—its production and its appreciation—is a secondary, but no less important, point of contention for the text. The Wilde scandal had a disastrous effect for many years not only on writers and artists, as W. H. Auden notes, but also upon the attitude of the general public towards the arts as a whole. The scandal allowed "the philistine man to identify himself with the decent man" ("An Improbable Life" 136). Literature, in the eyes of many in the decades following the trials, bore a dubious connection to Wilde, the infamous homosexual. The author makes breaking this connection a focus with the manly aesthete character Laurence Dayneford in the short story "Out of the Sun," in the collection *Her Enemy, Some Friends—and Other Personages: Stories and Studies Mostly of Human Hearts* (1913). Aschenbach battles in the name of art in *Der Tod in Venedig*, striving to transform the production of literature into a manly and heroic enterprise. In *Imre*, a similar battle is fought out no less tenaciously and with greater success for the protagonists. "We were both interested in art" (47), explains Oswald, and it is this shared interest in the arts that is the means through which the two characters initially form their friendship. It also signals to each other the possibility that they have more in common than these interests: their sexuality. Music and the plastic arts seem a safer conversational terrain to navigate, enabling them to disclose enough about their personalities without full confessions. Early on, Imre calls himself a "music-fiend" (40). His career, his commission in the Hungarian army, was chosen out of duty to his father and aristocratic, but impoverished, family rather than in fulfillment of his own wishes: "I wanted to study art, I didn't care what art: music, painting, sculpture, perhaps music more than anything" (50). Indeed, Oswald acknowledges that Imre is "a most excellent practical musician": "his musical enthusiasm, his musical insight and memory, they were all of a piece, the rich and perilous endowment of the born son of Orpheus" (56). This association with the legendary Greek musician and poet could point to homosexuality for anyone who had read Ovid. After attempting unsuccessfully to rescue Eurydice from Hades, he becomes the first pederast. "Orpheus now would have nothing to do / with the love of women . . . [and] even started the practice among the Thracian / tribes of turning for love to immature males and of plucking / the flower of a boy's brief spring before he had come to his manhood" (*Metamorphoses* 385–86). Imre's aesthetic enthusiasm does not extend to literature, though, at least not at this stage in the narrative, as this art form reveals too much about the face he conceals behind his mask. He feigns a "relative aversion to belles-lettres." "For novels, as for poetry, he cared almost nothing" (53–54), and he even detests letter writing. "As for sentiment—sentiment! in my letters to friends!—well, I simply cannot squeeze *that* out" (62). These aversions are at variance with "modest 'literary impulses'" manifest in an "emotional eloquence of phrase" which Oswald observes burst forth in "fountains of innermost feeling" when he is stirred (54). Oswald accounts for this apparent contradiction with reference to Imre's nationality, his "race": "Imre was a Magyar, one of a race in which sentimental eloquence is always lurking in the blood, even to a poetic passion in verbal utterance" (55). Imre, until just before he discloses his homosexuality to Oswald, projects a manly reserve, a mask, which occludes expression of emotion. In the third part of the novel, he consciously rejects this, as demonstrated first by the expressive letters he writes to Oswald from the military camp and second by his decision to confess his sexuality.

This more explicit correlation between literature and homosexuality in the novel is likely an after effect of Wilde, but this point of anxiety disappears once Imre decides to admit to Oswald that he too is homosexual. Both characters are upper class and passionate about the arts, but not effete aesthetes. Their interests indicate homosexuality but not effeminacy; thus *Imre* recoups and reclaims the arts for a distinctly manly, Uranian identity. Art and literature, with history and classical philosophy, cultural figures from Plato and Socrates, through Shakespeare, Marlowe, Winckelmann, and Platen, to Whitman (87), play a decisive role in the formation of this masculine homosexual role: they are tools which empower the protagonists to forge their Uranian identities. It is a Whitmanian brand of aestheticism, not Wildean aestheticism. The link between the arts, especially literature, and homosexuality is re-established in the text, while effeminacy is repudiated. In *Imre*, these interests are the domain of the super-male homosexual man, whereas the effeminate artists are merely bad artists, not to mention bad homosexuals.

Reacting to the effeminacy model and adopting an approach to depicting homosexuality which foregrounds masculine models is not unique to *Imre*. Indeed, this novel anticipates a struggle between depicting "normal" and "queer" images which remains a central issue in gay literature (see Brookes, *Male Fiction since Stonewall* 3; see also Stevens, "Normality and Queerness in Gay Fiction" 81–96). Prime-Stevenson's fiction and nonfiction works grapple with the societal image which received its figurehead the decade before, responding to this stereotype by distancing the manly Uranians from the Oscar Wilde sort and by attempting to disassociate art from effeminacy. A similar effort is undertaken in Forster's *Maurice* through the ostensibly normal and masculine hero of the novel who rejects both intellectual and effeminate discourses of same-sex desire. The two texts differ on two key points: first, in *Maurice* there is no attempt to portray the arts as manly; and second, more importantly, the effeminate figure in Forster's work is not a negative image merely for Maurice to distinguish himself against, but assists in furthering his education and the construction of his identity.

Not "one of the unspeakables of the Oscar Wilde sort"

In *Maurice*, as in *Imre*, the platform which maintains that the homosexual man is as masculine and "normal" as the heterosexual man is promoted over the effeminate model, thus advocating normality over queerness, assimilation over subversion. Forster's novel features four homosexual characters and three visions of homosexuality. Clive represents Hellenism while Risley is aristocratic, effete bohemianism. Although key figures through whose influence and against whom Maurice builds his identity, neither vision of same-sex subjectivity fits. Maurice and Alec represent an alternative model to those of intellectualism and effeminacy. Maurice is Suburbia, middle-class Edwardian England; instead of an element which could have been easily side-lined (e.g., a scholar with a fantasy of ancient Greece, or an ineffectual, effete aristocrat), Maurice is at the very heart of English national identity, a pillar of British society. The protagonist is exceptional only in that he is utterly average, "Hall was one of them, and they would never cease to feel him so"; middle-class Edwardian society "could celebrate itself in his image" (15). This casting of the protagonist speaks against the pathologization of homosexuality with Maurice as the literary embodiment of the sexual reform efforts spearheaded by Symonds and Carpenter. Additionally, he provides an image in opposition to the Wildean stereotype, depicting Symonds's assertion, which he makes in "A Problem in Modern Ethics," that most Uranians are "athletic, masculine in habit, frank in manner" and able to pass "through society year after year without arousing a suspicion of their inner temperament" (*Symonds and Homosexuality* 135). Unlike Prime-Stevenson's novel, which salvages an appreciation of the fine arts and claims these interests and pursuits for the Uranian identity, Maurice is what Forster would regard as the very likeness of British manliness: masculine, athletic, and a Philistine. However, the key difference between *Maurice* and the other work lies in the fact that this novel does not deem it necessary to denigrate effeminate homosexuality in order to valorize the manly model. Risley, the representative of the Wildean mode of sexual identity, is not discounted outright. This character plays an important role in the narrative as a catalyst in the eponymous character's trajectory toward self-understanding and self-acceptance.

Risley is a figure radically unlike those of Maurice's suburban, middle-class milieu. "Risley was dark, tall and affected. He made an exaggerated gesture when introduced, and when he spoke, which was continually, he used strong yet unmanly superlatives" (19). Maurice "was not sure that he loathed Risley, though no doubt he ought to, and in a minute should" (19–20). The "strong yet unmanly superlatives" suggest the key function language fulfills in this homosexual role. Conversation is Risley's forte and the only thing, so he claims, he cares about. His words are packed with performative power: "Words *are* deeds" (21). And yet behind this high camp sensibility of wit and frivolity rests a seriousness that does not escape Maurice's recognition (20). Risley deploys arguably the most potent weapon in the Wildean arsenal; Michael Bronski writes that Wilde taught homosexual men to use words against their adversaries, "to use wit and imagination to diffuse and deflate the attacks of serious society" (*Culture Clash* 60). With words, Risley stirs up and in turn disarms the other men in this scene. The norms and values inculcated in Maurice by his Edwardian upbringing and education tell him that he ought to loathe Risley for his effeminate loquacity. But he does not, for he recognizes his need for a homosexual mentor and recognizes the possibility of finding it in Risley. Risley has "stirred

Maurice incomprehensibly"; he knows that he must meet "this queer fish" again (23). "He was not attracted to the man in the sense that he wanted him for a friend, but he did feel he might help him—how, he didn't formulate. It was all very obscure, for the mountains still overshadowed Maurice. Risley, surely capering on the summit, might stretch him a helping hand" (23). Maurice attempts to be "bohemian," to adopt Risley's mode of parlance, his imperative to "talk, talk," and accept for himself the Wildean model; but this proves to be hopeless (23). Sedgwick writes that despite the middle-class gentleman having attended the same schools and universities as the leisure-class man, he "seems not to have had easy access to the alternative subculture, the stylized discourse, or the sense of immunity of the aristocratic/bohemian sexual minority" (*Between Men* 172–73). Despite this, Risley does offer "a helping hand," each time furthering, although indirectly, Maurice's process of building an identity as a man-loving man.

The protagonist's initial meeting with Risley helps him to identify his vague and disconcerting feelings in relation to this character. Not only does Risley further Maurice's recognition of his sexuality, but he serves a similar purpose for Clive as well. "In [Clive's] second year he met Risley, himself 'that way.' Clive did not return the confidence which was given rather freely, nor did he like Risley and his set. But he was stimulated. He was glad to know that there were more of his sort about" (56). Clive is "stimulated" by Risley, and Maurice is "stirred" by him. Prior to meeting Risley, both characters are isolated in their sexuality. After meeting him, the two begin to be able "to speak out." Clive explains to Maurice, "When I came to know Risley and his crew it seemed imperative to speak out. You know what a point they made of that—it's really their main point" (31). Although neither joins (or perhaps is able to join) this aristocratic, bohemian coterie, they receive consolation from knowing that they are not alone and they learn that their desire is not "unmentionable."

Risley's second appearance in the narrative is crucial because it results in relieving Maurice of the guilt under which he suffers after the two doctors' consultations have impressed upon him that he suffers from a psychological disorder or an "evil hallucination" (131–35). They meet by chance at a performance of Tchaikovsky's *Symphonie Pathétique*, and Risley comments, no doubt provocatively, that the composer dedicated the symphony to his nephew with whom he had fallen in love. Maurice feigns lack of interest in this information, but it leads him to a biography of the great queer composer, in which he reads of his unhappy marriage and love for his nephew "Bob." The biography proves to be "the one literary work that had ever helped him" because it demonstrates to him that marriage, Dr. Barry's recommendation which he has been seriously contemplating (137), could only spell disaster for him and the woman he would marry. And the third and final instance of Risley's influence upon the narrative is his recommendation of the hypnotist Lasker Jones (138). This is the most decisive push this character gives the plot. Hypnotism does not cure Maurice, but stimulates him, opening him to the possibility of "sharing" with Alec (to use the novel's euphemism for intercourse). Maurice calls out into the night; Alec, who is standing below his window, responds by climbing up a ladder into his room

(165–66). He does not find "repose" at the hands of the hypnotist, as he hoped (155), but the two sessions are a contributing factor to the novel's happy ending.

Risley's part in the narrative is relatively small, but his impact upon the plot is significant. He is responsible for effecting key events and indirectly contributes greatly to Maurice's identity formation. A degree of distance is maintained between the two characters; to Maurice, Risley is shrouded in inscrutability: "he always felt Risley knew too much" (138). The two characters are certainly not friends, but it could be read that Risley, behind his high-camp pose of disengagement, takes an interest in Maurice's search for identity. His confidences, dropping of hints, and knowing smile suggest Risley's willingness to help a member of his tribe. Risley, "capering on the summit" of the mountains of self-knowledge, stretches Maurice "a helping hand." *Maurice* depicts a manly model of same-sex identity and relations, as does Prime-Stevenson's *Imre*. It is, however, unfair to read Forster's novel as a rejection of the Wildean effeminacy model; instead it offers further choice, broader depictions of man-loving men. Although the author suppressed his text, the manuscript had a small, but important, readership, including Christopher Isherwood and Stephen Spender, whose own writings would offer readers the broader range of images of homosexuality that *Maurice*'s suppression denied them (see Isherwood, *Christopher and His Kind* 125–27; Zeikowitz, *Letters Between Forster and Isherwood* 3–4, 12–13, 20–21, 74–75, 149–51; Leeming *Stephen Spender* 76).

Conclusion

This chapter shows then that responding to the Wilde scandal was a central issue for early gay novels. The two English texts offer readers a more diverse range of images of homosexuality, namely images in opposition the Wildean effeminate stereotype, ones that seek to break the links between homosexuality and effeminacy that were cemented in the public's imagination after the Wilde trials. *Imre*, published a mere eleven years after the Wilde scandal, presents homo-masculinities which unambiguously reject the Wildean model of same-sex subjectivity. In *Maurice*, the Wildean character seems to be a figure against whom the protagonist defines his sense of self; but the novel's portrayal of effeminate Risley can, by no means, be called repudiation. Instead he serves as a valid option, one through which the protagonist can arrive at his own authentic identity as a manly homosexual. This insistence upon the conventional masculinity of the homosexual central characters is not without its subversiveness to mainstream stereotypes of heterosexual masculinity though. These works overturn these preconceptions by commandeering society's images of manliness. Take, for instance, the case of Maurice, who so fully epitomizes, externally at any rate, the English ideal of middle-class manliness. That he internally embodies a mode of sexual subjectivity which was cast as a countertype to normality works to undermine such normality and the naturalization of heterosexuality.

Chapter 7

Das Bildnis des Oskar Wilde

Looking back at the foundation of the *Wissenschaftlich-humanitäre Komitee*, in the 1902 edition of his treatise *Sappho und Sokrates; oder, Wie erklärt sich die Liebe der Männer und der Frauen zu Personen des eigenen Geschlechts?* (Sappho and Socrates; or, How Does One Explain the Love of Men and Women to Persons of Their Own Sex?, 1896), Hirschfeld cites the "lamentable" trials of the "English poet Oskar [*sic*] Wilde" as a major impetus toward organization (Hirschfeld 27–28; see also Herzer, *Magnus Hirschfeld* 53; Keilson-Lauritz, *Die Geschichte der eigenen Geschichte* 25; Ivory, "The Trouble with Oskar" 141–42). The Wilde scandal was not confined to the English-speaking world; indeed, it was an international phenomenon. A result of his notoriety is that, in Germany, Wilde experienced a literary renaissance. Sander Gilman writes that "Wilde's popularity in Germany grew almost in inverse proportion to its decline in Britain" ("Strauss, the Pervert, and Avant Garde Opera of the Fin de Siècle" 40). Before the trials, Wilde's aesthetic theories found some favorable reception, particularly in Austria (Bridgwater, "Some German Oscar Wildes" 237). The Austrian writer Hugo von Hofmannsthal can be counted amongst the early admirers of Wilde's aestheticism. By this point, though, only the essay in dialogue form "The Decay of Lying" (1891) had been translated into German. Yvonne Ivory points out that "Oscar Wilde was not a household name in Germany when the scandal broke," and therefore most of the journalists who reported on the scandal in the German press "found they needed to clarify who Wilde was" ("The Oscar Wilde Scandal in the German Press" 223). Only afterwards did the German-speaking world's fascination with Wilde truly begin (Kohlmayer and Krämer, "*Bunbury* in Germany" 189). Between 1900 and 1934, especially after André Gide's biographical essay "Hommage à Oscar Wilde" (1902, translated into German 1903) and the publication of *De Profundis* in German in 1905, there were more than 250 translations of Wilde's work, this totaling more than any other British writer except Shakespeare. During the 1903–04 theater season alone, there were 248 performances of his plays. The most widely performed was *Salomé*, with 111 performances, following Max Reinhardt's production in 1902 (Funke, *Oscar Wilde in Selbstzeugnissen und Bilddokumenten* 7). The Wilde estate became solvent and put in credit, writes H. Montgomery Hyde, in large part on account of "the royalties from German translations of his books and the receipts from productions of his plays in Germany." Hyde highlights the irony of this development: "The fact that Wilde's literary rehabilitation should have begun in so pronounced a manner in Germany would certainly have surprised the author, who was inclined to deride the Germans for being so serious-minded and lacking a sense of humour" (*Oscar Wilde* 380). Not only were the theater-going and reading public enthralled by Wilde, but many German-speaking writers were influenced by Wilde's aesthetic theories, explains Robert Vilain. "Wilde came to be seen in Germany and Austria as the very embodiment of one of the most fascinating aspects of the intellectual and aesthetic temper of his age, the aesthetic movement" ("Tragedy and the Apostle of Beauty" 174). These writers, including Mann, saw Wilde as an "apostle of beauty" and individualism challenging Victorian Philistinism (Vilain 187). Wilde became, writes Gilman, "the symbolic artist persecuted by the forces of aesthetic conservatism" (43).

In the wake of his trials and death, writers from across Europe, many of whom were man-loving men, began treating same-sex desire and homosexual characters in their fiction. In his essay, Wolfgang Popp examines the images of homosexuality the texts responding to Wilde's legacy create. The works he considers include, among others, André Gide's *L'Immoraliste* (*The Immoralist*, 1902), Stefan George's pederastic poetry, Mann's short story "Tonio Kröger" (1903), Herman Bang's novel *Mikaël* (Michael, 1904), Louis Couperus's novel *De berg van licht* (The Mountain of Light, 1905–06), and Mikhail Kuzmin's novel *Wings* (1906). For Popp, this moment of liberality was cut short by the Eulenburg Affair, Germany's own homosexual scandal. The denunciation of two leading advisors to Kaiser Wilhelm II, Prince Philipp zu Eulenburg-Hertefeld and Kuno Count von Moltke, in the journal *Die Zukunft* (*The Future*) by the editor Maximilian Harden in 1907 set off a series of court cases with an ensuing media circus (Steakley, "Iconography of a Scandal" 235). Like the Wilde trials, the Eulenburg affair made homosexuality a topic of public discourse, literally putting "homosexuality" into the dictionaries (Steakley, "Iconography" 251). Between these two events, the Wilde and Eulenburg affairs, Popp argues, "in this eleven year time frame, not only did the most eminent authors of the time engage with the topic of homosexuality more intensively than ever before, but they also formulated images of homosexual masculinity" ("In diesen gerade einmal elf Jahren haben sich nicht nur die bedeutendsten Autoren der Zeit intensiver als je zuvor mit dem Thema Homosexualität beschäftigt, sondern sie haben auch homosexuelle Männlichkeitsbilder entworfen"; "Zwischen Wilde-Prozess und Eulenburg-Affäre" 102). He identifies images of homo-masculinity ranging from reactions to the effeminacy model to rehabilitations of the homosexual aesthete and artist figure. An example of the latter is the character Ménalque in Gide's novel, a sort of nomad aesthete who speaks in epigrams (Gide, *The Immoralist* 74–78, 80–82, 83–86). Another is in Bang's novel, which has not been translated into English but is accessible to English-speaking audiences through Carl Theodor Dreyer's silent film adaptation, *Michael* (1924), in which the hero, the artist Claude Zoret, tragically loves Michael, his faithless muse/protégé. "The shock of the Wilde trials not only led, in the intellectual and literary milieux of Europe, to opposition to the discrimination and criminalization of homosexuality, but also produced in Germany the first emancipation movements of homosexual men. The Eulenburg Affair, which precipitated above all a political scandal, could only temporarily influence these developments" ("Der Schock der Wilde-Prozesse hat sich im Geistes- und Literaturleben ganz Europas nicht zuletzt dahin ausgewirkt, dass sich überall Widerstand gegen die Diskriminierung und Kriminalisierung der Homosexualität regt und in Deutschland die erste Emanzipationsbewegung homosexueller Männer entsteht. Die Eulenburg-Affäre, die vor allem einen politischen Skandal auslöste, konnte diese Entwicklungen nur vorübergehend beeinflussen"; Popp, "Zwischen Wilde-Prozess und Eulenburg-Affäre" 102). The recourse to coding and concealment of homosexual subject matter in literature published in the fallout of the second scandal was temporary, as is demonstrated, argues Popp, by the literary treatments of same-sex desire which flourished in the interwar era.

This chapter builds and expands on Popp's valuable claims. Since the timeframe his study considers, the period between 1895 and 1906, ends at the point when he argues that gay literature went temporarily back into the closet, it does not take into account the effect the later scandal had on further forming homosexual images and reinforcing homosexual roles. The Eulenburg Affair triggered wide-ranging shifts in and outside Germany. In France, for instance, homosexuality was called "le vice allemand" (the German vice) because it was perceived to be "more widespread there than in any other country in Europe" (Willy, *The Third Sex* 15). Berlin gained the appellation "Sodom-on-Spree," and Germans were called "Eulenbuggers." "In the men's toilets," Florence Tamagne writes, "homosexual come-ons took a new form: 'Do you speak German?'" (*A History of Homosexuality in Europe* 19). Both the Wilde trials and the affair, Steakley argues, "were labeling events that dramatically accelerated the emergence of the modern homosexual identity by stimulating and structuring public perceptions of sexual normalcy and abnormalcy" (Steakley, "Iconography" 235). Despite the backlash, "a subtle dialectic was at work tending to proliferate sexual practices and identities" (235). Not only did gay literature rebound, but the event certainly spurred greater literary treatments of homosexuality in much the same way that the Wilde scandal had done. One example of such a response is Gide's defense of the "normal pederast" in *Corydon* (1924), which makes reference to both the Wilde and Eulenburg scandals (Gide, *Corydon* 3, 8). This chapter considers the German responses to Wilde in Thomas Mann's *Der Tod in Venedig* and then John Henry Mackay's *Der Puppenjunge*, representing two different responses to the Wildean homosexual model. Whereas *Der Tod in Venedig* explores both the positive and negative sides of homosexual effeminacy, with its associations with aestheticism as a form of protest, Mackay's novel foregrounds masculine pederasty before other styles of same-sex sexuality.

Especially in Mann's early works, the ties that bind art with effeminacy and homoeroticism as products of decadence are recurrent themes. Amongst these works,

Der Tod in Venedig stands at the forefront, in which the exploration of decadence reaches its culmination. Hannelore Mundt writes that *Der Tod in Venedig* incorporates both the negative and the positive aspects of decadence: "decadence was presented as an artistic force that could produce art that transcends bourgeois norms and conventions. This ambivalence, bestowing both negative and positive meanings upon decadence, is a central key to our understanding of Aschenbach's departure from his bourgeois existence" (*Understanding Thomas Mann* 89). Wildean dandy-aestheticism figures prominently in this ambivalent treatment of decadence. Patrick Bridgwater and Robert Vilain, in their respective essays, discuss the importance of Oscar Wilde for Mann. Bridgwater points out that Mann's notebooks demonstrate the impact of Wilde and his aestheticism on the German writer's works. He writes that Mann certainly "had Wilde/Dorian Gray in mind when he produced the 'criminal' artist/aesthete figures (Tonio Kröger, Gustav von Aschenbach, Felix Krull) of whom Aschenbach is in a number of ways closest to Wilde/Gray, among them the fact that he illustrates Lord Henry's *mot* 'The only ways to get rid of a temptation is to yield to it'" ("Some German Oscar Wildes" 237). For Mann, writes Bridgwater, the dandy was an artist: both roles are necessarily egocentric, and like the artist, the dandy likes to relate to the public but prefers his own company. Mann was particularly fascinated by Wilde's dandyism. The idea that the artist/aesthete is not suited for ordinary life because the artistic temperament involves such a high degree of alienating self-awareness and narcissism, asserts Bridgwater, extends throughout Mann's oeuvre and is particularly important with regard to the portrayal of Aschenbach ("Some German Oscar Wildes" 238). Robert Vilain suggests that "Mann's homosexuality, largely suppressed throughout his life, may have been a factor in the fascination that Wilde exercised over him; he may have seen and admired a degree of courage in the face of public approbation that he could not himself muster" ("Tragedy and the Apostle of Beauty" 187). Their studies are valuable overviews which the first section of this chapter seeks to build upon by undertaking a close reading of Mann's classic in order to explore the manifestations of Wilde in the novella (see also Wilper "Wilde and the Model of Homosexuality in Mann's *Tod in Venedig*").

On the other hand, Mackay's designation of same-sex love as "nameless" in his writings suggests the influence of Wilde through his citation of "the Love that dare not speak its name" from Douglas's poem "Two Loves" (1894) (Douglas 297). Mackay explains in the introduction to *Die Bücher der namenlosen Liebe* that this form of love "since no name yet correctly names it today" (15) ("da kein Name sie heute recht noch nennt"; 13). And with this strategy, he circumvents the discursive baggage with which most contemporary names for love between males were laden. Mackay is not the only writer of the era to take up his pen in support of same-sex desire only to be confronted with a paucity of opprobrium-free nomenclature. Symonds writes in the introduction to "A Problem in Modern Ethics" by stating that he could "hardly find a name" for discussing same-sex love "which will not seem to soil this paper" (*Symonds and Homosexuality* 128), Carpenter coined the expression "homogenic love," and Elisar von Kupffer created "Lieblingminne." The term "pederasty" would carry with it connotations which Mackay would naturally have wanted to avoid (see J. Bauer, "On the Nameless Love and Infinite Sexualities" 9). Opting for namelessness was by no means an untested strategy (see Cocks, *Nameless Offences* 158–61), with Wilde's mobilization of Douglas's poem as perhaps the most famous instance. Wilde's highly publicized citation has "assumed quasi-mythic status," writes Richard Bozorth, as "a gesture of defiance against persecution" ("Naming the Unnameable" 203). Lawrence Danson writes that "In a century that could not name Wilde's love without making it 'unnatural,' the deferral of naming was a necessary act of resistance" ("Oscar Wilde, W. H., and the Unspoken Name of Love" 997). Walter Fähnders, Wolfgang Popp, and Hubert Kennedy write in reference to Mackay's works that the namelessness of homosexual love is a direct reference to Wilde (Fähnders, "Anarchism and Homosexuality in Wilhelmine Germany" 142; Popp, "Zwischen Wilde-Prozess und Eulenburg-Affäre" 95; Kennedy, *The Anarchist of Love* 11). J. Edgar Bauer, though, dissents from this assessment, arguing that "the motivation of Mackay's strategy of avoidance essentially differs from the one underlying Alfred Douglas's poetical periphrasis." He posits that "While Douglas stresses the shrinking back from daring to pronounce the 'true' name of homosexual love, Mackay refuses to name his love with the names offered to him by a Zeitgeist saturated by the displacements of Christian culture" ("On the Nameless Love and Infinite Sexualities" 10). Bauer distinguishes between two uses of namelessness: whereas Douglas is passive, "shrinking back" from articulating the name of same-sex love, Mackay is active in avoiding unsuitable naming systems. But read differently, "Two Loves" expresses, writes Bozorth, "the drive to put such love into language—to speak it in the face of forces that would make it *unspeakable* in every sense" (204). Even if Douglas does shrink back from naming homosexual love in the poem, as Bauer suggests, Wilde's citation most certainly does not. His courtroom defense deploys strategic namelessness in the same mode as Mackay; Wilde avoids the terms loaded with "the displacements of Christian culture," that is, sodomy, buggery, "gross indecency," as Mackay avoids similar terms, in addition to those that carry medico-psychopathological connotations, that is, "inversion," "homosexuality," "contrary sexual feeling."

Wilde's influence on the *Bücher der namenlosen Liebe* reaches beyond the designation of same-sex love as "nameless." In particular, *Der Puppenjunge* responds to Wilde's legacy in two key ways. On the one hand, the novel records a neophyte's entry into the homosexual underworld, coming across a wide range of homosexualities, including many that appear to be embodiments of the stereotypes of Wilde. Therefore, Wilde impacts the novel in regard to fictionalizing the models and archetypes of homosexuality coined during and in the wake of his trials. On the other hand, the novel responds to Wilde's aftermath in terms of reacting to effeminacy, taking this reaction further than Forster's and even Prime-Stevenson's novels. And thus it becomes evident in the second section of this chapter that there is a tension in the novel between its documentary navigation of Berlin's homosexual subcultures from Günther's perspective and the repudiation of these communities from Graff's perspective.

The Homosexual Rebels: Wilde and Aschenbach

Mann understood the seriousness that underlies dandyism and especially aestheticism, and this is why, in "Nietzsches Philosophie im Lichte unserer Erfahrung" ("Nietzsche's Philosophy in the Light of Recent History," 1947), he compares Wilde to Nietzsche. These two figures are leading voices in "the first head-on assault [of the European intelligentsia] upon the hypocritical morality of the middle-class Victorian age" (*Last Essays* 157) ("d[em] ersten Anrennen der europäischen Intelligenz gegen die verheuchelte Moral des viktorianischen, des bürgerlichen Zeitalters"; *Gesammelte Werke* 9: 691). Mann writes that many of Nietzsche's philosophical tenets could have appeared in Wilde's comedies, shocking and delighting audiences (158; 692), and, conversely, Wilde's epigrams are distinctively Nietzschen:

> When Wilde declares: "For, try as we may, we cannot get behind the appearance of things to reality. And the terrible reason may be that there is no reality in things apart from their appearances"; when he speaks of the "truth of masks" and the "decay of the lie"; when he bursts out: "To me beauty is the wonder of wonders. It is only shallow people who do not judge by appearances. The true mystery of the world is the visible, not the invisible"; when he calls truth something so personal that the same truth can never be recognized by two different minds; when he says: "Every impulse that we strive to strangle broods in the mind and poisons us . . . The only way to get rid of a temptation is to yield to it"; and: "Don't be led astray into paths of virtue!"—we cannot help seeing that all these quotations might have come from Nietzsche. (157–58)

> (Wenn Wilde erklärt: "For, try as we may, we cannot get behind the appearance of things to reality. And the terrible reason may be that there is no reality in things apart from their appearances"; wenn er von der "Wahrheit der Masken" und von dem "Verfall der Lüge" spricht, wenn er ausbricht: "To me beauty is the wonder of wonders. It is only shallow people who do not judge by appearances. The true mystery of the world is the visible, not the invisible"; wenn er die Wahrheit etwas so Persönliches nennt, daß niemals ein und dieselbe Wahrheit von zwei Geistern gewürdigt werden kann, wenn er sagt: "Every impulse that we strive to strangle broods in the minds and poisons us ... The only way to get rid of a temptation is to yield to it," und "Don't be led astray into paths of virtue!"—so könnte das alles sehr wohl bei Nietzsche stehen.; 691–92.)

For Mann, aestheticism is their protest against nineteenth-century moral hypocrisy. "It is curious, although comprehensible, that aestheticism was the first manifestation of the European mind's rebellion against the whole morality of the bourgeois age. Not for nothing have I coupled the names of Nietzsche and Wilde—they belong together as rebels, rebels in the name of beauty" (172) ("Es ist merkwürdig genug, obgleich wohl verständlich, daß die erste Form, in der der europäische Geist gegen die Gesamtmoral des bürgerlichen Zeitalters rebellierte, der Ästhetizismus war. Nicht umsonst habe ich Nietzsche und Wilde zusammen genannt—als Revoltierende, und zwar im Namen der Schönheit Revoltierende gehören sie zusammen"; 707). Although this essay was published thirty-five years after the novella, it gives the reader some indication of what may have been Mann's attitude to Wildean dandy-aestheticism when he created Aschenbach. Towards the end of the narrative, the protagonist, like Nietzsche and Wilde before him, becomes a "rebel in the name of beauty." But Aschenbach is not alone in this role. The first of these dandy-aesthete rebel characters is the old man whom Aschenbach encounters on the ship to Venice. This character is generally identified as a foreshadowing device which signals the protagonist's coming downfall, however, I argue here that the reader never receives an objective or unbiased description of this character. The narrative style is "erlebte Rede," or free indirect discourse, which means that the narrator reports immediately from Aschenbach's experience (Reed, Introduction 28), and thus our negative impression of him is as a result of Aschenbach's repulsion. His reaction to the dandy reflects more on the protagonist's gender and sexual identity, its potential to be undone, than it is an objective characterization of this figure. If the reader can assume that in the novella aestheticism is a form of rebellion, then Aschenbach's final transformation, rather than indicating his final disgrace before his death, could enact a will to freedom that challenges contemporary value systems. Death in this case is not Aschenbach's punishment for violating bourgeois norms, but instead his release from them.

    In the depictions of the two Wildean homosexuals, perception is skewed to the extent that the reader never can fully ascertain an unbiased sense of these characters. In the first instance, the reader experiences the aging dandy primarily through Aschenbach's perception and thus partakes in Aschenbach's disgust. In the second instance, the protagonist, the narrator, and the barber assess Aschenbach's transformation as a successful one, and yet the image persists that he has become a garishly made-up, maudlin old fool. The first scene occurs on the ship to Venice where Aschenbach feels a spasm of horror when he beholds that one of a group of young Italian men is not young at all, but instead that "the man's youth was false" (211) ("der Jüngling falsch war"; 79). "He was old, there was no mistaking it. There were wrinkles round his eyes and mouth. His cheeks' faint carmine was rouge, the brown hair under his straw hat with its coloured ribbon was a wig, his neck was flaccid and scrawny, his small stuck-on moustache and the little imperial on his chin were dyed, his yellowish full complement of teeth, displayed when he laughed, were a cheap artificial set, and his hands, with signet rings on both index fingers, were those of an old man" (211) ("Er war alt, man konnte nicht zweifeln. Runzeln umgaben ihm Augen und Mund. Das matte Karmesin der Wangen war Schminke, das braune Haar unter dem farbig umwundenen Strohhut Perücke, sein Hals verfallen und sehnig, sein aufgesetztes Schnurrbärtchen und die Fliege am Kinn gefärbt, sein gelbes und vollzähliges Gebiß, das er lachend zeigte, ein billiger Ersatz, und seine Hände, mit Siegelringen an beiden Zeigefingern, waren die eines Greises"; 79–80). This character differs to Aschenbach in some fundamental ways, first in clothing: the old dandy, "who wore a light yellow summer suit of extravagant cut, a scarlet necktie and a rakishly tilted Panama hat" (211) ("in hellgelbem, übermodisch geschnittenem Sommeranzug, roter Krawatte und kühn aufgebogenem Panama"; 79), contrasts to Aschenbach and his sober accoutrements. Second they differ in their public presence: of the high-spirited group of men, the dandy "was the most conspicuous of them all in his shrill hilarity" (211) ("tat sich mit krähender Stimme an Aufgeräumtheit vor allen andern hervor"; 79) which contrasts to the protagonist's dignified reserve. Finally, the dandy's unbounded sexuality, he was "full of wretched exuberance, clutching at everyone who approached him, . . . and licking the corners of his mouth with the tip of his tongue in a repellently suggestive way" (213) ("zeigte er einen jammervollen Übermut, hielt jeden, der sich ihm näherte, . . . und leckte auf abscheulich zweideutige Art mit der Zungenspitze die Mundwinkel"; 83), contrasts to Aschenbach's repression. The protagonist's strong emotional response indicates a reaction to a countertype to the form of manly austerity he has fashioned for himself. The text shows this character to be Aschenbach inverted. He haunts Aschenbach and twice causes him to feel a growing estrangement from the world. The first instance is after the protagonist discovers that "the man's youth was false". "He had a feeling that something not quite usual was beginning to happen, that the world was undergoing a dreamlike alienation, becoming increasingly deranged and bizarre" (211) ("Ihm war, als lasse nicht alles sich ganz gewöhnlich an, als beginne eine träumerische Entfremdung, eine Entstellung der Welt ins Sonderbare um sich zu greifen"; 80). And the second is after he notes the way in which the man licks the corners of his lips. "Aschenbach watched him with frowning disapproval, and once more a sense of numbness came over him, a feeling that the world war somehow, slightly yet uncontrollably, sliding into some kind of bizarre and grotesque derangement" (213) ("Aschenbach sah ihm mit finsteren Brauen zu, und wiederum kam ein Gefühl von Benommenheit ihn an, so, als zeige die Welt eine leichte, doch nicht zu hemmende Neigung, sich ins Sonderbare und Fratzenhafte zu entstellen"; 83). As Aschenbach disembarks onto the quay, the dandy accosts him with another suggestive sign (214; 84). But, as this character only seems to affect Aschenbach, there is the possibility that the character is not as horrifying as he perceives. After all, the man's companions not only tolerate him, but seem to accept his presence, and he causes no major concern for other passengers. His intense reaction indicates the threat this character poses to the protagonist as his antithesis. He represents decadence, aestheticism, dandyism, anti-bourgeois behaviors and values. The protagonist attempts to define himself against such a figure through his reverence for masculine virtues of self-sacrificing heroism, austerity, civic mindedness, and discipline, but this figure undermines his manly reserve. Aschenbach rejects a hidden potential, subconsciously recognized at most, the repressed elements of himself projected upon this figure (see also Webber, "Mann's Man's World" 74–75).

Aschenbach is insecure in his gender role, a fact which is made further evident by his attitude towards his profession, his calling as an artist. His art is described in terms of "a war, an exhausting struggle" (249) ("ein[em] Krieg, ein[em] aufreibende[n] Kampf"; 132), through which he attempts to justify his life. "A life of self-conquest and defiant resolve, an astringent, steadfast and frugal life which he had turned into the symbol of that heroism for delicate constitutions, that heroism so much in keeping with the times—surely he might call this manly, might call it courageous?" (249) ("Ein Leben der Selbstüberwindung und des Trotzdem, ein herbes, standhaftes und enthaltsames Leben, das er zum Sinnbild für einen zarten und zeitgemäßen Heroismus gestaltet hatte,—wohl durfte er es männlich, durfte es tapfer nennen?"; 132). The hallmark of Aschenbach's life and work is his effort to transform the production of art into a manly, proactive, and civic-minded undertaking by conquering its effeminate, egocentric, and asocial aspects. This was a site of anxiety, writes James Eli Adams, for many nineteenth-century writers. With intellectual labor during this century beginning to be characterized as an "unmanly" or "effeminate" pursuit, these writers drew upon modes of masculinity which were "understood as the incarnation of an ascetic regimen, an elaborately articulated program of self-discipline," one of which was that of the soldier (*Dandies and Desert Saints* 2). Aschenbach likens struggle in the name of art to the lives of Frederick the Great and Saint Sebastian. "For composure under the blows of fate, grace in the midst of torment—this is not only endurance: it is an active achievement, a positive triumph, and the figure of Saint Sebastian is the most perfect symbol if not of art in general, then certainly of the kind of art here in question" (205) ("Denn Haltung im Schicksal, Anmut in der Qual bedeutet nicht nur ein Dulden; sie ist eine aktive Leistung, ein positiver Triumph, und die Sebastian-Gestalt ist das schönste Sinnbild, wenn nicht der Kunst überhaupt, so doch gewiß der in Rede stehenden Kunst"; 72). Both are soldier figures (not to mention homosexual icons) who maintained their resolve in the face of adversity. Aschenbach idolizes the manliness "of a youth who clenches his teeth in proud shame and stands calmly on as the swords and spears pass through his body" (205) ("die in stolzer Scham die Zähne aufeinanderbeißt und ruhig dasteht, während ihr die Schwerter und Speere durch den Leib gehen"; 71–72). With these Olympian figures of manly virtue as his guides, Aschenbach produces civic-minded art which possesses moral weight. The style of its balanced classicism is held up as a model for German school boys.

In this struggle, his crowning achievement is his novel *Ein Elender* (*A Study in Abjection*), in which the "forthright words of condemnation . . . weighed vileness in the balance and found it wanting—they proclaimed their writer's renunciation of all moral scepticism, of every kind of sympathy with the abyss; they declared his repudiation of the laxity of that compassionate principle which holds that to understand all is to forgive all" (207) ("Die Wucht des Wortes, mit welchem hier das Verworfene verworfen wurde, verkündete die Abkehr von allem moralischen Zweifelsinn, von jeder Sympathie mit dem Abgrund, die Absage an die Laxheit des Mitleidssatzes, daß alles verstehen alles verzeihen heiße"; 74). Yet, as he pursues Tadzio through the labyrinth of Venice, Aschenbach is confronted with the conflict between his artistic nature and his paternal legacy. He gauges his life against his forebears' sobriety and manliness; they were "men who had spent their disciplined, decently austere life in the service of the King and the state" (202) ("Männer, die im Dienste des Königs, des Staates ihr straffes, anständig karges Leben geführt hatten"; 68). His ancestors, to him, represent the embodiment of moral and civic manliness. "And [Aschenbach] thought of them even here and now, entangled as he was in so impermissible an experience, involved in such exotic extravagances of feeling; he thought, with a sad smile, of their dignified austerity, their decent manliness of character. What would they say? But for that matter, what would they have said about his entire life, a life that had deviated from theirs to the point of degeneracy, this life of his in the compulsive service of art" (249) ("[Aschenbach] dachte ihrer auch jetzt und hier, verstrickt in ein so unstatthaftes Erlebnis, begriffen in so exotischen Ausschweifungen des Gefühls, gedachte der haltungsvollen Strenge, der anständigen Männlichkeit ihres Wesens und lächelte schwermütig. Was würden sie sagen? Aber freilich, was hätten sie zu seinem ganzen Leben gesagt, das von dem ihren so bis zur Entartung abgewichen war, zu diesem Leben im Banne der Kunst"; 132). This passage indicates that not only does Aschenbach fall short of his manly ideal whilst surrendering himself to his emotion and desire, but he has never, in his mind, been able to live up to it. That Aschenbach feels the need to clothe the production of art in notions of manliness and heroism indicates that he does not truly believe art to be an inherently masculine pursuit. The fact that he asks the question implies that the answer is no. If he believed it were true, then there would be no angst. And the struggle has been in vain. If Aschenbach is punished, it is not for his transgression of bourgeois norms, but for enslaving his emotions which take their revenge upon their master.

The second Wildean homosexual is Aschenbach himself after his metamorphosis at the hands of the hotel barber. Not long after he gives voice to his love, Aschenbach has a dream which is at the same time more than a dream, "a bodily and mental experience" (259) ("ein körperhaft-geistiges Erlebnis"; 146); he witnesses an orgy in honor of the foreign god, Dionysus, which Mann based on descriptions of Dionysian rites described by the classicist Erwin Rohde in his *Psyche: Seelencult und Unsterblichkeitsglaube der Griechen* (*Psyche: The Cult of Souls and the Belief in Immortality Among the Greeks*, 1894) (Lehnert, "Thomas Mann's Early Interest in Myth and Erwin Rohde's *Psyche*" 297, 299). Aschenbach is initially repulsed by and fears what he sees and hears: bare-breasted women entwined by snakes, hairy men with horns on their brows, smooth-skinned boys leading goats, chanting, shrieking, and drums beating a tattoo. "Great was his loathing, great his fear, honourable his effort of will to defend to the last what was his and protect it against the Stranger, against the enemy of the composed and dignified intellect" (260) ("Groß war sein Abscheu, groß seine Furcht, redlich sein Wille, bis zuletzt das Seine zu schützen gegen den Fremden, den Feind des gefaßten und würdigen Geistes"; 147). This dream is the point when he loses struggle that he has waged throughout his life: the struggle between reason and emotion, between intellect and intuition, between repression and sensuality. At first merely an observer, he yearns to join the rite like Pentheus in Euripides's *Bacchae*. "His heart throbbed to the drumbeats, his brain whirled, a fury seized him, a blindness, a dizzying lust, and his soul craved to join the round-dance of the god" (260) ("Mit den Paukenschlägen dröhnte sein Herz, sein Gehirn kreiste, Wut ergriff ihn, Verblendung, betäubende Wollust, und seine Seele begehrte, sich anzuschließen dem Reigen des Gottes"; 148). And when he finally releases the reins of self-control and joins them, "The dreamer now was with them and in them, he belonged to the stranger-god . . . and his very soul savoured the lascivious delirium of annihilation" (261) ("Mit ihnen, in ihnen war der Träumende nun und dem fremden Gotte gehörig . . . und seine Seele kostete Unzucht und Raserei des Unterganges"; 148), Aschenbach forsakes the last pretenses to the Apollonian intellect which had heretofore ordered his life, giving himself over to his darker, fierier urges.

After the dreams he embraces the dandy-aesthete role:

> Like any other lover, he desired to please and bitterly dreaded that he might fail to do so. He added brightening and rejuvenating touches to his clothes, he wore jewellery and used scent, he devoted long sessions to his toilet several times a day, arriving at table elaborately attired and full of excited expectation. As he beheld the sweet youthful creature who had so entranced him he felt disgust at his own ageing body, the sight of his grey hair and sharp features filled him with a sense of shame and hopelessness. He felt a compulsive need to refresh and restore himself physically; he paid frequent visits to the hotel barber. (261)

> (Wie irgendein Liebender wünschte er, zu gefallen und empfand bittere Angst, daß es nicht möglich sein möchte. Er fügte seinem Anzuge jugendlich aufheiternde Einzelheiten hinzu, er legte Edelsteine an und benutzte Parfums, er brauchte mehrmals am Tage viel Zeit für seine Toilette und kam geschmückt, erregt und gespannt zu Tische. Angesichts der süßen Jugend, die es ihm angetan, ekelte ihn sein alternder Leib, der Anblick seines grauen Haares, seiner scharfen Gesichtszüge stürzte ihn in Scham und Hoffnungslosigkeit. Es trieb ihn, sich körperlich zu erquicken und wiederherzustellen; er besuchte häufig den Coiffeur des Hauses; 149.)

The barber uses his art to transform Aschenbach, dying his hair and applying cosmetics to his skin: "with beating heart he saw himself as a young man in earliest bloom" (262) ("[er] erblickte mit Herzklopfen einen blühenden Jüngling"; 150). The barber declares, "Now the signore can fall in love as soon as he pleases" (263) ("Nun kann der Herr sich unbedenklich verlieben"; 150). It would seem, then, that Aschenbach's transformation has been a successful one. The protagonist, narrator, and barber seem to be pleased. For the reader, it is equivocal. For those of us influenced by the cinematic images of Luchino Visconti's 1971 film *Morte a Venezia* (*Death in Venice*), it is difficult not to be tempted to take Aschenbach's disgust projected at the dandified old man at face value and in turn interpret this physical transformation as a fulfilment of the prophecy embodied in that character. Visconti's vision is however only one interpretation. Was the man really so awful to behold? Does Aschenbach's transformation in the same way represent a horrid masquerade of youth? The equivocalness in the characterizations of both Wildean dandy figures makes these questions impossible to answer definitively.

The essay "The Painter of Modern Life" (1863), by Charles Baudelaire (1821–1867), can assist in interpreting Aschenbach's final transformation. The two figures, Baudelaire and Wilde, were not unconnected for Mann. He defends the aestheticism of both in his polemic *Betrachtungen eines Unpolitischen* (*Reflections of an Unpolitical Man*, 1918) (Vilain 238). Baudelaire characterizes dandyism as heroic, "the last flicker of heroism in decadent ages," and writes positively of the use of cosmetics ("The Painter of Modern Life" 39). Therefore, it might be possible to argue that, in similar terms, Aschenbach's use of this art form succeeds, as far as the protagonist, the narrator (at least at this point in the narrative), and the barber are concerned, in transcending nature, "to hide all the blemishes that nature has so outrageously scattered over the complexion" (46). He has "received at birth a spark of that sacred fire [he] would feign use to light up [his] whole being" (47), and in doing so he hopes to win the love of the divine Tadzio. Aschenbach makes his life into a work of art, although only briefly. The reader could view this embrace of his maternal legacy as a manner of liberation. "He no longer feared the observant eyes of other people; whether he was exposing himself to their suspicions he no longer cared" (261) ("Er scheute nicht mehr die beobachtenden Blicke der Menschen; ob er sich ihrem Verdacht aussetze, kümmerte ihn nicht"; 148). Suspicion for what, we might ask, for his homosexuality? He overcomes the shame he associates with the aspects of himself that he has worked to conquer, repress, and conceal from his conscious self and the world: his emotion, his intuition, his ability to love homosexually. At one level death is indeed a judgment upon Aschenbach, but on another level it is his liberator. And this may be a liberation he welcomes. For Baudelaire, "suicide is the supreme sacrament of dandyism" (Sartre, *Baudelaire* 140–41; see also Hiddleston, *Baudelaire and the Art of Memory* 67). When, in the frenzy of his intoxication, Aschenbach consumes "some fruit, some overripe soft strawberries" (264) ("einige Früchte, Erdbeeren, überreife und weiche"; 152) which are tainted, thereby infecting himself with cholera (Binion, *Sounding the Classics* 139), one could argue that he partakes of this final sacrament of the religion of dandyism.

Especially in the penultimate scene of the novella, the growing irony and distance toward the protagonist seems to condemn Aschenbach's liberation and discount the catharsis, which he reaches in the final Socratic monologue. It is the deranged product of "his half-asleep brain with its tissue of strange dream-logic" (264) ("sein[em] halb schlummernde[n] Hirn an seltsamer Traumlogik"; 153). Addressing his Tadzio/Phaedrus, Aschenbach repudiates the role of the artist as worthy citizen (264–65; 153), a repudiation which, as discussed in chapter 2, has significance for the Platonic relationship he imagines between himself and the boy. Moreover, this rejection speaks to the role of art and the artist in society. Aschenbach's art is utilitarian, civic, manly, but, at this point, he claims that art serves no moral function, art is amoral. "For I must tell you that we artists cannot tread the path of Beauty without

Eros keeping company with us and appointing himself as our guide" (265) ("Denn du mußt wissen, daß wir Dichter den Weg der Schönheit nicht gehen können, ohne daß Eros sich zugesellt und sich zum Führer aufwirft"; 153). The artist must follow where Eros leads, and thus the implication is that art is autotelic and divorced from utilitarianism or didacticism: art for art's sake. Hence, *Der Tod in Venedig* comments upon Wilde's legacy through its incorporation of dandy-aestheticism as well as by (at least in part) endorsing a Wildean understanding of art and the artist. Aschenbach, like Wilde, is a rebel in the name of beauty, undertaking an aestheticist rebellion against nineteenth-century moral hypocrisy, through which the novella conducts the most extensive treatment of the themes associated with Wilde's legacy of the four texts under discussion. And yet, the novella's treatment of the aesthetic homosexual model is an equivocal one. But it is this equivocal nature that invites the reader to reinterpret Aschenbach's apparent disgrace, downfall, and death. It opens the possibility of viewing this death not as a condemnation, but as liberation.

"Feasting with panthers" in Berlin

Eight years before Christopher Isherwood's camera-like gaze recorded Berlin tottering at the edge of an abyss, Mackay's novel offered vignettes of life in Berlin's gay bars. In an example of literary documentary, the novel captures a wide array of styles of homosexual subjectivity which had proliferated after the Wilde trials and the Eulenburg Affair, attesting to the impact of these scandals upon German homosexual subcultures and thus demonstrating their impact upon the novel. Kennedy writes that, in the course of 1924, Mackay frequented Berlin's gay bars to research male prostitute subcultures (*Anarchist of Love* 40–41). The styles that the novel captures are diverse; on one end of the social ladder is "the Count" ("der Herr Graf"), an aristocratic aesthete and homosexual voyeur. He collects Günther as an *objet d'art* and treats him to a life of idle, and uneventfully boring, luxury (*Hustler* 136–56; *Puppenjunge* 161–82). On the other end of said ladder is "the refined Atze" ("der feine Atze"), an interwar Berlin "panther" who lives for feasting and wrangling more money out of his clients. "There's no such thing as love," Atze instructs Günther, "At least it's never yet happened to me. But if it did—Chick, pay attention to what I'm telling you now—if one of them was to fall in love with me, I would really take advantage of him!" (75) ("Liebe gibt's überhaupt nicht. Mir wenigstens is se noch nich vorgekommen. Wenn es sie aber gibt—Hühnchen, pass' auf, was ich Dir jetzt sage:—wenn sich aber einal Einer in mich verlieben sollte, den würde ich schön hochnehmen!"; 84). Interaction in the subculture(s) occurs mostly in the gay lounges, the "Adonis Lounge" ("Adonis-Diele") being the most frequented in the novel, which was based on a real bar called the *Marienkasino* (Kennedy 40). Found there are homosexual pairs: "No one was allowed in without a necktie. Nor, of course, was any female admitted. Only toward evening, after nine, did it become really full. Many couples show up, always an older man and a younger. They sat together and no one approached them" (48) ("Ohne Kragen wurde Niemand hereingelassen.

Ebensoweinig natürlich ein weibliches Wesen. Erst gegen Abend, nach neun, wurde es richtig voll. Viele Paare, immer ein Älterer und ein Jüngerer, erschienen. Sie saßen zusammen und Keiner kam ihnen nah"; 53). These homosexual couples are part of this world, but, at the same time, they keep certain segments of this world, that is, the male prostitutes, at arm's length. They are a "respectable" element in this milieu, as is suggested by the emulation of heterosexual norms and the fact that they segregate themselves, they "sat together and no one approached them," in other words, the hustlers know that they are not interested in their services.

And, of course, there are the hustlers, the *Pupen-* or *Strichjungen*. "At mostly small tables sat more or less well-dressed, often over-elegant young men, many with affected manners and even wearing makeup, but others still quite vigorous and manly" (49) ("An den meist kleinen Tischen saßen mehr oder weniger gut, oft aber auch übermäßig elegant gekleidete junge Menschen, manche geziert in ihrem Wesen und sogar geschminkt, andere aber ganz frisch noch und männlich"; 53). On one end of a spectrum of hustler masculinity are the rough trade ("Kessen, Heißen, Starken"; 47), like "Karl the Great" ("Karl der Große"). He literary and figuratively towers over the other hustlers. "In a well-tailored suit of the best material, with his powerful, strong shoulders and his broad chest, his large, regular, handsome, and frank face, he stood there and, with a good-natured smile, looked down at the shrimps under him" (94) ("In gut gearbeitetem Anzug von besten Stoff, mit seinem mächtigen, starken Schultern und seiner bereiten Brust, mit seinem großen, regelmäßigen, hübschen und zugleich offenem Gesicht, stand er da und sah gutmütig lächelnd auf den Knirps unter ihm"; 107). There is also brutish "Sailor Otto" ("Matrosen-Otto"). "As his name indicated, he wore a sailor's uniform and one sensed under it his muscular and sinewy arms and legs. His exposed chest showed red and blue tattoos" (94) ("Er trug, wie sein Name es schon nicht anders zuließ, die Kuli-Kluft, und man fühlte unter ihr die muskulösen und sehnigen Arme und Beine. Die halbnackte Brust zeigte rote und blaue Tätowierungen"; 108). Even these masculine figures display an exaggerated quality, what was at this time in subcultures in English-speaking countries becoming known as a "camp" quality. For instance, "Sailor Otto had never been to sea" (94) ("Matrosen-Otto war nie zur See gewesen"; 108), his show of masculinity is all pretense concocted in order to attract a customer. While at the other end of this continuum are the "aunties" ("Tanten"). "An auntie," explains Atze, "well, that was just: 'Oooh nooo! an auntie—like girls when they're young and then just like old maids'" (47) ("Eine Tante—nun das war eben—huch nein!—eine Tante: 'wie die Mädchens, wenn se jung sind und dann ganz wie die ollen Weiber . . .'"; 51). Amongst the supporting cast, the *Tanten* greatly outnumber the rough trade. The novel contains a number of sketches and caricatures of effeminate characters. One of these is "Josie" ("Finchen"), an effeminate young man who works at a hotel in which Günther finds himself one morning. "In elegant pajamas, with leather slippers on his dainty feet, he came dancing in. . . . Josie's real name was Joseph, but since it would have been perverse to cal him Joe, he was more appropriately named Josie. He, or rather 'she,' occupied something like a confidential position at the hotel. She was porter and waiter at the same time, and was glad to be available (when paid, of course) as a substitute for the young guest, in case a gentleman arrived without one" (101) ("In einem hocheleganten Schlafanzug, Lederpantöffelchen an den zierlichen, nackten Füßen, kam er tänzelnd herein. . . . Finchen hieß eigentlich Joseph. Aber da es pervers gewesen ware, ihm Seppl zu rufen, wurde er zweckentsprechender Finchen genannt. Er, oder besser gesagt sie bekleidete hier so etwas wie einen Vertrauensposten, war Portier und Kellner zugleich, und vertrat gern und hingebend [wenn es sich lohnte natürlich] die Stelle der jungen Gäste, falls ein Herr einmal ohne einen solchen hier abstieg"; 116–17). These portrayals contribute to the documentary realism of the text and attest to how visible homosexual communities had become during the interwar period, but have little effect upon the story's plot. This ensemble represents a well-established stock of types, variations which came to be associated with the homosexual world through notable scandals, thus demonstrating their influence upon the formation of homosexual stereotypes held by the public at large as well as identities adopted and adapted by individuals within these communities.

The novella *Fenny Skaller: Ein Leben der namenlosen Liebe* also treats homosexual subcultures, but in contrast to the later novel merely peeps into the homosexual world beyond the narrow confines of the protagonist's liaisons. "What Skaller saw filled him with disgust and deep sadness" (150) ("Was Skaller sah, erfüllte ihn mit Ekel und tiefer Traurigkeit"; 266). The portrayal of the hubs of homosexual subcultures, the gay bars and the men who frequent them, is disparaging. Skaller's perception is reductionary and biased by his distaste for effeminacy. The portions of *Der Puppenjunge* narrated from Graff's perspective are also biased, but not to the same extent as Skaller's. Graff's reaction to one of the novel's *Tanten* demonstrates this. The character is a work colleague and everything that the reader knows about him is second hand, filtered through Graff's reaction to him—comparable to Aschenbach's response to the old dandy on the ship to Venice. This character has tried to befriend Graff, but his offers have been evaded. When the protagonist is convicted for violating Paragraph 175, this man again offers friendship and is the only one to show sympathy. A physical impression of him comes to the reader through his hand, which is soft and boneless. This hand is a synecdoche. He gripped Graff's hand "with a sympathetic pressure" (275) ("mit einem teilnehmenden Druck"; 318). "He could not even return the pressure of this hand, so soft and boneless did it lie in his" (275) ("Er konnte selbst den Druck dieser Hand nicht erwidern, so weich, so knochenlos lag sie in der seinen"; 318). Whereas harmlessly effete and effeminate characters are described by the narrator in other parts of the novel, the reader only experiences the work colleague through Graff. "He had something (not exactly slimy, but clinging), something specifically effeminate in his whole conduct, which he could not endure for the life of him" (274) ("Er hatte so etwas—(nicht grade Schleimiges, aber doch Anschmiegendes)—so etwas spezifisch Weibisches in seinem ganzen Wesen, das er nun einmal auf den Tod nicht vertragen konnte"; 317). The difference between this *Tante* and the others is that whereas the others are oddities with whom neither Günther nor Graff sense affinity or kinship, the work colleague recognizes, through unnamed signs, Graff's sexuality and pursues his friendship based on this. This connection, as well as the potential that he is giving off these signals, is threatening to Graff. The colleague offers support and shows solidarity with him, but his advances are rebuffed. So far Graff's interaction within the subculture has been limited to his liaison with Günther, sitting alone at the *Adonis-Diele*, and searching for Günther when he disappears with Pipel, another boy-prostitute. The work colleague could offer access to a circle of man-loving men with whom Graff might actually be able to relate as equals in terms of education, social class, tastes, and interests. But he resists an association with this character and the community to which he belongs. "He suspected a world in which he did not belong and with which he had nothing in common. A small world of its own—full of various connections, special and particular interests, and endless idle gossip" (282) ("Er ahnte eine Welt, in die er nicht gehörte, und mit der er Nichts gemein hatte. Eine kleine, eigene Welt—voll mannigfacher Beziehungen, besonderen und eigentümlichen Interessen, und endlosem Klatsch und Tratsch"; 326). Like Skaller's refusal to identify with the subjects of the sexological study (*Bücher der namenlosen Liebe* 214–15), Graff resists identifying himself and his desire with a community of men with whom the only commonality is their shared desire for their own sex.

The central characters of *Imre* are also averse to identifying with and participating in effeminate homosexual subcultures: "how sordid and debasing are the average associations of the homosexual kind, how likely to be wanting in idealism, in the exclusiveness, in those pure and manly influences which ought to be bound up in them and to radiate from them!" (*Imre* 120). Imre is as disparaging of other homosexuals as Fenny Skaller. Imre "had grown to have a horror of similisexual types, of all contacts with them" (120). It is not too different in *Maurice* either, the way that Clive and Maurice regard "Risley and his set" (*Maurice* 56). Where the aversion experienced by Graff differs from those shared by Oswald and Imre and Clive and Maurice is in how they employ this in forming the boundaries of their identities. Whereas, in the English-language texts, the characters distance themselves from the effeminacy model by arguing that homosexuals are not necessarily effeminate, in the books of the nameless love the protagonists' mode of desire and related identity are posited as simply different. In *Imre*, effeminate homosexuals are regarded begrudgingly as fellow tribesmen; and Maurice is able to begin to understand his desires by at first identifying them with Risley, the effeminate Wildean character. By contrast, in *Der Puppenjunge*, as well as in *Fenny Skaller*, this is not the case. The earlier text makes this claim more explicitly: "to seek to line up here men who differ from other men in nothing but that their inclination is for the younger of their own, instead of the other sex, and only for this reason, was an absurdity only still possible in a time like ours, which allows only doctors to have the word in this matter. A new error, fateful above all for those whom it touched" (*Books* 148) ("Männern, die sich in Nichts von anderen Männern unterschieden, als darin, daß ihre Neigung den Jüngeren ihres eigenen Geschlechtes galt, anstatt dem anderen, hier einzureihen zu versuchen, und nur deshalb, war eine Lächerlichkeit und möglich allein in einer Zeit noch, wie dieser, die nur Aerzten erst das Wort in dieser Sache gestallete. Ein neuer Irrthum, verhängnißvoll vor Allem für Die, welche er traf"; *Bücher* 263–64). Nonetheless the sentiment is common to both texts. The protagonists of Mackay's fiction resist being classified with other men based on same-sex desire. It is ironic then that a work of fiction that does so much to chronicle homosexual life during interwar Berlin's Golden Twenties is also a text which insists that the protagonist is not actually like those others. They may share attraction to their own sex, but the narrative consistently reinforces the difference between the desire "of the man with a feminine disposition, or perhaps better said, of the outwardly masculine female who is inclined to men" (148) ("des weiblich gearteten Mannes, oder, wohl besser gesagt, des äußerlich männlich gearteten Weibchens, das sich dem Manne gab"; 263) and that of the manly love of the protagonists, "the ancient love of the Greeks" (148) ("die alte Liebe der Hellenen"; 263). Thus the books of the nameless love go further than even *Imre* in their opposition to the effeminacy model. Whereas the protagonists of that text acknowledge their kinship with effeminate homosexuals as members of "the Race-Homosexual" (*Imre* 86), Skaller and Graff insist upon the recognition of the specificity of their love. Although the novel records and perpetuates homosexual images and stereotypes, it seeks to deconstruct the homosexual as a subspecies of human and instead to argue for divisions that are specific to the individuals concerned. The boy-lover is manly and "normal," not at all like those depraved effeminate beings. Indeed, theirs is a completely different mode of desire, and thus the nameless love deserves to be regarded as a love like any other and accepted by the mainstream.

Conclusion

Mann's portrayal of Aschenbach can be taken to read some of the aspects of a Wildean legacy—particularly effeminacy, dandyism, aestheticism—positively in a mode of social critique. In this reading, Aschenbach is a sort of Nietzschean renegade against the narrow standards of contemporary bourgeois morality. But this endorsement of the protagonist's will to liberation is balanced against his apparent punishment for his desire to transgress moralistic strictures. Above I consider Aschenbach the homosexual artist as a tragic hero who, although he may have failed in his attempt, makes fathomable at least the possibility of living at odds with or even outside of conventional moral structures. And thus, Mann's literary response to Wilde and what he came to represent is the most faceted of the texts explored in this section.

Although Mackay's *Der Puppenjunge* is a vivid documentation of Berlin's interwar homosexual world, the novel and the other nameless love writings take the strategy of foregrounding masculine models of same-sex subjectivity a step further than the English texts explored in the previous chapter. The protagonists in the books of the nameless love resist being placed alongside other men with whom their only commonality is same-sex desire. Instead they deconstruct the rubric "homosexual" and insist upon recognizing the specificity of the desire of a masculine man for a masculine youth within "the tremendous variety of love" (*Books* 125) ("der ungeheuren Verschiedenheit der Liebe"; *Bücher* 223). Hence, rather than argue that effeminacy is not indicative of moral, social, or physical disintegration—or alternately revel in the subversiveness of their crossing of genders, class divisions, and national barriers—*Der Puppenjunge* remains locked within the ideological framework offered to it by its heteronormative society. It accepts a manly/effeminate binary where the former embodies all that is good, vital, and healthy whereas the latter is bad, ineffectual, and morbid. The novel goes to great lengths to argue for the masculinity of the homosexual man and makes this argument to the point of misogyny. Similar to *Imre*, and somewhat to *Maurice*, the images of homo-masculinity on offer in *Der Puppenjunge* function to provide homosexual readers with affirmative images and to challenge the established stereotypes of mainstream readers. These aims are accomplished, especially in Prime-Stevenson's and Mackay's writings, at the cost of discounting effeminacy, censuring nongender-specific behaviors and interests, and thereby reifying the superior social worth of maleness and manliness.

Afterword

For much of the nineteenth century, homosexuality was the sin so terrible that it could not be mentioned and, when it was named, was designated by terms loaded with opprobrium: the Sin of Sodom, "gross indecency," and "widernatürliche Unzucht" ("unnatural sex act"). By the end of the century, there existed a plethora of rivaling sets of designations for these passions. "Greek love" was revived and reinvented, medico-scientific terms and concepts were conceived and theorized, and, as a result of his trials for gross indecency, "Oscar Wilde" became a signifier and stereotype. This study argues that, from this discursive landscape, the gay novel emerged. Despite their differences, the four works of fiction under scrutiny here were part of a movement that brought open and, above all, affirmative portrayals of same-sex passions into literary discourse. They adopt aspects of particular conceptual and taxonomical structures, oppose others, help to perpetuate and develop them, while challenging and expanding these cultural and scientific discursive formations. In the early twentieth century, this love dared to speak its name and did so openly for the first time in the novel.

There is a great deal of overlap, much exchange and interaction, between the discourses which this study scrutinizes. For starters, the religio-legal formation, the societies' default discourses, are a pervasive social force to which the formations of Greek love, sexology and the Wildean discourse react. As well, Greek love was to direct greatly sexological discourse in the form of nomenclature owing to Ulrichs. And Oscar Wilde drew upon Greek love, but employed it to reach different ends to John Addington Symonds and Edward Carpenter. While Symonds disapproved of "the morbid and perfumed manner of treating such psychological subjects" as Wilde had done in *The Picture of Dorian Gray* (qtd. in Grosskurth, *The Woeful Victorian* 267), Wilde was an admirer of Symonds. Wilde looked upon Symonds as an authority on Greek love; and, in his expanded version of "The Portrait of Mr. W. H.," Lawrence Danson points out, "Symonds actually makes an appearance" ("Oscar Wilde, W. H., and the Unspoken Name of Love" 993; see Wilde, *The Portrait of Mr W.H.* 43–44). Furthermore, there is also commonality between Wilde and the *Gemeinschaft der Eigenen* and Mackay in terms of philosophies of Individualism (Ivory, "The Trouble with Oskar" 146–47). And finally, Walt Whitman was an indispensable influence upon Symonds and Carpenter (and thus Forster by way of the English Uranians), Wilde, Prime-Stevenson, Mann, and the many writers associated with Adolf Brand's journal *Der Eigene* (including Mackay), who took from the "love of comrades" very different visions of love between men. In summation, this epilogue considers the ways in which the three cross-cultural discourses of male same-sex love explored separately in the study are interwoven in each of the four literary texts and thereby draw some larger conclusions about these works and the rise of the gay novel.

Aspects of both sexology and Wilde's writings belong to fin-de-siècle decadence. Despite the more progressive attitude that Richard von Krafft-Ebing assumed in his research of same-sex sexualities as the nineteenth century drew to a close, his *Psychopathia Sexualis* still regarded nonnormative sexual desire as disease, resultant from the degrading effects of modern life. Wilde, along with such writers as Charles Baudelaire, Théophile Gautier (1811–1872), and others, was a central figure in literary decadence of this period. Thus there is some overlap in my readings of Mann's *Der Tod in Venedig* in chapters 4 and 7, where I explore the novella's engagement with discourses of pathology and aestheticism, respectively. Degeneration and art, disease and beauty, and death and love go hand in hand. The impact of late nineteenth-century degenerationist sexology and that of Wildean aestheticism upon the novella are analyzed in two separate chapters. This treatment better allowed for the comparison with and contrast to the other works of fiction discussed here, but it would be possible to consider them one after the other. Sexual science provides for the formation of an intermediate-sexed individual, one with "an incorrigible and natural tendency toward the abyss" (265) ("eine[r] unverbesserliche[n] und natürliche[n] Richtung zum Abgrunde"; 153), one whose intermediacy in terms of gender and sexuality grants him, though, a "brilliant endowment in art, especially music, poetry" (Krafft-Ebing, *Psychopathia Sexualis* 223) ("glänzende Begabung für schöne Künste, besonders Musik, Dichtkunst"; Krafft-Ebing, *Psychopathia Sexualis* 243). This figure is a Wildean dandy-aesthete, a rebel in the name of beauty, whom Aschenbach becomes in the wake of his dream of the Dionysian orgy. Aschenbach's struggle has been waged equally against disease and unmanliness, his own delicate constitution and intermediate gender and sexuality being part and parcel of one another.

In the course of *Der Tod in Venedig*, Aschenbach attempts to draw upon discourses of Hellenism to channel his desire so as to render it compatible with his life as the revered and ennobled *Dichter*. But Greek love only proves to undermine his bourgeois manly reserve. Aschenbach concludes in his final Platonic monologue "that we artists cannot tread the path of Beauty without Eros keeping company with us and appointing himself as our guide" (265) ("daß wir Dichter den Weg der Schönheit nicht gehen können, ohne daß Eros sich zugesellt und sich zum Führer aufwirft"; 153). Aschenbach succumbs to this briefly in the narrative, creating a work of "exquisite prose" (240) ("erlesener Prosa"; 119) and then feels shame for his "debauch" (240) ("Ausschweifung"; 119). Attempts to repress or refashion desire only lead directly back to that desire and to the abyss. "We try to achieve dignity by repudiating that abyss, but whichever way we turn we are subject to its allurement"

(265) ("Wir möchten ihn wohl verleugnen und Würde gewinnen, aber wie wir uns wenden mögen, er zieht uns an"; 153–54). Repudiating the abyss by way of the pursuit of Beauty is no repudiation, but leads "to intoxication and lust" ("zum Rausch und zur Begierde"): "they lead a noble mind into terrible criminal emotions, which his own fine rigour condemns as infamous; they lead, they too lead, to the abyss" (265) ("[sie] führen den Edlen vielleicht zu grauenhaftem Gefühlsfrevel, den seine eigene schöne Strenge als infam verwirft, führen zum Abgrund, zum Abgrund auch sie"; 154). Greek love is not a means for containing same-sex desire, as Aschenbach attempts to employ it in the narrative. It is not a way of rendering such desire compatible with his identity as the author of manly, civic-minded prose; rather, Greek love releases this desire.

Comrade love, rejections of homosexual effeminacy, and the third-sex theory of homosexuality are as interlinked in Prime Stevenson's *Imre* as they are in Forster's *Maurice*. Whitman's belief in comradely "adhesiveness" which he communicates in his verse influences the same-sex partnership depicted in Prime-Stevenson's text between Oswald and Imre. Theirs is a love "between two manly souls [that] was no mere ideal; but instead, a possible crown of existence, a glory of life, a realizable unity that certain fortunate sons of men attained!" (78). Theirs is a love inspired by Whitman, "one of the prophets and priests of homosexuality" whose verse is pervaded with "neo-hellenic, platonic democracy" (*The Intersexes* 377). Carpenter and Merrill's partnership, which also took cues from Whitman, directs the relationship between Maurice and Alec. It was on Forster's "second or third visit to the shrine," to Millthorpe, that "the spark was kindled" that became *Maurice*. Forster writes in the novel's terminal note that the comrades "combined to make a profound impression on me and to touch a creative spring" (215; see also Moffat, *E. M. Forster* 113–14). In the novel, Carpenter and Merrill's love becomes Maurice's devotion to his "friend" that he dreams of as a boy and later realizes with Alec. "He could die for such a friend, he would allow such a friend to die for him; they would make any sacrifice for each other, and count the world nothing, neither death nor distance nor crossness could part them" (12). At the end of the novel, Maurice and Alec disappear into the greenwood; they, as well as Oswald and Imre, are like the comrades of Whitman's "Calamus" poem, "Long I thought that knowledge alone would suffice me": "It is to be enough for us that we are together—We never separate again" (Whitman, *The Complete Poems* 609).

Whitman also inspired, directly and indirectly, the masculine identities depicted in the novels. This influence is direct in *Imre*, and indirect, filtered through Carpenter, in *Maurice*. The health and manliness of the Uranians in the novels negate psychopathological conceptions of homosexuality (as are explored in chapter 5) as well as effeminate models (which are explored in chapter 6). The third-sex theory, which is based upon Ulrichs's hypothesis of a female psyche confined in a male body, would seem to be antithetical to the manly, Whitmanian program. Indeed, John Fletcher writes, in regard to *Maurice*, that it is ("Forster's Self-Erasure" 73–74). Yet this supposed "contradiction between Ulrichs and Whitman" (Fletcher 73) creates no dissonance in the work of Symonds, Carpenter, Prime-Stevenson, and Forster because for Ulrichs the soul, not the body, of the third-sex individual belonged to the other sex. In "A Problem in Modern Ethics," in which Symonds discusses Ulrichs and Whitman, one after the other, as "Literature—Polemical" (*Symonds and Homosexuality* 175–94) and "Literature—Idealistic" (194–202), he writes that "Ulrichs maintains that the body of an Urning is masculine, his soul feminine, so far as sex is concerned" (180). By soul he means the Uranian's "passions, inclinations, sensibilities, emotional characteristics," but primarily his "sexual desires" (181). The souls of the main characters of *Imre* and *Maurice*, despite the value the texts place upon manliness of these figures, betray elements which at this time were marked as "feminine," not only in the "sexual desires" of the characters. While Oswald narrates from the assumption that Imre is heterosexual, the eponymous protagonist seems "a striking example of contradictions and inequations" (53): he is sensitive to aesthetic stimulation, particularly to music, but at the same time he is a military officer, renowned for his physical and martial abilities, the possessor of a "Hellenic exterior" (52). When he relinquishes his "mask" and admits to his homosexuality, he explains that he bears "the psychic trace of the woman" (125). He suffers from his belief that being a man and being "more feminine in impulse" are mutually exclusive. Oswald reproves Imre for this (125) because his gender and sexuality is a source of strength rather than something "base and vile" "to be crushed out" (119). And yet, in this novel, while affirming the importance of so-called "feminine virtues" in the protagonists, the deranged and "womanish" types of homosexuals are feared; Oswald says: "Those, *those*, terrified me, Imre!" (86). This terror, in contrast, is not present in Forster's *Maurice*. Carpenter's work on the intermediate sex is remarkably similar to Prime-Stevenson's, especially in regard to its use of Whitman and Greek love legacies and its incorporation of the third sex theory to argue the worth of intersexed Uranians. Although Maurice does not consciously conceive of himself as belonging to the third sex in the way that Oswald does, there are subtle indicators in the text which suggest the influence of Carpenter's theory of sexual intermediaries. These include Maurice's sensitive nature and his willingness to sacrifice for his "friend." The novel does not affirm the protagonist's masculinity by devaluing effeminacy in others. Unlike the "womanish beings" against which Oswald marks the boundaries of his identity, the Wildean figure, Risley, in *Maurice* is an essential point of reference for the protagonist as he gropes his way toward an authentic identity.

Mackay's nameless love writings depict same-sex love as "self-evident" and "natural": the protagonist Graff "did not trouble himself for an explanation where there was nothing to explain. What was self-evident, natural, and not in the least sick did not require an excuse through an explanation" (*Hustler* 158) ("[Graff] bemühte sich aber nicht um Erklärung, wo es Nichts zu erklären gab.—Was selbstverständlich, natürlich und nicht im Geringsten krankhaft war bedurfte nicht der Entschuldigung durch eine Erklärung"; *Puppenjunge* 184). Because it is a love like any other, the nameless love needs neither an excuse nor an explanation from Greek love (as is discussed in chapter 2) or from science (as discussed in chapter 4). Mackay argues in the introduction to *Die Bücher der namenlosen Liebe*, "Die Geschichte eines Kampfes um die namenlose Liebe," that the two failing points of homosexual liberation, up to that point, were turning to the ancient past and science for answers and defense.

> Mistakes and errors have been made that must absolutely be avoided. *Two above all.* In reaction to a persecution that had increased until it was unbearable, it has been sought to represent this love as special, as "nobler and better." It is not. This love is a love like any other love, not better, but also not worse. . . . A second mistake has been made that, in my eyes, is more disastrous than these others. This love, persecuted by judges and cursed by priests, has fled to the medical doctors as if it were a sickness that could be cured by them. But it is no sickness. Doctors have as little to look for and examine here as judges, and those who have accepted it as a sickness are mistaken if they believe they can free themselves from the clutches of power by making a pact with this power. (44–45)

> (Fehler und Irrthümer sind begangen worden, die unbedingt vermieden werden müssen. Zwei vor Allen. Man hat, im Umschlag gegen eine bis zur Unerträglichkeit gesteigerte Verfolgung, versucht, diese Liebe als eine besondere hinzustellen, als eine "edlere und bessere." Das ist sie nicht. Diese Liebe ist eine Liebe, wie jede andere Liebe, nicht besser, aber auch nicht schlechter. . . . Endlich aber ist ein Irrthum begangen worden, verhängnißvoller in meinen Augen, als alle anderen. Diese Liebe, verfolgt von den Richtern und verflucht von den Priestern hat sich zu den Ärzten geflüchtet, als sei sie eine Krankheit, die von ihnen geheilt werden könne. Aber sie ist keine Krankheit. Ärzte haben hier so wenig zu suchen und zu untersuchen, wie Richter, und die sich ihrer angenommen haben wie keiner Kranken, irren sich, wenn sie glauben, sie könnten sie aus den Fängen der Gewalt befreien, indem sie mit dieser Gewalt paktieren; 62–63.)

Mackay states plainly that turning to science is "more calamitous" ("verhängnißvoller") than the other. The third-sex theory, in particular, seems threatening in Mackay's writings because of its implication of effeminacy. In this way, *Der Puppenjunge* rejects the Victorian notion that love for a man is an essentially feminine drive. This contrasts this novel to Prime-Stevenson's. For all of Oswald's affirmations that the homosexual man represents the apex of manliness, there is "one thing which keeps such a 'man' back from [the] possibility of ever becoming integrally male" (96), which is his desire for other men. Mackay rejects this most contentious aspect of the third-sex theory: its reification of gender norms by accepting society's assumption that love for a man is essentially a feminine impulse. Mackay was not alone in this rejection but, unlike many of his contemporaries in the GdE, he did not argue against sexology through a revived form of Greek love, the renaissance of *Lieblingminne*. His fiction presents not a universalizing, but a minoritizing vision of love between males. Mackay's fiction progresses further than the others in depicting love and desire between men beyond cultural-historical and medical paradigms. The point where this writing program fails is his repudiation of other styles of same-sex sexuality, such as Wildean models that are distinguished by effeminacy, which although is less prevalent in *Der Puppenjunge* than in the earlier work *Fenny Skaller*, nevertheless directs the portrayals of homosexual identity in the nameless love writings. They, similar to *Imre* and even to some extent to *Maurice*, promote conformity to traditional gender roles by reifying, rather than challenging, the social worth of masculinity.

There was a movement underway in the late nineteenth and early twentieth centuries that made the heretofore "unspeakable" speakable and a subject of serious discourse. The four works of fiction explored in this study—Prime-Stevenson's *Imre*, Mann's *Der Tod in Venedig*, Forster's *Maurice*, and Mackay's *Der Puppenjunge*—stand at the vanguard of the corresponding literary movement that not only demanded to speak the name of this love, but made it the focus of influential and even great art. The literary texts thematize, problematize, and react to societal, scientific, and literary discourses, creating a broader space for depicting love between men. These novels are four prominent examples of the emergence of the gay novel. They set the stage for the next generation of homosexual writings in which many of the same issues and discourses would be fictionalized. Indeed, the discourses explored in these four works of fiction continue to impact gay writings: from efforts to reconcile religion and homosexuality, especially the fight for marriage equality, to (re)connections with and (re)constructions of a gay past in historical fiction and nonfiction, to scientific endeavors to discover the "gay gene," to the radical "queer" and assimilative dialectic. As long as these discourses are a part of our culture, they will continue to influence and direct the stories we tell about ourselves.

Works Cited

Ackerley, J. R. *My Father and Myself*. London: Bodley Head, 1968.
Adams, James Eli. *Dandies and Desert Saints: Styles of Victorian Manhood*. London: Cornell UP, 1995.
Adams, Stephen D. *The Homosexual as Hero in Contemporary Fiction*. London: Vision Press, 1980.
Aldrich, Robert. *Colonialism and Homosexuality*. London: Routledge, 2003.
---. *Seduction of the Mediterranean: Writing, Art, and Homosexual Fantasy*. London: Routledge, 1993.
Aldrich, Robert, and Gary Wotherspoon, eds. *Who's Who in Gay and Lesbian History: From Antiquity to World War II*. 2001. London: Routledge, 2002.
Allen, Robert H. *The Classical Origins of Modern Homophobia*. London: McFarland, 2006.
Ammerer, Heinrich. *Am Anfang war die Perversion: Richard von Krafft-Ebing: Psychiater und Pionier der modernen Sexualkunde*. Vienna: Styria, 2011.
Archer, John, and Barbara Lloyd. *Sex and Gender*. Cambridge: Cambridge UP, 2002.
Ardis, Ann. "Hellenism and the Lure of Italy." *The Cambridge Companion to E. M. Forster*. Ed. David Bradshaw. Cambridge: Cambridge UP, 2007. 62–76.
Auden, W. H. "An Improbable Life." *Oscar Wilde: A Collection of Critical Essays*. Ed. Richard Ellmann. London: Allen, 1970. 116–37.
Austen, Roger. *Playing the Game: The Homosexual Novel in America*. Indianapolis, IN: Bobbs-Merrill, 1977.
Bailey, Quentin. "Heroes and Homosexuals: Education and Empire in E. M. Forster." *Twentieth Century Literature* 48.3 (2002): 324–47.
Bakshi, Parminder Kaur. *Distant Desire: Homoerotic Codes and the Subversion of the English Novel in E. M. Forster's Fiction*. New York: Peter Lang, 1996.
Bartlett, Neil. *Who was that Man? A Present for Mr Oscar Wilde*. London: Serpent's Tail, 1988.
Baudelaire, Charles. *The Painter of Modern Life*. Trans. P. E. Charvet. London: Penguin, 2010.
Bauer, Heike. *English Literary Sexology: Translations of Inversion, 1860–1930*. Basingstoke: Palgrave Macmillan, 2009.

---. "'Not a translation but a mutilation': The Limits of Translation and the Discipline of Sexology." *The Yale Journal of Criticism* 16.2 (2003): 381–405.

---. "'Race,' Normativity and the History of Sexuality: Magnus Hirschfeld's *Racism* and Early Twentieth-Century Sexology." *Psychology and Sexuality* 1.3 (2010): 239–49.

Bauer, J. Edgar. "On the Nameless Love and Infinite Sexualities." *Journal of Homosexuality* 50.1 (2005): 1–26.

Beachy, Robert. "The German Invention of Homosexuality." *The Journal of Modern History* 82.4 (2010): 801–38.

Beccalossi, Chiara. *Female Sexual Inversion: Same-Sex Desires in Italian and British Sexology, 1870–1920*. Basingstoke: Palgrave Macmillan, 2012.

Beemyn, Brett Genny. "The Americas: From Colonial Times to the 20th Century." *Gay Life and Culture: A World History*. Ed. Robert Aldrich. London: Thames & Hudson, 2006. 145–65.

Beerbohm, Max. "1880." *The Works of Max Beerbohm*. Project Gutenberg, 2008. Kindle edn.

Binion, Rudolph. *Sounding the Classics: From Sophocles to Thomas Mann*. London: Praeger, 1997.

Blazek, Helmut. *Rosa Zeiten für rosa Liebe: Zur Geschichte der Homosexualität*. Frankfurt a.M.: Fischer, 1996.

Boa, Elizabeth. "Global Intimations: Cultural Geography in *Buddenbrooks*, *Tonio Kröger*, and *Der Tod in Venedig*." *Oxford German Studies* 35.1 (2006): 21–33.

Böhm, Karl Werner. *Zwischen Selbstzucht und Verlangen: Thomas Mann und das Stigma Homosexualität: Untersuchungen zu Frühwerk und Jugend*. Würzburg: Königshausen & Neumann, 1991.

Boes, Maria R. "On Trial in Early Modern Germany." *Sodomy in Early Modern Europe*. Ed. Tom Betteridge. Manchester: Manchester UP, 2002. 27–45.

Booth, Howard J. "Maurice." *The Cambridge Companion to E. M. Forster*. Ed. David Bradshaw. Cambridge: Cambridge UP, 2007. 173–87.

Boswell, John. *Christianity, Social Tolerance, and Homosexuality: Gay People in Western Europe from the Beginning of the Christian Era to the Fourteenth Century*. Chicago: U of Chicago P, 1980.

Bowden, James. "Education, Ideology, and the Ruling Class: Hellenism and English Public Schools in the Nineteenth Century." *Rediscovering Hellenism: The Hellenic Inheritance and the English Imagination*. Ed. G. W. Clarke. Cambridge: Cambridge UP, 1989. 161–86.

Bozorth, Richard R. "Naming the Unnameable: Lesbian and Gay Love Poetry." *The Cambridge Companion to Gay and Lesbian Writing*. Ed. Hugh Stevens. Cambridge: Cambridge UP, 2011. 202–17.

Brady, Sean, ed. Introduction. *John Addington Symonds and Homosexuality: A Critical Edition of Sources*. Basingstoke: Palgrave Macmillan, 2012. 1–38.

---. *Masculinity and Male Homosexuality in Britain, 1861–1913*. Basingstoke: Palgrave Macmillan, 2005.

Bray, Alan. "Homosexuality and the Signs of Male Friendship in Elizabethan England." *Queering the Renaissance*. Durham: Duke UP, 1994. 40–61.

Breen, Margaret. "Homosexual Identity, Translation, and Prime-Stevenson's *Imre* and *The Intersexes*." *CLCWeb: Comparative Literature and Culture* 14.1 (2012): <http://dx.doi.org/10.7771/1481-4374.1786>.

Bremmer, Jan. "Greek Pederasty and Modern Homosexuality." *From Sappho to De Sade: Moments of the History of Sexuality*. Ed. Jan Bremmer. London: Routledge, 1989. 1–14.

Bridgwater, Patrick. "Some German Oscar Wildes." *The Importance of Reinventing Oscar: Versions of Wilde During the Last 100 Years*. Ed. Julie Hibbard. Amsterdam: Rodopi, 2002. 237–48.

Brinkley, Edward S. "Fear of Form: Thomas Mann's *Der Tod in Venedig*." *Monatshefte* 91.1 (1999): 2–27.

Brinkschröder, Michael. *Sodom als Symptom: Gleichgeschlechtliche Sexualität im christlichen Imaginären—eine religionsgeschichtliche Anamnese*. Berlin: De Gruyter, 2006.

Bristow, Joseph. "'A Complex and Multiform Creature': Wilde's Sexual Identities." *The Cambridge Companion to Oscar Wilde*. Ed. Peter Raby. Cambridge, Cambridge UP, 1997. 195–218.

---. *Effeminate England: Homoerotic Writing After 1885*. New York: Columbia UP, 1995.

---. "Homosexual Writing on Trial: from *Fanny Hill* to *Gay News*." *The Cambridge Companion to Gay and Lesbian Writing*. Ed. Hugh Stevens. Cambridge: Cambridge UP, 2011. 17–33.

---, ed. Introduction. *Wilde Writings: Contextual Conditions*. Toronto: U of Toronto P, 2003. 1–38.

---. "Picturing His Exact Decadence: The British Reception of Oscar Wilde." *The Reception of Oscar Wilde in Europe*. Ed. Stefano Evangelista. London: Continuum, 2010. 20–50.

---. *Sexuality*. 1997. London: Routledge, 2011.

---. "Symonds's History, Ellis's Heredity: Sexual Inversion." *Sexology in Culture: Labelling Bodies and Desires*. Ed. Lucy Bland and Laura L. Doan. Chicago: U of Chicago P, 1998. 79–99.

Bronski, Michael. *Culture Clash: The Making of Gay Sensibility*. Boston: South End Press, 1984.

Brookes, Les. *Gay Male Fiction since Stonewall: Ideology, Conflict, and Aesthetics*. London: Routledge, 2009.

Brown, Catherine. "What Is 'Comparative' Literature?" *Comparative Critical Studies* 10.1 (2013): 67–88.

Bruns, Claudia. *Politik des Eros: Der Männerbund in Wissenschaft, Politik und Jugendkultur (1880–1934)*. Cologne: Böhlau, 2008.

"Buggery of a Mare." *The Proceedings of the Old Bailey, 1674–1913*. April 2013. 18 June 2014. <http://www.oldbaileyonline.org/browse.jsp?id=t16770711-2-of-f7&div=t16770711-2#highlight>.

"Buggery with a certain Mungril Dog." *The Proceedings of the Old Bailey, 1674–1913*. April 2013. 18 June 2014. < http://www.oldbaileyonline.org/browse.jsp?id=t16770711-1-off4&div=t16770711-1#highlight >.

Busch, Frank. *August Graf von Platen, Thomas Mann: Zeichen und Gefühle*. Munich: Fink, 1987.

Bush, Jeff. "'I'd rather be dirty': The Queering of the Greenwood in E. M. Forster's *Maurice*." *Dandelion: Postgraduate Arts Journal & Research Network* 4.1 (2013): 1–13 <http://dandelionjournal.org/index.php/dandelion/article/view/104>.

Calloway, Stephen. "Wilde and the Dandyism of the Senses." *The Cambridge Companion to Oscar Wilde*. Ed. Peter Raby. Cambridge, Cambridge UP, 1997. 34–54

Carpenter, Edward. *The Intermediate Sex: A Study of Some Transitional Types of Men and Women*. London: Swan Sonnenschein, 1908.

---. *Ioläus: An Anthology of Friendship*. London: Swan Sonnenschein, 1906.

---. *My Days and Dreams, Being Autobiographical Notes*. London: Allen & Unwin, 1916.

Casper, Johann Ludwig. "Über Nothzucht und Päderastie und deren Ermittlung seitens des Gerichtsarztes." *Vierteljahrschrift für gerichtliche und öffentliche Medizin* 1.1 (1852): 21–78. Repr. in *Der unterdrückte Sexus: Historische Texte zur Homosexualität*. Ed. Joachim S. Hohmann. Lollar: Achenbach, 1977.

Cavafy, C. P., *Collected Poems*. Trans. Edmund Keelcy and Philip Sherrard. London: Chatto & Windus, 1990.

Chauncey, George. *Gay New York: Gender, Urban Culture, and the Makings of the Gay Male World, 1890–1940*. New York: Basic Books, 1994.

Chester, Lewis, David Leitch, and Colin Simpson. *The Cleveland Street Affair*. London: Weidenfeld & Nicolson, 1977.

Cocks, H. G. *Nameless Offences: Homosexual Desire in the Nineteenth Century*. London: Tauris, 2003.

---. "Secrets, Crimes, and Diseases: 1800-1914." *A Gay History of Britain: Love and Sex Between Men since the Middle Ages*. Ed. Matt Cook, Randolph Trumbach, and H. G. Cocks. Oxford: Greenwood World Publishing, 2007. 107–44.

Cohen, Ed. *Talk on the Wilde Side: Toward a Genealogy of a Discourse on Male Sexualities*. London: Routledge, 1992.

---. "Writing Gone Wilde: Homoerotic Desire in the Closet of Representation." *PMLA: Publications of the Modern Language Association of America* 102.5 (1987): 801–13.

Cohn, Dorrit. "The Second Author of *Der Tod in Venedig*." *Critical Essays on Thomas Mann*. Ed. Inta M. Ezergailis. Boston: G. K. Hall, 1988. 124–43.

Connon, Bryan. *Beverley Nichols: A Life*. Portland: Timber Press, 2000.

Cook, Matt. *London and the Culture of Homosexuality, 1885–1914*. Cambridge: Cambridge UP, 2003.

Works Cited

Copley, Anthony. *A Spiritual Bloomsbury: Hinduism and Homosexuality in the Lives and Writing of Edward Carpenter, E. M. Forster, and Christopher Isherwood.* Oxford: Lexington Books, 2006.

Crompton, Louis. *Homosexuality & Civilization.* London: Belknap, 2003.

Crozier, Ivan D., ed. "Introduction: Havelock Ellis, John Addington Symonds and the Construction of *Sexual Inversion.*" Havelock Ellis and John Addington Symonds, *Sexual Inversion: A Critical Edition.* Basingstoke: Palgrave Macmillan, 2008. 1–86.

---. "The Medical Construction of Homosexuality and Its Relation to the Law in Nineteenth-Century England." *Medical History* 45.1 (2001): 61–82.

---. "Pillow Talk: Credibility, Trust and the Sexological Case History." *History of Science* 46.4 (2008): 375–404.

Curr, Matthew. "Recuperating E. M. Forster's *Maurice.*" *Modern Language Quarterly* 62.1 (2001): 53–69.

Danson, Lawrence. "Oscar Wilde, W. H., and the Unspoken Name of Love." *English Literary History* 58.4 (1991): 979–1000.

---. "Wilde as Critic and Theorist." *The Cambridge Companion to Oscar Wilde.* Ed. Peter Raby. Cambridge, Cambridge UP, 1997. 80–95.

Davenport-Hines, R. P. T. *Sex, Death and Punishment: Attitudes to Sex and Sexuality in Britain since the Renaissance.* London: Collins, 1990.

Davidson, James N., *The Greeks and Greek Love: A Radical Reappraisal of Homosexuality in Ancient Greece.* London: Weidenfeld & Nicolson, 2007.

Death in Venice. Dir. Luchino Visconti. Perf. Dirk Bogarde and Björn Andrésen. 1971. Warner Home Video, 2004. DVD.

Dellamora, Richard. *Masculine Desire: The Sexual Politics of Victorian Aestheticism.* Chapel Hill: U of North Carolina P, 1990.

---, ed. *Victorian Sexual Dissidence.* Chicago: U of Chicago P, 1999.

D'Emilio, John, and Estelle B. Freedman. *Intimate Matters: A History of Sexuality in America.* Chicago: U of Chicago P, 1988.

Denisoff, Dennis. *Aestheticism and Sexual Parody, 1840–1940.* Cambridge: Cambridge UP, 2001.

Derks, Paul. *Die Schande der heiligen Päderastie: Homosexualität und Öffentlichkeit in der deutschen Literatur 1750–1850.* Berlin: Rosa Winkel, 1990.

Detering, Heinrich. *Das offene Geheimnis: Zur literarischen Produktivität eines Tabus von Winckelmann bis zu Thomas Mann.* Göttingen: Wallstein, 1994.

Deuse, Werner. "'Besonders ein antikisierendes Kapitel scheint mir gelungen': Griechisches in *Der Tod in Venedig.*" *Heimsuchung und süßes Gift : Erotik und Poetik bei Thomas Mann.* Ed. Gerhard Härle. Frankfurt a.M.: Fischer, 1992. 41–66.

Dierks, Manfred. "Thomas Mann und die Tiefenpsychologie." *Thomas-Mann-Handbuch.* Ed. Helmut Koopmann. 1990. Stuttgart: Kröner, 2001. 284–300.

Different from the Others (Anders als die Andern). Dir. Richard Oswald. Perf. Conrad Veidt and Fritz Schulz. 1919. Kino International, 2004. DVD.

Dines, Martin. *Gay Suburban Narratives in American and British Culture: Homecoming Queens*. Basingstoke: Palgrave Macmillan, 2010.

Dollimore, Jonathan. "Perversion, Degeneration, and the Death Drive." *Sexualities in Victorian Britain*. Ed. Andrew H. Miller and James E. Adams. Bloomington: Indiana UP, 1996. 96–117.

---. *Sexual Dissidence: Augustine to Wilde, Freud to Foucault*. Oxford: Clarendon Press, 1991.

Dose, Ralf. "The World League for Sexual Reform: Some Possible Approaches." Trans. Pamela Selwyn. *Sexual Cultures in Europe: National Histories*. Ed. Franz Eder, Lesley A. Hall, and Gert Hekma. Manchester: Manchester UP, 1999. 242–59.

Douglas, Alfred. "Two Loves." *The Columbia Anthology of Gay Literature: Readings from Western Antiquity to the Present Day*. Ed. Byrne R. S. Fone. New York: Columbia UP, 1998. 295–97.

Dover, Kenneth J. *Greek Homosexuality*. Cambridge: Harvard UP, 1978.

Dowling, Linda. *Hellenism and Homosexuality in Victorian Oxford*. Ithaca: Cornell UP, 1994.

Doylen, Michael R. "Oscar Wilde's *De Profundis*: Homosexual Self-Fashioning on the Other Side of Scandal." *Victorian Literature and Culture* 27.2 (1999): 547–66.

Dyer, Richard. *Now You See It: Studies in Lesbian and Gay Film*. 2nd ed. London: Routledge, 2003.

Duberman, Martin B., Martha Vicinus, and George Chauncey, Jr. eds. *Hidden from History: Reclaiming the Gay and Lesbian Past*. Ed. London: Penguin, 1991.

Duc, Aimée. *Sind es Frauen? Ein Roman über das dritte Geschlecht*. Berlin: Amazonen-Frauenverlag, 1976.

Duggan, Lisa. *Sapphic Slashers: Sex, Violence, and American Modernity*. Durham: Duke UP, 2001.

Eder, Franz X. "Sexual Cultures in Germany and Austria, 1700–2000." *Sexual Cultures in Europe: National Histories*. Ed. Franz X. Eder, Lesley A. Hall, and Gert Hekma. Manchester: Manchester UP, 1999. 138–72.

"Edgar Miller, Sexual Offences > sodomy, 3rd May 1886." *The Proceedings of the Old Bailey, 1674–1913*. April 2013. 18 June 2014. <http://www.oldbaileyonline.org/browse.jsp?id=t18860503-541-offence-1&div=t18860503-541#highlight>.

Elfenbein, Andrew. *Romantic Genius: The Prehistory of the Homosexual Role*. New York: Columbia UP, 1999.

Ellem, Elizabeth Wood. "E. M. Forster's Greenwood." *Journal of Modern Literature* 5.1 (1976): 89–98.

Ellis, Havelock. *My Life*. London: Heinemann, 1940.

---. *Studies in the Psychology of Sex, Vol. 2, Sexual Inversion*. 3rd edn. Philadelphia: F.A. Davis, 1924.

Ellis, Havelock, and John Addington Symonds. *Sexual Inversion: A Critical Edition*. Ed. Ivan D. Crozier. Basingstoke: Palgrave Macmillan, 2008.

Ellmann, Richard, ed. "Introduction: The Critic as Artist as Wilde." *The Artist as Critic: Critical Writings of Oscar Wilde*. London: Allen, 1970. ix–xxviii.

---. *Oscar Wilde*. London: Penguin, 1987.

Endres, Nikolai. "Failures of Love: Plato and Platonism in E. M. Forster, Thomas Mann, and André Gide." Diss. University of North Carolina, Chapel Hill, 1999.

Eskridge, William N. *Dishonorable Passions: Sodomy Laws in America, 1861– 2003*. New York: Viking, 2008.

Euripedes. *Bakkhai*. Trans. Anne Carson. London: Oberon Books, 2015.

Evangelista, Stefano. "'Lovers and Philosophers at Once': Aesthetic Platonism in the Victorian 'Fin de Siècle.'" *The Yearbook of English Studies* 36.2 (2006): 230–44.

Fähnders, Walter. "Anarchism and Homosexuality in Wilhelmine Germany: Senna Hoy, Erich Mühsam, John Henry Mackay." *Journal of Homosexuality* 29.2 (1995): 117–53.

Feuerlicht, Ignace. "Thomas Mann and Homoeroticism." *Germanic Review* 57.3 (1982): 89–97.

Fitzroy, A. T. [Rose Allatini] *Despised and Rejected*. Ed. Brett Rutherford. Providence: Yogh & Thorn, 2010.

Fletcher, John. "Forster's Self-Erasure: *Maurice* and the Scene of Masculine Love." *Sexual Sameness: Textual Differences in Lesbian and Gay Writing*. Ed. Joseph Bristow. London: Routledge, 1992. 64–90.

Fone, Byrne R. S., ed. "The Criminal Law Amendment Act of 1885." *The Columbia Anthology of Gay Literature: Readings from Western Antiquity to the Present Day*. New York: Columbia UP, 1998. 335.

---. *Homophobia: A History*. New York: Metropolitan, 2000.

---. *A Road to Stonewall: Male Homosexuality and Homophobia in English and American Literature, 1750–1969*. New York: Twayne Publishers, 1995.

Forster, Bill. [Herman Breuer] *Anders als die Andern*. Hamburg. Männerschwarm. 2009.

Forster, E. M. *Howards End*. Ed. David Lodge. London: Penguin, 2000.

---. *The Life to Come, and Other Stories*. London: Norton, 1987.

---. *Maurice*. Ed. Philip Gardner. London: Deutsch, 1999.

---. *A Passage to India*. Ed. by Oliver Sallybrass. London: Penguin, 2000.

---. *Selected Short Stories*. Ed. David Leavitt and Mark Mitchell. London: Penguin, 2001.

Foucault, Michel. *The History of Sexuality, Volume 1, The Will to Knowledge*. Trans. Robert Hurley. London: Penguin, 2008.

---. "On the Genelogy of Ethics: An Overview of Work in Progress." *The Foucault Reader: An Introduction to Foucault's Thought*. Ed. Paul Rabinow. Harmondsworth: Penguin, 1984. 340–72.

Fout, John C. "Sexual Politics in Wilhelmine Germany: The Male Gender Crisis, Moral Purity, and Homophobia." *Journal of the History of Sexuality* 2.3 (1992): 388–421.

Freedman, Jonathan. *Professions of Taste: Henry James, British Aestheticism, and Commodity Culture.* Stanford: Stanford UP, 1990.

Freud, Sigmund. *Drei Abhandlungen zur Sexualtheorie.* Ed. Lothar Bayer and Hans-Martin Lohmann. Stuttgart: Reclam, 2010.

---. *On Sexuality: Three Essays on the Theory of Sexuality and Other Works.* Ed. Angela Richards. London: Penguin, 1991.

Friedländer, Benedict, *Renaissance des Eros Uranios: Die physiologische Freundschaft, ein normaler Grundtrieb des Menschen und eine Frage der männlichen Gesellungsfreiheit: in naturwissenschaftlicher, naturrechtlicher, culturgeschichtlicher und sittenkritischer Beleuchtung.* Berlin: Renaissance, 1904.

Funke, Peter. *Oscar Wilde in Selbstzeugnissen und Bilddokumenten.* Reinbeck: Rowohlt, 1969.

Furbank, P. N. *E. M. Forster: A Life.* 2 vols. London: Secker & Warburg, 1979.

Gardner, Philip, ed. *E. M. Forster: The Critical Heritage.* London: Routledge and Kegan Paul, 1973.

Garton, Stephen. *Histories of Sexuality.* London: Equinox, 2004.

"gay, *adj.*, *adv.* and *n.*" OED Online. OED Third Edition, March 2008. Oxford UP. 18 June 2014. <http://www.oed.com/view/Entry/77207>.

George, Stefan. *Gedichte.* Ed. Ernst Osterkamp. Frankfurt a.M.: Insel, 2005.

Gide, André. *Corydon.* Trans. Richard Howard. Swaffham: Gay Men's Press, 1998.

---. *The Immoralist.* Trans. David Watson. London: Penguin, 2000.

Gifford, James J. *Dayneford's Library: American Homosexual Writing, 1900-1913.* Amherst: U of Massachusetts P, 1995.

---, ed. Introduction and Notes. Edward Prime-Stevenson. *Imre: A Memorandum.* Peterborough: Broadview Press, 2003. 13–26.

---. "What Became of *The Intersexes*?" *The Gay & Lesbian Review Worldwide*, 18.5 (2011): 18 June 2014. <http://www.glreview.org/article/what-became-of-the-intersexes/ >.

Gilman, Sander L. "Strauss, the Pervert, and Avant Garde Opera of the Fin de Siècle." *New German Critique* 43 (1988): 35–68.

Grau, Günter, ed. *Hidden Holocaust?: Gay and Lesbian Persecution in Germany 1933–45.* Trans. Patrick Camiller. London: Cassell, 1995.

Green, Martin. *Children of the Sun: A Narrative of "Decadence" in England After 1918.* 1976. London: Pimlico, 1992.

Greenberg, David F. *The Construction of Homosexuality.* Chicago: U of Chicago P, 1988.

Greenberg, David F., and Marcia H. Bystryn. "Christian Intolerance of Homosexuality." *American Journal of Sociology* 88.3 (1982): 515–48.

Greenslade, William P. *Degeneration, Culture, and the Novel, 1880–1940.* Cambridge: Cambridge UP, 1996.

---. "Fitness and the Fin de Siècle." *Fin de Siècle/ Fin du Globe: Fears and Fantasies of the Late Nineteenth Century.* Ed. John Stokes. Basingstoke: Macmillan, 1992. 37–51.

Works Cited

Grosskurth, Phyllis. *The Woeful Victorian: A Biography of John Addington Symonds*. New York: Holt, Rinehart, and Winston, 1964.

Guldin, Rainer. *Lieber ist mir ein Bursch ... Zur Sozialgeschichte der Homosexualität im Spiegel der Literatur*. Berlin: Rosa Winkel, 1995.

---. *Verbrüderung: J. A. Symonds, E. Carpenter, E. M. Forster: Literarische Porträts*. Berlin: Rosa Winkel, 1991.

Guy, Josephine M. "'The Soul of Man under Socialism': A (Con) Textual History." *Wilde Writings: Contextual Conditions*. Ed. Joseph Bristow. Toronto: U of Toronto P, 2003. 59–85.

Guy, Josephine M., and Ian Small. *Studying Oscar Wilde: History, Criticism, and Myth*. Greensboro: ETL Press, 2006.

Härle, Gerhard. *Männerweiblichkeit: Zur Homosexualität bei Klaus und Thomas Mann*. Frankfurt a.M.: Athenäum, 1988.

Hall, Lesley A. *Sex, Gender, and Social Change in Britain since 1880*. London: Macmillan, 2000.

---. "Sexual Cultures in Britain: Some Persisting Themes." *Sexual Cultures in Europe: National Histories*. Ed. Franz X. Eder, Lesley A. Hall, and Gert Hekma. Manchester: Manchester UP, 1999. 38–42.

Hall, Radclyffe. *The Well of Loneliness*. London: Virago, 2001.

Halperin, David M. "Forgetting Foucault: Acts, Identities, and the History of Sexuality." *Representations* 63 (1998): 93–120.

---. *One Hundred Years of Homosexuality: And Other Essays on Greek Love*. London: Routledge, 1990.

Hammond, Paul. *Love Between Men in English Literature*. Basingstoke: Macmillan, 1996.

Harned, Jon. "Becoming Gay in E. M. Forster's *Maurice*." *Papers on Language and Literature* 29.1 (1993): 49–66.

Hartland, Claude. *The Story of a Life: For the Consideration of the Medical Fraternity*. San Francisco: Grey Fox Press, 1985.

Hays, Richard B. *The Moral Vision of the New Testament: A Commentary Introduction to New Testament Ethics*. London: T&T Clark, 1996.

Heilbut, Anthony. *Thomas Mann: Eros and Literature*. London: Macmillan, 1996.

Heine, Gert and Paul Schommer. *Thomas Mann Chronik*. Frankfurt a.M.: Vittorio Klostermann, 2004.

Hekma, Gert. "'A Female Soul in a Male Body': Sexual Inversion as Gender Inversion in Nineteenth-Century Sexology." In *Third Sex, Third Gender: Beyond Sexual Dimorphism in Culture and History*. Ed. Gilbert Herdt. New York: Zone Books, 1994. 213–40.

Helminiak, Daniel A. *What the Bible Really Says about Homosexuality*. San Francisco: Alamo Square, 1994.

Henry, Seán. "August Graf von Platen und *Der Tod in Venedig*." *Thomas Manns "Der Tod in Venedig": Wirklichkeit, Dichtung, Mythos*. Ed. Frank Baron and Gert Sautermeister. Lübeck: Schmidt-Römhild, 2003. 27–50.

Herrero-Brasas, Juan A. *Walt Whitman's Mystical Ethics of Comradeship: Homosexuality and the Marginality of Friendship at the Crossroads of Modernity.* Albany: SUNY Press, 2010.

Herzer, Manfred. "Communists, Social Democrats, and the Homosexual Movement in the Weimar Republic." *Journal of Homosexuality* 29.2 (1995): 197–226.

---. "Kertbeny and the Nameless Love." *Journal of Homosexuality* 12.1 (1986): 1–26.

---. *Magnus Hirschfeld: Leben und Werk eines jüdischen, schwulen, und sozialistischen Sexologen.* Frankfurt a.M.: Campus, 1992.

"homosexuality, *n.*" *OED Online.* OED Second Edition, 1989. Oxford UP. 18 June 2014. <http://www.oed.com/view/Entry/88111>.

Hichens, Robert Smythe. *The Green Carnation.* Ed. Stanley Weintraub. Lincoln, NE: U of Nebraska P, 1970.

Hiddleston, J. A. *Baudelaire and the Art of Memory.* Oxford: Clarendon, 1999.

Hirschfeld, Magnus. *Die Homosexualität des Mannes und des Weibes.* 1914. Berlin: Marcus, 1920.

---. *The Homosexuality of Men and Women.* Trans. Michael A. Lombardi-Nash. Amherst: Prometheus, 2000.

---. *Sappho und Sokrates; oder, Wie erklärt sich die Liebe der Männer und der Frauen zu Personen des eigenen Geschlechts?* 1896. Leipzig: Spohr, 1902. Repr. in *Documents of the Homosexual Rights Movement in Germany, 1836–1927.* New York: Arno Press, 1975.

Homunkulus. *Zwischen den Geschlechtern: Roman einer geächteten Leidenschaft.* Ed. Albert Knoll and Wolfram Setz. Hamburg: Männerschwarm, 2012.

Hubbard, Thomas K. "Pederasty and Democracy: The Marginalization of a Social Practice." *Greek Love Reconsidered.* Ed. Thomas K. Hubbard. New York: Wallace-New Hampton, 2000. 1–11.

Hull, Isabel V. *Sexuality, State, and Civil Society in Germany, 1700–1815.* Ithaca: Cornell UP, 1996.

Hutter, Jörg. "The Social Construction of Homosexuals in the Nineteenth Century: The Shift from the Sin to the Influence of Medicine on Criminalizing Sodomy in Germany." *Journal of Homosexuality* 24.3/4 (1993): 73–93.

Hyde, H. Montgomery. *The Cleveland Street Scandal.* London: W.H. Allen, 1976.

---. *Oscar Wilde: A Biography.* London: Penguin, 1976.

---. *The Trials of Oscar Wilde.* New York: Dover Publications, 1973.

Irvine, Janice M. *Disorders of Desire: Sex and Gender in Modern American Sexology.* Philadelphia: Temple UP, 1990.

Isherwood, Christopher. *Christopher and His Kind.* Minneapolis: U of Minnesota P, 2001.

Ivory, Yvonne. "'Aus Anlass eines Sensationsprozesses': The Oscar Wilde Scandal in the German Press." *Seminar: A Journal of Germanic Studies* 48.2 (2012): 218–39.

---. *The Homosexual Revival of Renaissance Style, 1850–1930.* Basingstoke: Palgrave Macmillan, 2009.

---. "The Trouble with Oskar: Wilde's Legacy for the Early Homosexual Rights Movement in Germany." *Oscar Wilde and Modern Culture: The Making of a Legend*. Ed. Joseph Bristow. Athens, OH: Ohio UP, 2008. 133–53.

---. "The Urning and His Own: Individualism and the Fin-de-Siècle Invert." *German Studies Review* 26.2 (2003): 333–52.

---. "Wilde's Renaissance: Poison, Passion, and Personality." *Victorian Literature and Culture* 35.2 (2007): 517–36

Jellonek, Burkhard. *Homosexuelle unter dem Hakenkreuz: Die Verfolgung von Homosexuellen im Dritten Reich*. Paderborn: Schöningh, 1990.

Jenkyns, Richard. *The Victorians and Ancient Greece*. Oxford: Blackwell, 1980.

Jennings, Theodore W., Jr. *Plato or Paul?: The Origins of Western Homophobia*. Cleveland: Pilgrim Press, 2009.

Jofen, Jean. "A Freudian Commentary on Thomas Mann's *Death in Venice*." *Journal of Evolutionary Psychology* 6.3/4 (1985): 238–49.

Jonas, Ilsedore B. *Thomas Mann and Italy*. Trans. Betty Crouse. Tuscaloosa: U of Alabama P, 1979.

Jones, James W. *"We of the Third Sex": Literary Representations of Homosexuality in Wilhelmine Germany*. New York: Peter Lang, 1990.

Jones, Norman W. *Gay and Lesbian Historical Fiction: Sexual Mystery and Post-Secular Narrative*. Basingstoke: Palgrave Macmillan, 2007.

Jordan, Mark D. *The Invention of Sodomy in Christian Theology*. Chicago: U of Chicago P, 1997.

Kane, Michael. *Modern Men: Mapping Masculinity in English and German Literature, 1880–1930*. London: Cassell, 1999.

Kaplan, Morris B. *Sodom on the Thames: Sex, Love, and Scandal in Wilde Times*. Ithaca: Cornell UP, 2005.

Katz, Jonathan Ned. *Gay American History: Lesbians and Gay Men in the U.S.A.: A Documentary History*. New York: Meridian, 1992.

Kaufmann, Arthur, ed. *Die peinliche Gerichtsordnung Kaiser Karls V. von 1532 (Carolina)*. Stuttgart: Reclam, 1980.

Keilson-Lauritz, Marita. *Die Geschichte der eigenen Geschichte: Literatur und Literaturkritik in den Anfängen der Schwulenbewegung am Beispiel des "Jahrbuchs für Sexuelle Zwischenstufen" und der Zeitschrift "Der Eigene"*. Berlin: Rosa Winkel, 1997.

Kellogg, Stuart, ed. "Introduction: The Uses of Homosexuality in Literature." *Literary Visions of Homosexuality*. New York: Haworth Press, 1983. 1–12.

Kennedy, Hubert. *The Anarchist of Love: The Secret Life of John Henry Mackay*. San Francisco: Peremptory Publications, 2002.

---. "Karl Heinrich Ulrichs, First Theorist of Homosexuality." *Science and Homosexualities*. Ed. Vernon A. Rosario. London: Routledge, 1997. 26–45.

---. "Research and Commentaries on Richard von Krafft-Ebing and Karl Heinrich Ulrichs." *Journal of Homosexuality* 42.1 (2002): 165–78.

---. "Who was Sagitta? An Introduction to the Books of the Nameless Love." John Henry Mackay, *Sagitta's Books of the Nameless Love*. Trans. Hubert Kennedy. Concord: Peremptory Publications, 2005. 1–11.

Kinna, Ruth. 'The Mirror of Anarchy: The Egoism of John Henry Mackay and Dora Marsden'. *Max Stirner*. Ed. Saul Newman. Basingstoke: Palgrave Macmillan, 2011. 42–63.

Kitcher, Philip. *Deaths in Venice: The Cases of Gustav von Aschenbach*. New York: Columbia UP, 2013.

Koelb, Clayton. "Death in Venice." *A Companion to the Works of Thomas Mann*. Ed. Herbert Lehnert and Eva Wessell. Rochester: Camden House, 2004. 95–114.

Kohlmayer, Rainer, and Lucia Krämer. "*Bunbury* in Germany: Alive and Kicking." *The Reception of Oscar Wilde in Europe*. Ed. Stefano Evangelista. London: Continuum, 2010. 189–202.

Krafft-Ebing, Richard von. *Psychopathia Sexualis, mit besonderer Berücksichtigung der conträren Sexualempfindung: Eine medicinisch-gerichtliche Studie für Ärzte und Juristen*. 12 edn. Stuttgart: Enke, 1903.

---. *Psychopathia Sexualis, with Especial Reference to the Antipathic Sexual Instinct: A Medico-Forensic Study*. Trans. Franklin S. Klaf. London: Staples Press, 1965.

---. "Vorwort." Albert Moll. *Die Conträre Sexualempfindung*. Berlin: Fischer, 1891. iii–viii.

Kupffer, Elisarion von. "The Ethical-Political Significance of *Lieblingminne*." *Homosexuality and Male Bonding in Pre-Nazi Germany*. Ed. Harry Oosterhuis. Trans. Hubert Kennedy. London: Haworth Press, 1991. 35–48.

---. *Lieblingminne und Freundesliebe in der Weltliteratur: Eine Sammlung mit einer ethisch-politischen Einleitung*. Ed. Marita Keilson-Lauritz. Berlin: Rosa Winkel, 1995.

Kurzke, Hermann. *Thomas Mann: Epoche – Werk – Wirkung*. Munich: Beck, 1985.

---. *Thomas Mann: Das Leben als Kunstwerk*. Munich: Beck, 1999.

Kuzmin, Mikhail. *Wings*. Trans. Hugh Aplin. London: Hesperus, 2007.

Lane, Christopher. "Forsterian Sexuality." *The Cambridge Companion to E. M. Forster*. Ed. David Bradshaw. Cambridge: Cambridge UP, 2007. 104–19.

Lauritsen, John. "Edward Prime-Stevenson." *Before Stonewall: Activists for Gay and Lesbian Rights in Historical Context*. Ed. Vern L. Bullough. London: Routledge, 2002. 35–40.

Lawrence, D. H. "The Prussian Officer." *Pages Passed from Hand to Hand: The Hidden Tradition of Homosexual Literature in English from 1748 to 1914*. Ed. Mark Mitchell and David Leavitt. London: Chatto & Windus, 1998. 404–23.

Leeming, David. *Stephen Spender: A Life in Modernism*. London: Duckworth, 1999.

Lehnert, Herbert. "Thomas Mann's Early Interest in Myth and Erwin Rohde's *Psyche*." *PMLA: Publications of the Modern Language Association of America* 79.3 (1964): 297–304.

Lesér, Esther H. *Thomas Mann's Short Fiction: An Intellectual Biography*. Ed. Mitzi Brunsdale. London: Associated University Presses, 1989.

Works Cited

Levin, James. *The Gay Novel: The Male Homosexual Image in America*. New York: Irvington Publishers, 1983.

Lewis, Chester, David Leitch, and Colin Simpson. *The Cleveland Street Affair*. London: Weidenfeld & Nicolson, 1977.

Lilly, Mark. *Gay Men's Literature in the Twentieth Century*. Basingstoke: Palgrave Macmillan, 1993.

Livesey, Matthew J. "From This Moment On: The Homosexual Origins of the Gay Novel in American Literature." Diss. University of Wisconsin, Madison, 1997.

Looby, Christopher. "The Gay Novel in the United States, 1900–1950." *A Companion to the Modern American Novel 1900–1950*. Ed. John T. Matthews. Oxford: Wiley-Blackwell, 2009. 414–36.

Lücke, Martin. "Beschmutzte Utopien. Subkulturelle Räume, begehrte Körper und sexuelle Identität in belletristischen Texten über männliche Prostitution 1900–1933." *Verhandlungen im Zwielicht: Momente der Prostitution in Geschichte und Gegenwart*. Ed. Sabine Grenz and Martin Lücke. Bielefeld: Transcript, 2006. 301–18.

Maar, Michael. *Das Blaubartzimmer: Thomas Mann und die Schuld*. Frankfurt a.M.: Suhrkamp, 2000.

Mackay, John Henry. *Autobiographical Writings*. Trans. Hubert Kennedy. Philadelphia: Xlibris, 2000.

---. *Die Bücher der namenlosen Liebe*. Berlin: Rosa Winkel, 1979.

---. *The Hustler: The Story of a Nameless Love from the Friedrichstrasse*. Trans. Hubert Kennedy. Philadelphia: Xlibris, 2002.

---. *Der Puppenjunge: Die Geschichte der namenlosen Liebe aus der Friedrichstraße*. Ed. Hubert Kennedy. Berlin: Rosa Winkel, 1999.

---. *Sagitta's Books of the Nameless Love*. Trans. Hubert Kennedy. Concord: Peremptory Publications, 2005.

Mader, D. H. "The Greek Mirror: The Uranians and Their Use of Greece." *Same-Sex Desire and Love in Greco-Roman Antiquity and in the Classical Tradition of the West*. Ed. Beert C. Verstraete and Vernon Provencal. New York: Harrington Park Press, 2005. 377–420.

Mancini, Elena. *Magnus Hirschfeld and the Quest for Sexual Freedom: A History of the First International Sexual Freedom Movement*. Basingstoke: Palgrave Macmillan, 2010.

Mann, Thomas. *Briefe, 1889–1936*. Ed. Erika Mann. Frankfurt a.M.: Fischer, 1961.

---. *Essays of Three Decades*. Trans. H. T. Lowe-Porter. London: Secker & Warburg, 1947.

---. *Death in Venice and Other Stories*. Trans. David Luke. London: Vintage, 1998.

---. *Gesammelte Werke*, 12 vols. Frankfurt a.M.: Fischer, 1960.

---. *Last Essays*. Trans. Richard Winston and Clara Winston. London: Secker & Warburg, 1959.

---. *Letters of Thomas Mann, 1889–1955*. Trans. Richard Winston and Clara Winston. Los Angeles: U of California P, 1975.

---. *Der Tod in Venedig*. Ed. T. J. Reed. London: Oxford UP, 1971.
---. "Tonio Kröger." *Death in Venice and Other Stories*. Trans. David Luke. London: Vintage, 1998. 135–94.
Markley, A. A. "E. M. Forster's Reconfigured Gaze and the Creation of a Homoerotic Subjectivity." *Twentieth Century Literature* 47.2 (2001): 268–92.
Martin, Robert K. "Edward Carpenter and the Double Structure of *Maurice*." *Journal of Homosexuality* 8.3/4 (1983): 35–46.
---. "Gender, Sexuality, and Identity in Mann's Short Fiction." *Approaches to Teaching Mann's Death in Venice and Other Short Fiction*. Ed. Jeffrey B. Berlin. New York: Modern Language Association of America, 1992. 57–67.
---, and George Piggford, eds. "Introduction: Queer Forster?" *Queer Forster*. Chicago: U of Chicago P, 1997. 1–28.
Maurice. Dir. James Ivory and Ismail Merchant. Perf. James Wilby, Hugh Grant, Rupert Graves. 1987. Criterion Collection, 2004. DVD.
Meyers, Jeffrey. *Homosexuality and Literature 1890–1930*. London: Athlone, 1977.
---. *Thomas Mann's Artist-Heroes*. Evanston: Northwestern UP, 2014.
Michael. Dir. Carl Theodor Dreyer. Perf. Benjamin Christensen and Walter Slezak. 1924. Kino International, 2004. DVD.
Minton, Henry L. *Departing from Deviance: A History of Homosexual Rights and Emancipatory Science in America*. Chicago: U of Chicago P, 2002.
Moeller, Robert G. "Private Acts, Public Anxieties, and the Fight to Decriminalize Male Homosexuality in West Germany." *Feminist Studies* 36.3 (2010): 528–52.
---. "'The Homosexual Man Is a "Man," the Homosexual Woman is a "Woman"': Sex, Society, and the Law in Postwar West Germany." *Journal of the History of Sexuality* 4.3 (1994): 395–429.
Moffat, Wendy. *E. M. Forster: A New Life*. London: Bloomsbury, 2010.
---. "E. M. Forster and the Unpublished 'Scrapbook' of Gay History: 'Lest We Forget Him!'" *English Literature in Transition, 1880–1920* 55.1 (2012): 19–31.
Moran, Leslie J. *The Homosexual(ity) of Law*. London: Routledge, 1996.
Morgan, Thaïs E. "Victorian Effeminacies." *Victorian Sexual Dissidence*. Ed. Richard Dellamora. Chicago: U of Chicago P, 1999. 109–25.
Morrow, Ross. "Sexuality as Discourse—Beyond Foucault's Constructionism." *Journal of Sociology* 31.1 (1995): 15–31.
Mosse, George L. *The Image of Man: The Creation of Modern Masculinity*. London: Oxford UP, 1996.
---. *Nationalism and Sexuality: Respectability and Abnormal Sexuality in Modern Europe*. New York: Fertig, 1985.
Mort, Frank. *Dangerous Sexualities: Medico-Moral Politics in England Since 1830*. London: Routledge & Kegan Paul, 1987.
Müller, Stefan. *Ach, nur 'n bisschen Liebe: Männliche Homosexualität in den Romanen deutschsprachiger Autoren in der Zwischenkriegszeit 1919 bis 1939*. Würzburg: Königshausen & Neumann, 2011.

Mullins, Marie. "Sexuality." *A Companion to Walt Whitman*. Ed. Donald K. Kummings. Malden: Blackwell, 2006. 164–79.

Mundt, Hannelore. *Understanding Thomas Mann*. Columbia, SC: U of South Carolina P, 2004.

"Mustapha Pochowachett, Sexual Offences > sodomy, 24th May 1694." *The Proceedings of the Old Bailey, 1674–1913*. April 2013. 18 June 2014. <http://www.oldbaileyonline.org/browse.jsp?id=t16940524-20-off83&div=t16940524-20#highlight>.

Naphy, William. *Born to Be Gay: A History of Homosexuality*. Stroud, Gloucestershire: Tempus, 2006.

Nordau, Max. *Degeneration*. London: U of Nebraska P, 1993.

---. *Entartung*. 2 vols. Berlin: Dunder, 1892.

Norton, Rictor. *The Myth of the Modern Homosexual: Queer History and the Search for Cultural Unity*. London: Cassell, 1997.

Oaks, Robert F. "Defining Sodomy in Seventeenth-Century Massachusetts." *Journal of Homosexuality* 6.1/2 (1980–81): 79–83.

Oosterhuis, Harry. "The Dubious Magic of Male Beauty: Politics and Homoeroticism in the Lives and Works of Thomas and Klaus Mann." Trans. Ton Brouwers *Queering the Canon: Defying Sights in German Literature and Culture*. Ed. Christoph Lorey and John Plews. Columbia, SC: Camden House, 1998. 181–206.

---. "Medicine, Male Bonding and Homosexuality in Nazi Germany." *Journal of Contemporary History* 32.2 (1997): 187–205.

---. "Richard von Krafft-Ebing's 'Step-Children of Nature': Psychiatry and the Making of Homosexual Identity." *Science and Homosexualities*. Ed. Vernon A. Rosario. London: Routledge, 1997. 67–88.

---. *Stepchildren of Nature: Krafft-Ebing, Psychiatry, and the Making of Sexual Identity*. Chicago: U of Chicago P, 2000.

Ovid. *Metamorphoses*. Trans. David Raeburn. London: Penguin, 2004.

Page, Norman. *Auden and Isherwood: The Berlin Years*. Basingstoke: Macmillan, 1998.

Pater, Walter. *The Renaissance: Studies in Art and Poetry*. Ed. Adam Phillips. Oxford: Oxford UP, 1986.

Peakman, Julie, ed. "Sexual Perversion in History: An Introduction." *Sexual Perversions, 1670–1890*. Basingstoke: Palgrave Macmillan, 2009. 1–49.

Pearl, Monica B. *AIDS Literature and Gay Identity: The Literature of Loss*. London: Routledge, 2013.

Picart, Caroline Joan. *Thomas Mann and Friedrich Nietzsche: Eroticism, Death, Music, and Laughter*. Amsterdam: Rodopi, 1999.

Platen, August von. "Tristan." *German Poetry from 1750 to 1900*. Ed. Robert M. Browning. Trans. Herman Salinger. New York: Continuum, 1984. 172–75.

Plato. *Symposium*. Trans. Christopher Gill. London: Penguin, 2005.

Popp, Wolfgang. *Männerliebe: Homosexualität und Literatur*. Stuttgart: Metzler, 1992.

---. "Zwischen Wilde-Prozess und Eulenburg-Affäre: Das Tabu Homosexualität." *Abschied vom Mythos Mann: kulturelle Konzepte der Moderne*. Ed. Karin Tebben. Göttingen: Vandenhoeck & Ruprecht, 2002. 79–102.

Porter, Kevin, and Jeffrey Weeks, eds. *Between the Acts: The Lives of Homosexual Men, 1885–1967*. London: Routledge, 1991.

Prickett, David James. "Defining Identity via Homosexual Spaces: Locating the Male Homosexual in Weimar Berlin." *Women in German Yearbook* 21 (2005): 134–62.

Prime-Stevenson, Edward. *Imre: A Memorandum*. Ed. James J. Gifford. Peterborough: Broadview Press, 2003.

---. *The Intersexes: A History of Similisexualism as a Problem in Social Life*. New York: Arno Press, 1975.

---. "Letter from Edward Prime-Stevenson to Paul Elmer More." *Imre: A Memorandum*. Ed. James J. Gifford. Peterborough: Broadview Press, 2003. 132–40.

---. "Out of the Sun." *Pages Passed from Hand to Hand: The Hidden Tradition of Homosexual Literature in English from 1748 to 1914*. Ed. Mark Mitchell and David Leavitt. London: Chatto & Windus, 1998. 392–403.

Puff, Helmut. *Sodomy in Reformation Germany and Switzerland, 1400–1600*. Chicago: U of Chicago P, 2003.

Raby, Peter. *Oscar Wilde*. Cambridge: Cambridge UP, 1988.

Rahman, Tariq. "Edward Carpenter and E. M. Forster." *E. M. Forster: Critical Assessments*. Ed. John Henry Stape, Vol. 4. Robertsbridge, East Sussex: Helm Information, 1998. 40–57.

---. "Ephebophilia: The Case for the Use of a New Word." *Forum for Modern Language Studies* 24.2 (1988): 126–41.

Raschke, Debrah. "Breaking the Engagement with Philosophy: Re-envisioning Hetero/Homo Relations in *Maurice*." *Queer Forster*. Ed. Robert K. Martin and George Piggford. Chicago: U of Chicago P, 1997. 151–65.

Rector, Frank. *The Nazi Extermination of Homosexuals*. New York: Stein and Day, 1981.

Reed, T. J. *Death in Venice: Making and Unmaking a Master* (New York: Twayne Publishers, 1994.

---. "The Frustrated Poet: Homosexuality and Taboo in *Der Tod in Venedig*." *Taboos in German Literature*. Ed. David Jackson. Oxford: Berghahn, 1996. 119–34.

---, ed. Introduction and Notes. Thomas Mann, *Der Tod in Venedig*. London: Oxford UP, 1971. 1–43 and 158–80.

---. *Thomas Mann: The Uses of Tradition*. Oxford: Clarendon, 1974.

Reid, Forrest. *The Garden God: A Tale of Two Boys*. Ed. Michael Matthew Kaylor. Richmond: Valancourt Books, 2007.

Richards, Jeffrey. "'Passing the Love of Women': Manly Love and Victorian Society." *Manliness and Morality: Middle-Class Masculinity in Britain and America, 1800–1940*. Ed. J. A. Mangan and James Walvin. Manchester: Manchester UP, 1987. 92–121.

Works Cited

Riley, Thomas A. *Germany's Poet-Anarchist: John Henry Mackay: A Contribution to the History of German Literature at the Turn of the Century, 1880–1920*. New York: Revisionist Press, 1972.

Robb, Graham. *Strangers: Homosexual Love in the Nineteenth Century*. London: Picador, 2003.

Roberts, Celia. "Medicine and the Making of a Sexual Body." *Handbook of the New Sexuality Studies*. Ed. Steven Seidman, Nancy Fischer and Chet Meeks. London: Routledge, 2006. 88–96.

Robertson, Michael. *Worshipping Walt: The Whitman Disciples*. Oxford: Princeton UP, 2008.

Robertson, Ritchie. "Classicism and Its Pitfalls: *Death in Venice*." *The Cambridge Companion to Thomas Mann*. Ed. Ritchie Robertson. Cambridge: Cambridge UP, 2002. 95–106.

Robinson, Christopher. *Scandal in the Ink: Male and Female Homosexuality in Twentieth-Century French Literature*. London: Cassell, 1995.

Roden, Frederick S. "Marc-Andre [*sic*] Raffalovich: A Russian-French-Jewish-Catholic Homosexual in Oscar Wilde's London." *Jewish/Christian/Queer: Crossroads and Identities*. Ed. Frederick S. Roden. Farnham, Surrey: Ashgate, 2009. 127–38.

Rogers, Jack. *Jesus, the Bible, and Homosexuality: Explode the Myths, Heal the Church*. Louisville: Westminster John Knox, 2009.

Rowbotham, Sheila. *Edward Carpenter: A Life of Liberty and Love*. London: Verso, 2008.

Sacher-Masoch, Leopold. *Die Liebe des Plato*. Ed. Michael Gratzke. Hamburg: Männerschwarm, 2012. Kindle edn.

Sartre, Jean-Paul. *Baudelaire*. Trans. Martin Turnell. London: Horizon, 1949.

Schaffner, Anna Katharina. *Modernism and Perversion: Sexual Deviance in Sexology and Literature, 1850–1930*. Basingstoke: Palgrave Macmillan, 2012.

---. "Richard von Krafft-Ebing's *Psychopathia sexualis* and Thomas Mann's *Buddenbrooks*: Exchanges between Scientific and Imaginary Accounts of Sexual Deviance." *Modern Language Review* 106.2 (2011): 477–94.

Schaub, Hanns. *John Henry Mackay: Dichter des Namenlosen*. Basel: Privately printed, 1970.

Sedgwick, Eve Kosofsky. *Between Men: English Literature and Male Homosocial Desire*. New York: Columbia UP, 1985.

---. *Epistemology of the Closet*. 1990. Berkley: U of California P, 2008.

"sexology, *n.*" *OED Online*. OED Third Edition, September 2008. Oxford UP. 18 June 2014. <http://www.oed.com/view/Entry/177033>.

Shookman, Ellis. *Thomas Mann's "Death in Venice": A Novella and Its Critics*. Rochester: Camden House, 2003.

---. *Thomas Mann's "Death in Venice": A Reference Guide*. Westport, CT: Greenwood Press, 2004.

Sibalis, Michael. "Male Homosexuality in the Age of Enlightenment and Revolution, 1680–1850." *Gay Life and Culture: A World History*. Ed. Robert Aldrich. London: Thames & Hudson, 2006. 103–23.

Sigusch, Volkmar. *Auf der Suche nach der sexuellen Freiheit: über Sexualforschung und Politik*. Frankfurt a.M.: Campus, 2011.

Sinfield, Alan. *On Sexuality and Power*. New York: Columbia UP, 2004.

---. *The Wilde Century: Effeminacy, Oscar Wilde, and the Queer Moment*. London: Cassell, 1994.

Small, Ian. "Love-Letter, Spiritual Autobiography, or Prison Writing? Identity and Value in *De Profundis*." *Wilde Writings: Contextual Conditions*. Ed. Joseph Bristow. Toronto: U of Toronto P, 2003. 86–100.

---. *Oscar Wilde Revalued: An Essay on New Materials and Methods of Research*. Greensboro: ELT Press, 1993.

Solneman, K. H. Z. *Der Bahnbrecher John Henry Mackay: Sein Leben und Sein Werk*. Freiburg im Breisgau: Verlag der Mackay-Gesellschaft, 1979.

Somerville, Siobhan B. *Queering the Color Line: Race and the Invention of Homosexuality in American Culture*. London: Duke UP, 2000.

Spencer, Colin. *Homosexuality: A History*. London: Fourth Estate, 1995.

Springett, Ronald M. *Homosexuality in History and the Scriptures: Some Historical and Biblical Perspectives on Homosexuality*. Washington: Biblical Research Institute, 1988.

Stableford, Brian, ed. Introduction. *The Dedalus Book of Decadence: Moral Ruins*. Kindle edn. Sawtry, Dedalus, 2011. 1–83.

Stadion, Emerich von. *Drei seltsame Erinnerungen*. Bochnia: Pisz, 1868.

Steakley, James D. "Cinema and Censorship in the Weimar Republic." *Film History* 11.2 (1999): 181–203.

---. *The Homosexual Emancipation Movement in Germany*. Salem, NH: Ayer Publishers, 1975.

---. "Iconography of a Scandal: Political Cartoons and the Eulenburg Affair in Wilhelmine Germany." *Hidden from History: Reclaiming the Gay and Lesbian Past*. Ed. Martin B. Duberman, Martha Vicinus, and George Chauncey, Jr. London: Penguin, 1991. 233–57.

---. "Per Scientiam ad Justitiam: Magnus Hirschfeld and the Sexual Politics of Innate Homosexuality." *Science and Homosexualities*. Ed. Vernon A. Rosario. London: Routledge, 1997. 133–54.

Stevens, Hugh. "Normality and Queerness in Gay Fiction." *The Cambridge Companion to Gay and Lesbian Writing*. Ed. Hugh Stevens. Cambridge: Cambridge UP, 2011. 81–96.

Still, Judith. "Not Really Prostitution: The Political Economy of Sexual Tourism in Gide's *Si le grain ne meurt*." *French Studies* 54.1 (2000): 17–34.

Stümke, Hans-Georg. *Homosexuelle in Deutschland: Eine politische Geschichte*. Munich: Beck, 1989.

Summers, Claude J. *E. M. Forster*. New York: Ungar, 1983.

---. *Gay Fictions: Wilde to Stonewall, Studies in a Male Homosexual Literary Tradition.* New York: Continuum, 1990.
Symington, Rodney, "The Eruption of the Other: Psychoanalytic Approaches to *Death in Venice*." Thomas Mann: *Death in Venice*. Ed. Naomi Ritter. Boston: Bedford, 1998. 127–41.
Symonds, John Addington. *John Addington Symonds and Homosexuality: A Critical Edition of Sources*. Ed. Sean Brady. Basingstoke: Palgrave Macmillan, 2012.
---. *The Letters of John Addington Symonds*. Ed. Herbert M. Schueller and Robert Peters. 3 vols. Detroit: Wayne State UP, 1967.
---. *The Memoirs of John Addington Symonds*. Ed. Phyllis Grosskurth. London: Hutchinson, 1984.
---. *Walt Whitman: A Study*. London: Routledge, 1893.
Tamagne, Florence. *A History of Homosexuality in Europe, Berlin, London, Paris, 1919–1939*. New York: Algora, 2006.
Tatchell, Peter. *Europe in the Pink: Lesbian & Gay Equality in the New Europe*. London: Gay Men's Press, 1992.
"Thomas Davis, Sexual Offences > Sodomy, 11th October 1699." *The Proceedings of the Old Bailey, 1674–1913.* April 2013. 18 June 2014. <http://www.oldbaileyonline.org/browse.jsp?id=t16991011-29-off145&div=t16991011-29#highlight>.
Tobin, Robert D. "Kertbeny's 'Homosexuality' and the Language of Nationalism." *Genealogies of Identity: Interdisciplinary Readings on Sex and Sexuality*. Ed. Margaret Sönser Breen and Fiona Peters. Amsterdam: Rodopi, 2005. 3–18.
---. "The Life and Work of Thomas Mann: A Gay Perspective" *Thomas Mann: Death in Venice*. Ed. Naomi Ritter. Boston: Bedford Books, 1998. 225–44.
---. "Making Way for the Third Sex: Liberal and Antiliberal Impulses in Mann's Portrayal of Male-Male Desire in His Early Short Fiction." *A Companion to German Realism, 1848-1900*. Ed. Todd C. Kontje. Rochester: Camden House, 2002. 307–38.
---. "Twins! Homosexuality and Masculinity in Nineteenth-Century Germany." *Masculinity, Senses, Spirit*. Ed. Katherine Faull. Lewisburg: Bucknell UP, 2011. 131–51.
---. "Queering Thomas Mann's *Tod in Venedig*." *Thomas Mann. Neue kulturwissenschaftliche Lektüren*. Ed. Stefan Börnchen, Georg Mein, and Gary Schmidt. Paderborn: Wilhelm Fink, 2012. 67–80.
---. "Why is Tadzio a Boy: Perspectives on Homoeroticism in *Death in Venice*." Thomas Mann, *Death in Venice: A New Translation, Background, and Contexts, Criticism*. Ed. Clayton Koelb. London: Norton, 1994. 207–32.
Tosh, John. "The Old Adam and the New Man: Emerging Themes in the History of English Masculinities: 1750–1850." *Manliness and Masculinities in Nineteenth Century Britain: Essays on Gender, Family, and Empire*. Ed. John Tosh. Harlow: Pearson Longman, 2005. 61–82.

Trumbach, Randolph. "Renaissance Sodomy, 1500–1700." *A Gay History of Britain: Love and Sex Between Men Since the Middle Ages*. Greenwood World Publishing, 2007. 45–76.

---. *Sex and the Gender Revolution, vol. 1, Heterosexuality and the Third Gender in Enlightenment London*. Chicago: U of Chicago P, 1998.

Ulrichs, Karl Heinrich. *Forschungen über das Räthsel der Mannmännlichen Liebe*. Ed. Hubert Kennedy. 12 separately paginated essays in 4 vols. Berlin: Rosa Winkel, 1994.

---. *The Riddle of "Man-Manly" Love: The Pioneering Work on Male Homosexuality*. Trans. Michael A. Lombardi-Nash. 2 vols. Buffalo: Prometheus, 1994.

Upchurch, Charles. *Before Wilde: Sex Between Men in Britain's Age of Reform*. London: U of California P, 2009.

Vaget, Hans Rudolf. "Confession and Camouflage: The Diaries of Thomas Mann" *The Journal of English and Germanic Philology* 96.4 (1997): 567–90

Vanggaard, Thorkil. *Phallós: A Symbol and Its History in the Male World*. London: Cape, 1972.

Verstraete Beert C., and Vernon Provencal, eds. Introduction. *Same-Sex Desire and Love in Greco-Roman Antiquity and in the Classical Tradition of the West*. New York: Harrington Park Press, 2005. 1–12.

Vicinus, Martha. "The Adolescent Boy: Fin-de-Siècle Femme Fetale?" *Victorian Sexual Dissidence*. Ed. Richard Dellamora. Chicago: U of Chicago P, 1999. 83–108.

Vilain, Robert. "Tragedy and the Apostle of Beauty: The Early Literary Reception of Oscar Wilde in Germany and Austria." *The Reception of Oscar Wilde in Europe*. Ed. Stefano Evangelista. London: Continuum, 2010. 173–188.

Wanrooij, Bruno P. F. "Italy: Sexuality, Morality and Public Authority." *Sexual Cultures in Europe: National Histories*. Ed. Franz X. Eder, Lesley A. Hall, and Gert Hekma. Manchester: Manchester UP, 1999. 114–37.

Webber, Andrew J. "Mann's Man's World." *The Cambridge Companion to Thomas Mann*. Ed. Ritchie Robertson. Cambridge: Cambridge UP, 2002. 64–83.

Weeks, Jeffrey. *Coming Out: Homosexual Politics in Britain from the Nineteenth Century to the Present*. London: Quartet Books, 1977.

---. "Inverts, Perverts, and Mary-Annes: Male Prostitution and the Regulation of Homosexuality in England in the Nineteenth and Early Twentieth Centuries." *Hidden from History: Reclaiming the Gay and Lesbian Past*, Ed. Martin B. Duberman, Martha Vicinus, and George Chauncey, Jr. London: Penguin, 1991. 195–211.

---. *Making Sexual History*. Cambridge: Polity Press, 2000.

---. *Sex, Politics, and Society: The Regulation of Sexuality since 1800*. London: Longman, 1981.

Westphal, Carl. "Conträre Sexualempfindung." *Archiv für Psychiatrie und Nervenkrankheiten* 2.1 (1869): 73–108. Repr. in *Der unterdrückte Sexus: Historische Texte zur Homosexualität*. Ed. Joachim S. Hohmann. Lollar: Achenbach, 1977.

White, Chris, ed. "General Introduction: Strategies for Liberation." *Nineteenth-Century Writings on Homosexuality: A Source Book*. London: Routledge, 1999. 1–8.

Whitman, Walt. *The Complete Poems*. Ed. Francis Murphy. London: Penguin, 2004.

Widmaier-Haag, Susanne. *Es war das Lächeln des Narziss: Die Theorien der Psychoanalyse im Spiegel der literaturpsychologischen Interpretationen des "Tod in Venedig"*. Würzburg: Königshausen & Neumann, 1999.

Wilde, Oscar. *The Complete Works of Oscar Wilde*. Ed. Ian Small, et al. 7 vols. Oxford: Oxford UP, 2000–13.

---. *The Portrait of Mr W.H*. London: Hesperus, 2003.

Willy. *The Third Sex*. Trans. Lawrence Schehr. Chicago: U of Illinois P, 2007.

Wilper, James P. "Sexology, homosexual history, and Walt Whitman: The 'Uranian' identity in *Imre: A Memorandum*." *Critical Survey* 22.3 (2010): 52–68.

---. "Wilde and the Model of Homosexuality in Mann's *Tod in Venedig*." *CLCWeb: Comparative Literature and Culture* 15.4 (2013): <http://dx.doi.org/10.7771/1481-4374.2305>.

Winkler, John J. *The Constraints of Desire: The Anthropology of Sex and Gender in Ancient Greece*. London: Routledge, 1990.

Wisskirchen, Hans. "Republikanischer Eros: Zu Walt Whitmans und Hans Blühers Rolle in der politischen Publizistik Thomas Manns." *"Heimsuchung und süßes Gift": Erotik und Poetik bei Thomas Mann*. Ed. Gerhard Härle. Frankfurt a.M.: Fischer, 1992. 17–40.

Woodhouse, Reed. *Unlimited Embrace: A Canon of Gay Fiction, 1945–1995*. Amherst: U of Massachusetts P, 1998.

Wolff, Charlotte. *Magnus Hirschfeld: A Portrait of a Pioneer in Sexology*. London: Quartet, 1986.

Woods, Gregory. *A History of Gay Literature: The Male Tradition*. London: Yale UP, 1998.

Wright, Thomas. *Oscar's Books*. London: Chatto & Windus, 2008.

Wysling, Hans. "Thomas Manns Rezeption der Psychoanalyse." *Probleme der Moderne: Studien zur deutschen Literatur von Nietzsche bis Brecht*. Ed. Benjamin Bennett, Anton Kaes, and William J. Lillyman. Tübingen: Niemeyer, 1983. 201–22.

Zeikowitz, Richard E., ed. *Letters Between Forster and Isherwood on Homosexuality and Literature*. Basingstoke: Palgrave Macmillan, 2008.

Index

Achilles, 74
Ackerley, 8, 177, 200
Adonis, 44, 132, 165, 168
aestheticism, 10, 72, 138, 140, 142, 146, 149, 153, 155, 156, 158, 159, 160, 164, 165, 169, 172
Aesthetic Movement, 140, 141
Agathon, 53, 71
Alcibiades, 59
Allatini, 4
anarchist, 45, 108, 165
anarchy/anarchism, 7, 45, 69, 93, 108
Antinous, 132
Aphrodite, 53, 54, 119
Apollo/Apollonian, 37, 105, 163
Aquinas, 17
Aristogeiton, 74, 85

Bang, 154
Baudelaire, 164, 172
berdache, 24
Berlin, 3, 4, 6, 7, 24, 45, 46, 47, 68, 120, 155, 157, 165, 169
 gay bars, 165, 167
Bloch, 97
Blüher, 52, 57
bohemianism, 150
Bosie, 37. *See also* Douglas
Boulton and Park case, 137
Brand, 52, 56, 69, 82, 105, 107, 172
Breuer, 4
buggery, 18, 19, 24, 25, 157. *See also* sodomy/sodomite; Sin of Sodom
Byron, 37, 81, 146

Cambridge, 3, 72, 84, 85, 139. *See also* Oxbridge
Carpenter, 5, 8, 9, 29, 41, 42, 72-74, 75, 76, 77, 80, 82, 85-88, 101, 116-18, 122-24, 132, 133-34, 140, 142, 143, 150, 156, 171-74

Casper, 95
Cavafy, 65
Cleveland Street Scandal, 20, 30, 137
Couperus, 154
Critobulus, 59

Damian, 17
dandy/dandyism, 10, 92, 101, 140, 141, 142, 143, 146, 156, 158, 159, 160, 163, 164, 165, 167, 169, 172
dandy-aesthete, 140, 141, 143, 159, 163, 172
Danson, 157, 171
Dionian, 118, 119, 125, 128
Dionysian, 37, 41, 162, 172
Dionysus, 41, 105, 162
Diotima, 54, 55, 56, 71
Douglas, 1, 42, 137, 156, 157. *See also* Bosie
Dreyer, 154

effeminacy, 75, 81, 92, 97, 125, 138, 139, 140, 143, 144, 145-50, 152, 154, 155, 157, 167-70, 173-76
Ellis, 9, 27, 29, 61, 71, 77, 115, 117, 118, 121-24, 143
Eros, 35, 37, 53, 56, 57, 58, 60-64, 69, 74, 75, 80, 85, 99, 106, 123, 165, 172
Eulenburg, 23, 30, 154, 155, 165

Foucault, 55, 94, 118
Frederick the Great, 97, 103, 161
Freud, 67, 91, 113
Friedländer, 52, 56, 57, 58, 69, 80, 105, 106

Gardener, 26
Gautier, 172
Gemeinschaft der Eigenen, 52, 56, 69, 75, 94, 105, 171
George, 65, 91, 97, 98, 99, 154

Gide, 9, 15, 65, 82, 141, 153, 154, 155
Goethe, 36, 37, 103
Greek love apologia, 7, 8, 51, 52, 63, 69, 78, 80
Griesinger, 95
gross indecency, 1, 8, 10, 15, 18, 19, 20, 40, 47, 84, 122, 137, 143, 157, 171

Hall, Lesley, 19
Hall, Radclyffe, 2, 117
Harden, 23, 154
Harmodius, 74, 85
Hartland, 115
Hauptmann, 23
Heliogabalus, 146
Hellenism, 8, 52, 58, 63, 66, 70, 72, 73, 74, 83-86, 88, 118, 129, 131, 150, 172
Hermes, 100
Hichens, 142
Hiller, 99
Hirschfeld, 2, 9, 22, 23, 27, 28, 92, 93, 96, 98, 99, 101, 104-06, 108, 111, 118, 119, 120-24, 126, 132, 134, 153
Hofmannsthal, 153
Holy Roman Empire, 21
homogenic love, 42, 117, 156
homosexual artist, 102, 104, 105, 169

impurity, 21
Individualism, 7, 141, 142, 143, 171
Institute for Sexual Research (*Institut für Sexualwissenschaft*), 120
intermediate sex, 9, 98, 123, 133, 174. See also sexual intermediaries; third sex
Isherwood, 5, 120, 152, 165
Ivory, James, 40
Ivory, Yvonne, 7, 10, 34, 35, 153

Joux, 116

Kaiserreich, 21, 28
Kertbeny, 3
Knabenliebe, 42, 57. See also Päderastie; paiderastia; pederast/pederasty
Krafft-Ebing, 1, 2, 9, 67, 91-93, 95, 96, 97-99, 102, 106, 108, 112, 113, 115, 117, 123-24, 127-28, 172
Kupffer, 42, 56, 57, 69, 80, 105, 106, 156
Kuzmin, 154

Labouchère, 19, 20
lad-lover, 107, 112
Lawrence, D. H., 4
Lesley Hall, 19, 139
Leviticus, 6, 16

Lieblingminne, 42, 56, 57, 69, 70, 80, 105, 106, 156, 175
London, 18, 20, 76, 120, 125, 140

Marlowe, 78, 81, 82, 149
Martial, 78, 83
Merrill, 41, 72, 76, 87, 123, 173
Michelangelo, 51, 78, 97, 145
middle-class manliness, 142, 152
Millthorpe, 76, 173
Mitchell, 27
Moll, 97, 99

Napoleon, 131
Napoleonic, 7, 19, 21
Nazi, 28, 29
New York, 2, 26, 27, 30
Nichols, 15
Nietzsche, 158, 159
Nietzschean, 169
Nordau, 96, 113, 126, 138

Oswald, 4, 7, 10, 23, 24, 31, 32-34, 37, 43, 46, 77-82, 87, 101, 112, 116, 124-30, 133, 146-49, 168, 173-75
Ovid, 148
Oxbridge, 72, 73
Oxbridge Hellenism, 72, 73
Oxford, 73, 84, 85, 140, 141. See also Oxbridge

Päderastie, 42, 57, 95
paiderastia, 62, 64
Paragraph 175, 22, 29, 68, 96, 101, 111, 119, 167
Pater, 141
Patroclus, 74
Pausanias, 52, 53, 54, 56, 61, 71, 119
pederast/pederasty, 42, 56, 57, 88, 145, 148, 155, 156. See also *Päderastie*; *paiderastia*; *Knabenliebe*
pederastic, 37, 53, 54, 55, 78, 99, 154
perversion (*Perversion*), 58, 95, 122, 145
perversity (*Perversität*), 95
Phaedrus, 52, 55, 60, 62, 70, 71, 83
Philistine/ Philistinism, 139, 143, 150, 154
Platen, 36, 37, 58, 63, 64, 78, 81, 82, 97, 104, 146, 149
Plato, 38, 51-56, 70, 71-74, 78, 81, 83, 119, 121, 145, 146, 149
Platonic, 40, 41, 53, 60, 61, 71, 73, 80, 84, 85, 87, 164, 172
Psychopathia Sexualis, 67, 92, 95, 108, 109, 111, 112, 124, 172

Index

Queensberry, Marquis of, 137

Rachilde, 15
racialized discourse, 103
Raffalovich, 143, 145
Rais, 146
Reid, 4, 39
Reinhardt, 153
Rilke, 23
Rohde, 162

Sacher-Masoch, 56
Sacred Band of Thebes, 74, 86. *See also* Theban Band
Sade, 146
Saint Paul, 16
Saint Sebastian, 103, 161
schools of sexology, 8-9, 92-93, 95-96, 113
Scientific-Humanitarian Committee, 22. *See also Wissenschaftlich-humanitäre(s) Komitee*
sexology, 4, 8, 30, 48, 77, 80, 93, 94, 96, 101, 106-11, 113, 116, 118, 121, 123, 124, 128, 129, 133, 134, 171, 172, 175
sexual intermediaries (*sexuelle Zwischenstufen*), 96, 99, 104, 105, 120, 132, 174. *See also* intermediate sex; third sex
sexual science (*Sexualwissenschaft*), 9, 94, 107, 120, 121, 128
Shakespeare, 51, 78, 81, 82, 145, 149, 153
Shepard, 25
Sin of Sodom, 31, 51, 124, 171. *See also* buggery; sodomy/sodomite
socialism, 29, 142
Socrates, 52, 54, 55, 59, 62, 83, 119, 146, 149
Socratic, 35, 59, 145, 164
sodomy/sodomite, 17, 18, 19, 20, 21, 22, 23, 24, 25, 26, 28, 30, 31, 47, 95, 122, 126, 130, 137, 157. *See also* buggery; Sin of Sodom
Stadion, 4
Stirner, 69
Strachey, 87, 133, 139
Symonds, 8, 9, 27, 37, 42, 71-77, 79, 82, 85, 88, 116-18, 121-24, 133, 134, 140, 150, 156, 171, 172, 174
Symposium, 52, 53, 54, 55, 70, 71, 83, 86, 119

Tchaikovsky, 78, 151
Theban Band, 85, 86. *See also* Sacred Band of Thebes

third sex (*das dritte Geschlecht*), 2, 9, 96, 98, 105, 106, 109, 110, 116, 118, 119, 120, 122, 127, 134, 174. *See also* intermediate sex; sexual intermediaries
third-sex theory, 93, 101, 105, 107, 110, 117, 118, 121, 129, 132, 133, 173, 175
"Two Loves," 1, 156, 157

Ulrichs, 9, 96, 101, 104, 106, 117, 118, 119, 121, 123, 124, 132, 133, 134, 171, 173, 174
unchastity, 21
Uranian, 8, 28, 34, 53, 54, 57, 72-76, 78, 79, 81, 82, 86, 96, 117, 119, 122, 123-29, 133, 144, 146-50, 174. *See also* Urning; urnish
Urning, 7, 74, 118, 119, 132, 174
urnish, 27

Visconti, 163

Ward, 27
Weber, 97, 98, 101, 104
Wedekind, 23
Weimar Republic, 23, 66
Westphal, 95, 97, 119
Wettstein-Adelt, 2
Whitman, 8, 71-77, 81, 82, 85, 116, 117, 122, 133, 140, 144, 146, 147, 149, 171, 173, 174
Wilbrandt, 4
Wildean
  (effeminate) stereotype, 9, 139, 145, 150, 152, 168
  homosexual, 138, 143, 146, 162
  homosexual model, 10, 140, 144, 151, 155, 156, 176
Winckelmann, 36, 37, 97, 149
Wissenschaftlich-humanitäre(s) Komitee, 22, 101, 119, 153. *See also* Scientific-Humanitarian Committee
Wolfenden, 29
Woods, 1
World League for Sexual Reform, 120

Xenophon, 59